MARVELLOUS!

MARVELLOUS!

The Trans-Antarctic Expedition Diary of
MAJOR 'ROY' HOMARD
1955-58

Abridged & Edited by
DUNCAN KNIGHT & STEPHEN HADDELSEY

With a Foreword by
RAINER GOLDSMITH

REME MUSEUM

2022

Dedicated to the memory of Roy Homard and his companions on
the Commonwealth Trans-Antarctic Expedition, 1955-58

First published 2022

REME MUSEUM
PRINCE PHILIP BARRACKS,
LYNEHAM,
CHIPPENHAM SN15 4XX

ISBN 978-1-915292-52-0

Printed and bound by Biddles, King's Lynn

CONTENTS

FOREWORD

The last great journey in the world, as the Crossing of Antarctica was dubbed at the time, was completed over sixty years ago. Much has been written about this adventure, and nearly all of those who took part have passed on – but now we can have a final, revealing look at one of the real heroes of the enterprise. A knighthood was awarded to the leader and orders and decorations given to those who were seen to have played a prominent part. But one man was left out of the official recognition. We are fortunate now to have the personal diary of Roy Homard, assistant engineer on the crossing and during the dramatic first year of base building. His diary reminds us who kept the whole enterprise on the rails, ensuring success.

So much has happened in the decades since four very sick Sno-cats arrived in McMurdo Sound after an epic journey of over 2000 miles across Antarctica. Now we think nothing of going to the moon, admittedly assisted by a bank of computers, connected to the base and indeed to the world by television and having instant communication with all and sundry should anything go wrong, all of which alleviate the challenge of a journey.

In contrast, in 1955 eight men were landed on the inhospitable shore of the Filchner Ice Shelf. They were left with no means of communication and minimal shelter, and a number of frail vehicles, to prepare a base for the final journey the following year. Of the eight one man tended the more or less sick vehicles and did much to maintain the relative comfort of his companions in so many ways. In the second year he was the mainstay of keeping the vehicles going over the many miles of rough terrain on the long journey over the Antarctic plateau.

It is now our privilege to be able to read his account of what he did and how he managed the near-impossible task with which he was faced. That man, Warrant Officer Roy Homard of the Royal Electrical and Mechanical Engineers, was a highly trained soldier, having joined the army as an apprentice. For over two years, he used his outstanding skills and initiative to ensure that his brood of reluctant babies, a curious mixture of old and second-hand vehicles, not only served in the mundane tasks of reconnaissance and building a base from scratch – the challenge of the Advance Party – but also kept going for the ninety-nine days of the Crossing itself. The work was unremitting, and much of it had to be done in the open air, with no garage for shelter available during the first year, nor on the trans-continental journey.

In both years Roy had to work exceptionally hard and for long hours. He was naturally a poor sleeper but his work schedule and discomfort in his tent in the first year and during the Crossing meant that his rest was further interrupted. But the surprising fact is that in his diary there are few complaints, either of the conditions forced on him, or of the amateur assistance that he received from his non-engineering colleagues.

It seems that he was sustained by love for his wife, Enid, and it is remarkable that a man so on top of his job and seemingly making his own work schedule should ask his wife for permission to stay for a second year. The support he received from Enid, particularly from the short communications that she was able to send him during his time away from home, were the mainstay of the outstandingly successful fulfilment of his tasks.

It is interesting to note that this remarkably competent and inventive man who showed such exceptional concentration when dealing with the challenges that were his everyday experience should on his retirement make firm friends with the foxes in his garden, feeding them by hand and nourishing their cubs. This was the soft, humane side of a remarkable man, the unrecognised number-one hero of this extraordinary enterprise, the last great journey on Earth.

Professor Rainer Goldsmith

ACKNOWLEDGEMENTS

Above all, this publication is a testament to the courage, conscientiousness and determination of Roy Homard who, through two almost unimaginably arduous years in the Antarctic, maintained his handwritten diary with a degree of lucidity and detail that is quite astonishing and deeply admirable. He knew that his diary would form a vital part of the record of the Commonwealth Trans-Antarctic Expedition, and we, as editors, consider it a privilege to have played a part in enabling its release to a wider audience.

In addition, we would like to applaud the work done by Roy's wife, Enid, who died in 2010. Quite apart from her support of Roy's adventures in Greenland and Antarctica, which took him away from home for such protracted periods, Enid undertook the mammoth task of typing up his expedition diaries from the numerous manuscript notebooks. The original typescript was then reviewed and corrected by Roy himself.

Shirleyann Clark, Roy's long-time friend (and ultimate carer) has played a key role in pursuing Roy's wish to have the diary published, and she has enthusiastically supported the editors throughout the process. We are also grateful to Roy's sons, Richard and Kent, for allowing publication.

Dr Peter Clarkson, Emeritus Associate of the Scott Polar Research Institute in Cambridge, has been very generous with his time, patiently providing a wide range of helpful advice and information, and Professor Rainer Goldsmith, the last surviving member of the expedition, has very kindly provided a foreword. .

Finally, we would like to thank the REME Museum for funding this publication and for giving us the opportunity to work on such a fascinating and historically important document.

Duncan Knight and Stephen Haddelsey

EXPEDITION PERSONNEL

Advance Party

Ken Blaiklock	Base leader and surveyor
Rainer Goldsmith	Medical officer and physiologist
Roy Homard	Mechanical engineer
Peter Jeffries	Meteorologist
Hannes La Grange	Meteorologist
Ralph Lenton	Deputy leader and carpenter
Tony Stewart	Meteorologist
Ellis Williams	Radio operator

Crossing Party

Ken Blaiklock	Surveyor
Vivian Fuchs	Leader
Roy Homard	Mechanical Engineer
Hannes La Grange	Meteorologist
Ralph Lenton	Handyman
Hal Lister	Glaciologist
George Lowe	Photographer and cameraman
David Pratt	Senior engineer
Geoffrey Pratt	Geophysicist
Allan Rogers	Medical officer and physiologist
Jon Stephenson	Geologist
David Stratton	Deputy leader and surveyor

Trans-Antarctic Flight Crew

Gordon Haslop	Pilot (RNZAF)
John Lewis	Pilot (RAF)
Peter Weston	Aircraft mechanic (RAF)
Ellis Williams	Radio Operator (RAF)

INTRODUCTION

There was once a boy whose love of adventure led him to become a soldier. But wartime service with the army did not satisfy his desire for new experiences, and he obtained permission from the military authorities to go on two polar expeditions, one to Greenland and one to Antarctica. He did well, being awarded the Polar Medal (twice), and having an Antarctic mountain named after him. By any standards, his career was a remarkable one.

Roy Homard wrote a diary when he was in Antarctica, the very last word of which is 'marvellous', the title of this book – though it wasn't all marvellous, of course. Far from it. The diary was often penned in appalling conditions, yet it is detailed and well-written. One of its joys is that it is not the work of an expedition leader or scientist or surveyor, but of someone who worked with his hands – and it reveals what a polar expedition was like on a day-to-day basis, both at base and out on the trail.

Roy wanted his diary published in full, and for this reason he remained reluctant to grant access to historians and researchers, who, he feared, might 'steal his thunder'. As a result, very little of the narrative published here for the first time has ever been seen by any but a very small and select group of family and friends. Unfortunately, the sheer size of the original manuscript has rendered it impracticable to publish it in its entirety, but every effort has been made to ensure that what is presented here is an accurate and representative sample. An explanatory linking narrative has also been added, so that Roy's experiences can be seen within the wider context of the expedition as a whole. The original diary is held by the Royal Electrical and Mechanical Engineers' Museum at Lyneham in Wiltshire, where a full typescript is available for inspection.

*

Christened Desmond Edgar Lemuel Homard, Roy was born in Dover on 18 January 1921, the middle child of five. His father was state-registered blind and the family remained impoverished throughout his childhood. After leaving school he worked first as a delivery boy and then in an aircraft factory but that wasn't the sort of life he wanted, so when a friend applied to join the army as an apprentice technician, Roy followed suit, enlisting as boy soldier B3011. At the Army Technical School in Chepstow, he mused so much about travel and exploration that he became known as 'Roy the Romancer' to his peers, and the name 'Roy' stuck ever after.

His man-service in the army began in 1939 as a general fitter with the Royal Army Ordnance Corps, just in time for the beginning of the Second World War. He moved up the ranks and by the time of his automatic transfer into the Royal Electrical and Mechanical Engineers (REME) upon its formation on 1 October 1942 he was a sergeant working on coastal defence guns. Soon afterwards he received his first posting abroad, initially to Algeria, then to the Middle East, Sicily, Italy and Austria. In October 1945 he married, but his wife, Vicky, died the following year of tubercular meningitis.

After the war, the army needed men who could repair vehicles rather than guns, so Roy re-trained and soon his REME work embraced both vehicle recovery and repairs. Promoted to Warrant Officer Class 2 in 1949, the following year he married his second wife, Enid. Some years later (after his Antarctic adventure) they adopted two boys.

In early 1953 Roy saw a notice seeking an artificer staff sergeant or WO2 used to working on tracked vehicles who would be willing to join the British North Greenland Expedition (BNGE) as a vehicle mechanic to replace one of two REME men already on secondment. Roy applied, was accepted, and served with the expedition in Greenland from August 1953 to August 1954 gaining excellent experience of working on vehicles in cold weather conditions and of the dangers of polar travel. He kept a diary during this expedition, which is also held by the REME Museum.

On the expedition's return, Roy resumed a more mundane life as a staff instructor, but that didn't last long. In January 1955 he learned that the Commonwealth Trans-Antarctic Expedition (TAE) was planning the first vehicular crossing of Antarctica. Although he had been back from Greenland for only a few months he somehow gained his wife's approval and with a nod from the army, he completed his application.

In later years, Roy liked to tell the story of how, when presented with the Polar Medal for his BNGE work, he asked the Queen if she would put in a good word for him with the expedition committee. Though it seems unlikely that Her Majesty could accede to this unconventional request, the story reveals both his enthusiasm and his boldness.

Applications for places with the expedition poured in from the UK and from Commonwealth countries around the world, but the expedition leader, Dr Vivian 'Bunny' Fuchs, naturally favoured those with previous polar experience, giving Roy a distinct advantage over his rivals. Fuchs also required his men to be physically fit, to have an 'equable nature', to be qualified in their area of expertise, and to be flexible with regard to taking on other duties that would include cooking and cleaning, as well as other heavy or unpleasant work. Roy's excellent army record and his recent experiences with the BNGE meant that he could confidently tick all those boxes. In addition – and of no small significance when considering personnel for an expedition that would require men to live and work together for many months in cramped and uncomfortable conditions – Fuchs and Roy got along. And so, despite the Queen's detachment from the decision-making process, he was appointed as number two to David Pratt, a D-Day tank-commander and Cambridge graduate who had been selected as the expedition's senior engineer.

The first stage of Fuchs's ambitious plan was to establish a foothold on the Weddell Sea coast of Antarctica, where an Advance Party of eight men would land. Their primary task would be to build the main expedition hut, though they would also be expected to conduct a limited programme of meteorological and exploratory work and to lay supply depots. Some members of the main expedition team would accompany them, but these men would stay only briefly before returning to the UK to work on the preparations for the continental crossing. An expanded team would return to the Antarctic during the following austral summer (1956-57) to take possession of the newly-completed hut. This enlarged team would broaden the scientific programme and prepare for the traverse, which would take place the summer after that. Finally, an RAF contingent would complete the first-ever aerial crossing of the continent in a single-engine aircraft.[1]

Meanwhile, on the Ross Sea side of the continent, a team from New Zealand would be responsible for route surveying and depot-laying between their base on Ross Island and the South Pole. These depots of food and fuel would be used by the main Crossing Party once they passed the South Pole, the midway point on their epic journey. The New Zealanders would be led by Sir Edmund Hillary, the conqueror of Mount Everest: a man whose worldwide celebrity had done much to raise support for the expedition in the southern hemisphere.

The expedition's plans included the completion of an extensive scientific programme, involving studies of glaciology, tides, meteorology, magnetism, and geology – but the undoubted jewel in the crown would be a running seismic survey that would resolve once and for all the question of whether Antarctica was a single continental landmass or a group of islands set in a permanently frozen sea. However, for all his championship of polar science, Fuchs knew that it was the gruelling challenge of the crossing itself that would grab the headlines, capture public interest and thereby enable him to raise the essential funds. No-one had driven a motor vehicle to the South Pole before, and no-one had crossed Antarctica from side to side. Both Wilhelm Filchner and Sir Ernest Shackleton had planned to cross but ran into insuperable difficulties before getting properly started. Success now would serve to underpin the values and determination of what politicians were repeatedly calling a new 'Elizabethan Age'. At the same time, it would help to bolster faltering British confidence in an uncertain post-war world. All of this would depend to no small degree on the competence and resilience of the two mechanical engineers who would keep the vehicles moving.

Roy's diary tells the story of his time with the TAE, both in the Advance Party and the Crossing Party. He played a crucial role in readying the vehicles for the work and in keeping them going over 2000 miles of difficult, unknown and bitterly cold terrain. He became the second serving soldier ever to reach the South Pole by surface crossing – the first being Captain Oates in 1912 – and the

---

[1] The first trans-Antarctic flight had been completed by Lincoln Ellsworth and Herbert Hollick-Kenyon in 1935, using a twin-engine Northrop Gamma named 'The Polar Star'.

first to complete a crossing coast to coast. In his honour, Mount Homard in the Shackleton Range is named after him[2] and for his contributions in Greenland and Antarctica, he was awarded the Polar Medal with clasps 'Arctic 1953-54' and 'Antarctic 1956-58'.

Upon his return Roy became a technical author at the Ministry of Defence's School of Electronic & Aeronautical Engineering at Arborfield in Berkshire, being granted a Short Service Commission on 28 October 1960. As a REME captain, he held various posts including a spell in the jungles of British Guiana in South America. He retired from REME with the rank of major at the end of March 1972. Thereafter, he worked for various organisations including the Ministry of Defence before being medically retired in June 1985. He died on 20 May 2015.

While there are more comprehensive accounts of the TAE than Roy's diary, there is probably no better *personal* record of the trials and tribulations faced and overcome by this small band of intrepid explorers. The newly-knighted Sir Vivian Fuchs and Sir Edmund Hillary co-wrote the official narrative, *The Crossing of Antarctica*,[3] and other accounts have followed, written by both expedition veterans and polar historians. All have their merits, but perhaps none is as close to the action as Roy's diary, written with numbed fingers in a wind-whipped tent amid the wastes of the Polar Plateau.

---

[2] Mount Homard (80°40'S, 29°50'W) is a mountain 1200 metres (3900 feet) high, close to the head of Blaiklock Glacier, 4 km (2 nautical miles) south of the Trey Peaks in the western part of the Shackleton Range, Antarctica. It was first mapped by the Commonwealth Trans-Antarctic Expedition in 1957.
[3] Fuchs and Hillary, *The Crossing of Antarctica: The Commonwealth Trans-Antarctic Expedition, 1955-58* (London: Cassell, 1958).

EDITORS' NOTE

The conditions under which Roy's diary was written have made it necessary to make a number of minor alterations to the text in order to facilitate reading. Square brackets enclose words added to assist clarity while round brackets are original. Occasional spelling errors and minor grammatical errors have been corrected. Paragraphs and punctuation have been adjusted where necessary and words and names abbreviated in the original have usually been given in full. The singular first-person pronoun 'I' has also been added where appropriate – usually at the beginning of sentences.

Temperatures have been changed from Fahrenheit to the nearest round number in Celsius, but measurements in feet and inches have not been converted to metric. Roy used a variety of formats for the times of day, and these have been retained throughout.

1

GETTING THERE

Monday 14 November, 1955

Last minute packing in the office. Last minute phone calls. Stephen Harper, Daily Express, *took me with trunk to Millwall Dock... Hundreds of people... Dozens of press cameras. Telephone books torn up for confetti. Small boy with copper trumpet. Last minute loadings... Ships' sirens! Stopped at Gravesend to pick up explosives. Slept well.*

After many months of preparation the expedition's ship, MV *Theron*, finally sailed from Millwall Dock a little after 4 p.m., loaded with 350 tons of provisions, vehicles, coal, hut components, twenty-four huskies, tents, and an Auster reconnaissance aircraft.

The vessel worked its way down the North Atlantic Ocean to the Cape Verde Islands, across the equator and then to Montevideo in Uruguay. During the voyage all members of the expedition took their turn in the unpleasant task of cleaning out the dogs' kennels, but otherwise they had plenty of spare time to relax, to read, to get to know one another, and, in Roy's case, to observe the unfamiliar wildlife.

In the bustling and colourful city of Montevideo Sir Edmund Hillary and his second-in-command, Bob Miller, joined the vessel. Roy and the other expeditionaries had often wondered what the world famous mountaineer would be like, but their introduction proved to be distinctly anticlimactic.

Friday 9 December, 1955
... Sir Edmund and Bob Miller of the New Zealand Party came aboard early, George[4] introduced me and of course I said, 'How do you do Sir Edmund?' and he just said, 'Hello' and was about to dash off. As he did so he turned half round and said, 'Call me Ed'...

Hillary's informality made him popular on the voyage south – but later events would have a profoundly negative impact on the perceptions of many members of the expedition.

The *Theron* sailed for South Georgia on the 10th, reaching the island six days later. On the 20th, with her oil and freshwater tanks replenished and with her rails festooned with whale meat to feed the dogs, Captain Harald Marø turned her bow southwards, towards the Weddell Sea and Antarctica.

It was at this point that Fuchs decided to take a calculated risk. He knew that two voyages into the ice-strewn Weddell Sea had met with unusually benign conditions. The first was that of Captain James Weddell, after whom the sea was named, in 1823. The second had been that of the Argentinian icebreaker, *General San Martin*, as recently as the austral summer of 1954-55. In his ship, the *Jane*, Weddell had reached a latitude of 74°S almost unhindered. The Argentinians had been less fortunate, but they had still sailed further south in a direct course than anyone since Weddell. What linked these two expeditions was that both had sailed much further to the west than was commonly the case, with the vast majority of navigators preferring the security of a south-easterly 'coastal lead' discovered by William Bruce on board the *Scotia* in 1904. This coastal lead could usually be relied upon to provide access to the southern ice shelf but its grave disadvantage, in Fuchs's eyes at least, was that it added a considerable mileage to his route. He now reasoned that, if his luck held, he might be able to replicate the success of the *Jane* and the *General San Martin*, and reach his destination in Vahsel Bay much sooner than would otherwise be the case. This would allow him a much greater window of opportunity to conduct building and survey work before he was forced to leave the Advance Party to its own devices.

---

[4] George Lowe: a veteran of the 1953 Everest expedition and a close friend of Hillary's. He would serve as photographer and cameraman travelling with the Crossing Party.

Unfortunately, his luck did not hold and from 22 December onwards, the *Theron* was engaged in a constant battle with ice.

Thursday 22 December, 1955
Through the night it snowed and got a bit swelly... During the early afternoon we started to see bergy bits floating past and they gradually became more frequent. From then on conditions improved from the heavy starboard swell we'd been having all morning and most of the afternoon. I had a sea sickness pill and went to sleep. I managed to wake up well enough to get up for supper at a quarter to six; now we were getting a whole lot of sea-ice float by. A few times we've had to push into some pieces and at 7.45 p.m. this evening, reduced speed to ride onto and push away some heavy sea-ice for a distance. Now we're in a lead again and going 'full'. Captain Marø is up in the crow's nest steering from there... Some of the ice is quite big and seems to be bergs from glaciers. Some that have been well broken up and washed over and over by the waves have formed many weird shapes, some like swans. Again we slowed right down to ride over some ice. A thump and some crunching and swirling waters and the big flat pieces split and get pushed along under our bows then slide out to the side.

Friday 23 December, 1955
... there were times when the ship didn't split and push the ice away. Then it would continue pushing for a few minutes and the engines [were] ordered to go into reverse to take another run... Some of the thumping jarred hard right through the ship but the chaps in the fo'castle got the worst shaking...

The ice has become more dense during the day and we don't get many runs of clear water. We have seen several seals from a distance lying on the ice and an emperor penguin was seen. Once, whilst we were stopped for better conditions a few of us saw a seal playing in the water alongside the ship. We've had a few silver grey petrels and snow petrels about and some Antarctic petrels, whilst the cape pigeons have now left us...

On 26 December Fuchs decided to launch the Auster, so that the pilot, Squadron Leader John Lewis AFC, could seek out the best route to follow. He subsequently reported that although they had been passing through a bad area, he could see good leads to the south-east. This promising report proved inaccurate and in the days and weeks ahead the ship regularly got stuck and it became necessary for the crew and expedition members to lend their muscle in the increasingly desperate attempts to break her free.

Tuesday 3 January, 1956

... During the afternoon some of our chaps and a few of the crew started 'digging' the ship out. It was very hard work digging the snow and slush and breaking up the ice with axes and crowbars. The crowbars could break up the ice binding the ship for five feet down but a lot of ice is further than that...

A four pound charge was placed about thirty feet in front of the bows and... produced a fair-sized broken-up area of ice but didn't crack it up all over the floe. So we carried on picking at the ice on the starboard side and had that just about as clear as we could when the second officer got the bo'sun to rig up the winch and fix the steel cable to a firm hummock of ice.

The engines went full astern and the forward winch took in the cable. There was a squealing and a creaking with the strain on the cable and then suddenly it went slack, for it had parted near the winch. So the engine... packed in, together with the rest of us, who were hungry. I and a few others were wet and cold too, through dropping through the slush into water underneath. At one point I had to crawl in water and slush on hands and knees...

At about 7.45 p.m. tonight four pounds of Nobel 704 were detonated in the ice near our stern and did a fine job bringing up some heavy slabs from under us. Since then the engines have been running but we can't move. We're going to have some more bangs...

With the constant disappointments, the physical and mental exhaustion, and the fact that Fuchs's choice of route now seemed more likely to reduce rather than increase the time during which the Advance Party would be supported in their work, morale began to suffer – though Roy's experiment with his home-made snow-shoes provided some much-needed comic relief.

Friday 6 January, 1956

The poor old ship kept up its struggles through the night but this morning we were in the same spot as last night and this evening we... got free but are firmly jammed again...

I produced the biggest laugh of the day by trying out my snow-shoes. I got onto the snow and tied the shoes securely to my boots and strode off... I should have kept my eyes open and trodden warily for, after about four paces, I sank into water up past my knees. I had to flounder out on all fours in the slush. If I'd known that so many people were watching me from the bridge, I'd have gone more carefully...

Adding to frustration over the delay was the fact that another vessel, the *Tottan*, carrying a scientific expedition for the Royal Society, had left home over a week later than the *Theron*, but having employed a longer, more prudent route had already made landfall. In theory, the TAE might locate its base at the same place as the Royal Society's expedition, and the diary entry for 6 January continues:

We heard this morning that Tottan *has found a spot where the ice cliff runs smoothly down to the sea ice and they have landed, although they might not settle there.*
In any case it might not be suitable for us as it is north of... Dawson Lambton Glacier – which we would have to travel over, or find a way round. We would be better off at, or near, Vahsel Bay...

In the meantime, the *Theron* could only battle on. Sometimes she escaped and made progress, but the problems with ice were proving insurmountable. The vessel steamed backwards and forwards, and round and back on itself. Ultimately, little could be done but to retreat northwards and find a different route. This decision was rendered easier when Captain Marø's radio operator made contact with HMS *Protector*, a Royal Navy ice-patrol ship, whose captain offered helicopter support to find a way forward. A rendezvous was arranged, but the events of 18 January, Roy's birthday, made the meeting seem a very distant prospect.

Wednesday 18 January, 1956
What a terrible day to have a birthday. I don't feel like celebrating because the ship is temporarily out of action. This morning we were stuck again although we had done about four miles in the night. The ship took a hell of a thumping as we got into some very thick ice...

I was on dogs again with John Lewis and Peter Jeffries and after cleaning and putting in snow for them, we helped poling. Some of the most magnificent work was done today in getting free. Great masses of ice were winched free and poled away. Some as big as twenty feet square and fifteen feet thick... Then we crashed through thinner ice to another lead and then ran into some more very thick and heavy stuff that, after repeated head-on attacks, failed to give. We were stuck... Four explosive charges have failed to free her although the last, at about 8 p.m., loosened some great chunks of ice so it was decided to winch one very big piece clear from the stern. The ship's engine was going to sweep the ice debris that was on the surface away, when suddenly the steel cable and hand rope were torn out of Bob Miller's hands up near the starboard bow and he shouted, 'It's got the propeller!' I yelled to the bridge, 'Stop the engine,' and everyone seemed to be spellbound...

This happened at 8.10 p.m. and now at 9.15 p.m. we await developments. The cable has been cut and they are trying to work it back from the propeller with the engine turning slowly on the starter...

At about 9.20 p.m. the engine was run and a rhythmic grating noise came up from the propeller. Then the engine stopped. Five minutes later it was run again and after a minute of grating it quietened to its normal sound.

About this point I took a bottle of beer that I had saved since New Year and put on my pullover. We all had a good session and then another 'bang'. We still didn't move but a couple of bits of ice went through the Auster wing which caused much gloom to Peter Weston. At last, at about 12.25 a.m., a new big bang loosened the ship and everyone was happy...

We are now charging to-and-fro at the ice but what terrible ogres rear their ugly heads. Peter Weston this morning was disenchanted, after nine weeks, to find that [the] dogs have been urinating on the spare Auster crate and Bunny has [only] just brought it up. Oh dear! ...

The next day another potentially disastrous situation arose when a collision with the ice bent the ship's rudder but, in a remarkable and daring gamble, Marø deliberately backed the vessel into an ice floe and managed to straighten it sufficiently to continue.

Many weeks of summer had been lost but when they finally rendezvoused with HMS *Protector* on 23 January they made better progress by heading south-east along the coast. Four days later the expedition members set foot on Antarctica for the first time, at the Royal Society's newly established base at Halley Bay.

The Royal Society was taking part in the forthcoming International Geophysical Year (IGY). The programme involved sixty-seven countries and some 30,000 scientists working on projects right across the world, including oceanography, meteorology and the launching of satellites into orbit. An important element focused on Antarctica and the base at Halley Bay constituted the UK's contribution. The IGY was entirely separate from the TAE and while the two teams co-operated, the expeditions remained distinct projects, independently funded.

The *Theron* left Halley Bay the next day and continued along the coast to Vahsel Bay where, with the assistance of the Auster, they eventually found a suitable place to land. Thus, many weeks later than intended, they had finally arrived.

Sunday 29 January, 1956
Here at last. We steamed through the night (in daylight) sometimes with a lead near the shore of several miles and at one or two spots only a ship's length to go through...

At 6 a.m. we were drifting one mile off the coast and at 0740 the plane took off for a recce, returning at 0830. It took off again at 0945 and the ship moved towards Vahsel Bay going through loose pack. At around midday we arrived at Vahsel Bay and the plane went up, then came down at 1345... The recce showed Vahsel Bay to be badly crevassed behind and not suitable generally, so we moved on.

We went full ahead along the ice shelf until we came to a likely spot earlier seen from the air. At about 1930 we arrived at the place we've now found to be suitable – somewhere about seventeen miles north east of the Argentinian Base, Belgrano...

[We] took off after putting ice anchors in to have a look at the terrain which sloped up about 1:6 behind our bay ice. Pretty good with a couple of rugged ridges up the hill and some old filled-in crevasses...

Aside from the fact that they were six weeks behind schedule, it must have been a great relief to make landfall – though, strictly speaking, they were not on land at all but on the Filchner Ice Shelf, a vast body of floating ice permanently fixed to the continental landmass. After a brief survey Fuchs chose what he felt was a safe location for 'Shackleton Base', about three quarters of a mile uphill from the sea.

Until the ship left, the men of the Advance Party could continue to eat and sleep on board, but their late arrival meant that the vessel could stay for only a few days, so unloading must be expedited.

Monday 30 January, 1956
... We will be working 8 a.m. to 11.30 p.m.

Today we started off at -14°C and a 15 knot wind so it was quite biting to the face... Unloading went well with dogs off the ship and put on lines and a lot of deck cargo such as oxygen and acetylene bottles, three ton sledges, aircraft cradle and floats, seals, etc., unloaded...

This evening... the sun was shining brightly, well up at midnight. All dogs howling madly all day...

Roy's particular task during the expedition would be the maintenance of the assorted motor vehicles, with the Advance Party's fleet including two specially adapted Ferguson farm tractors, two Studebaker 'Weasel' tracked vehicles, and one state-of-the-art Tucker 'Sno-Cat'. The next day he had his first taste of just how onerous his responsibility would be with the clutch of one tractor completely frozen and all but the Sno-Cat requiring constant coaxing and attention. Once they were running satisfactorily – at least for the time being – Roy could visit the site of the new base for the first time, though he could see little bar the flags which marked the intended locations for stores and equipment.

The unloading work continued apace, while everyone – particularly Fuchs and Marø – kept a keen eye on the weather. When it deteriorated, they came close to disaster.

Wednesday 1 February, 1956
... We knew that the barometer was dropping... About 3 p.m. this afternoon I began to find it a little difficult to find the route [to base] as a bit of a blizzard had sprung up... when we got to the ship we found that the wind was battering the ship against the ice and bergy bits were surrounding it, while the sea slopped up round the stern and up over the ice and was beginning to flow amongst our stores. Everything stopped for recovery. Theron's stern

mooring parted at 1715hrs and she had to get away from the ice edge, disappearing in thick spray, wind and snow.

We shifted several loads a good way in and then things began to look desperate. The pool of sea water was swirling in still and had covered quite a large area so that now a good number of boxes were in the water. I waded in up to my ankles to try to recover some boxes and found that they were very heavy and were boxes of spares for the vehicles. I managed to shift a few and Hannes waded in and helped but some others didn't intend doing anything...

At this time the Sno-Cat was in danger of getting into deep water... so decided to go and drive it clear if we could get it going. Unfortunately the 2x 12v batteries were down... but eventually... I got it running... By this time the sea water was lapping around... I got it turned round and moved away about 150 yards... My fingers were frozen and my trousers were frozen and burning into my icy knees and my boots were full of freezing water and the blizzard was pretty thick and strong...

By then the ship had reappeared and we were supposed to get on it as best we could while five others up at the base site would have to do their best in a Weasel or tent with no extra clothing or bedding and nothing to cook with. I know that they had plenty of pickles and milk though...

Great bergy bits had washed up where the ship had been and parts of the ice edge had broken away so the ship had difficulty enough without the wind, snow and rough sea. Capt. Marø on the bridge starboard wing calmly signalled into the bridge and magnificently brought the ship along a firm head of ice and one by one we jumped and scrambled onto the side on the two rope ladders that the crew were holding onto.

I grabbed the side of the ship and hauled myself on the six inch ledge against the Auster crate whose top I could just reach for steadying myself. Big Fred[5] got on top and hauled me up and I was able to get down into the ship...

There was a grave danger of losing a lot of stores with large pieces of ice breaking off, but we don't know for the ship has had to put to sea with those of us who had been on the ice and cruise around. It will be a heavy blow to lose any hut or vehicle parts, tools, etc., as they are vital. Of food we have an extra year's total supply, so, for instance, sausages can always be eaten instead of

---

[5] A member of the ship's crew.

bacon but a spare dynamo will never make a gearbox, nor a roof section into a truss.

I was jolly glad to get into warm dry clothing... I've got a touch of frostbite on my knees from the wet trousers...

Naturally there was much concern for the five men who had been unable to reach the ship before her unplanned departure. In the event, they survived a cramped and chilly night huddled together in a Weasel but, uncertain as they must have been as to whether the ship would ever return, their plight had been profoundly unenviable.

By the time the vessel returned on 2 February everything left near the sea lay partially submerged, but nothing had been lost and the unloading could continue. By 7 February, the vessel was empty – and not a moment too soon. The sea had begun the inexorable process of freezing over, meaning that the *Theron* must depart at once or risk being trapped for the winter.

Tuesday 7 February, 1956
... It was decided that the ship must leave so we took off our last things and handed back all that we'd borrowed...

Cine-cameras were out and lots of other cameras and there were very cheerful and sincere goodbyes and handshakes going on all over the place. There should be some good movie stuff. At about five past three, or quarter of an hour after the ship had left us, the ice rushed in with a loud whispering and rustling, pushing along and rafting the new 'frazzle' ice[6] into slushy heaps. And then there was this great mass of pack-ice tight up against the fixed ice where Theron *has been. As the ship left she turned round and then blew a signal of three siren blasts and someone fired off some coloured signals, one of which I got on Kodachrome. Waving went on for ages...*

We came up to base in the Sno-Cat at 8 p.m. and found the Sno-Cat crate erected and being made into a hut inside and with floor and door. All the tents were up and sleeping bags in them and Primuses filled. All Ken's work. So we had our first Antarctic supper, communally, in the Sno-Cat crate. Sausage, bacon and tomato all mixed up and then cocoa. Ralph brought out a very large home-made cake and we all had a large slice...

---

[6] Frazzle ice: a collection of loose plate- or disc-shaped ice crystals.

2

SURVIVAL

The eight men were now left to fend for themselves. Things could have been different had the ship arrived sooner as the rest of the team would have helped make a proper start on the main hut. Instead they had departed after just nine days without starting the job at all. They hadn't even managed to transport all the supplies to the hut site, with some 300 tons still on the ice at the landing point.

With hindsight, it seems reasonable to ask whether the Advance Party should have been left in this way to face an Antarctic winter with its fierce winds, bitter cold, and darkness – and with absolutely no hope of rescue in the event of an accident. At the time, however, no-one considered abandoning the project: to have done so would have been humiliating for all concerned, and the establishment of a toe-hold on Antarctica was integral to Fuchs's plans for future success. It also appears that each member of the Advance Party felt he had a job to do and that he was going to get on with it no matter what.

Who were the men left on the ice? Ken Blaiklock, a professional surveyor, was their leader – though he always considered himself, at least among the experienced team members, as more of a first among equals. His second in command, Ralph Lenton, was both radio operator and carpenter, and the man tasked with leading the construction of the hut. Roy, meanwhile, as sole engineer, had accepted responsibility not only for the five motor vehicles but also for resolving whatever mechanical and electrical problems might arise. All three men possessed previous polar experience and were holders of the prestigious Polar Medal.

Of the less experienced expeditionaries, three, R.H.A. (Tony) Stewart, Peter Jeffries (Jeff) and the South African, Johannes (Hannes) La Grange, were meteorologists; Dr Rainer (Rhino) Goldsmith would serve as medical officer and physiologist; while Sergeant Ellis (Taffy) Williams, a member of the TAE's RAF contingent, was the radio operator. Also requiring food and accommodation were twenty-four huskies, needed to haul sledges for exploratory work early the next summer, plus the pups they had whelped on the voyage down.

The Advance Party's first concern, of course, must be shelter – but there could be no question of their simply throwing up the main hut. That task would take many weeks of hard work to complete. Instead, they turned their attention to a wooden crate – the one in which the Sno-cat had completed its voyage south, lashed to the deck of the *Theron*. Measuring 21' x 9' and 8' high, the crate was quite large – but it was still just a box, without doors, windows, or any other form of modification to render it more comfortable – at least, that is, until Ralph Lenton began work on essential alterations. Too small for anyone but the duty cook to sleep in, this flimsy structure would serve as kitchen, radio shack and mess-room; at night the remaining seven explorers would be forced to retreat to their two-man tents. Surely there could be no better motivation for expediting hut-building operations.

Wednesday 8 February, 1956
... The Sno-Cat 'hut' (crate) is coming along fine with window and floor and tomorrow, Ralph said he'll have a table. We stopped early tonight to recuperate and so just moved some food cases to correct places. The ice is thick and heavy all round us now, so it is a good job Theron *did not stay a minute longer.*

Attempts were made right away to make contact with the outside world but the radio lacked power. For Roy's part, vehicle problems challenged him from the start, with tracks needing to be changed, throttles jamming and steering brakes failing.

Friday 10 February, 1956
... I've stripped down the brakes on one Fergy that had no brake steering and found the drums and shoes coated with ice where snow had entered and melted.[7] I've made some patent Homard

---

[7] The TAE's Ferguson tractors had been converted to 'full track' for use on snow and ice. Conversion involved locking the tractors' front wheels so that a caterpillar-type track could be passed around them and the large rear drive wheels. This modification rendered the steering wheel

Snow Excluders which I'm sure will work. It was a big job on my own removing and re-fitting tracks and wheels...

Ralph has done all the work and all the cooking too... producing some jolly good food on the Primuses and [he] strives for variety – even to making custard to go with the dried peaches. But we miss salt as it hasn't yet been located.

If working in polar conditions was proving difficult, sleeping in tents was no less so. Each man's bag rested on a sheepskin which in turn lay on a ground-sheet. This approach would provide insulation and a moisture barrier for the sleeping-bag's occupant when lying on snow – or so the theory went.

Monday 20 February, 1956
... As my bed has got so damp from moisture collected between the rubber ground sheet and the sheepskin, I had it all out and I had my double sleeping bag and canvas cover to pieces. From the sheepskin in its centre panel, I could and did, wring out streams of water, although it must sound impossible... I have rolled the rubber ground sheet out of it and have put my sheepskin on top of some canvas and old sack. Let my perspiration stick to the ice instead of soaking my bed...

Meanwhile, day-to-day tasks continued. Ralph Lenton started on the main hut, the meteorologists carried out regular observations between other more physical work and Roy patiently worked on his vehicles, while also helping in other ways whenever necessary.

Saturday 25 February, 1956
... I did quite a lot of welding today [for the base of the hut] which should have been done in UK... The grillage is going on quite well...

We each received our three month's chocolate ration today, two dozen two-ounce bars of milk Cadbury's and two dozen two-ounce bars of Caramello filled. One bar every second day...

---

redundant, making it necessary to steer by braking the left and right tracks independently.

In Antarctica, drift snow presents an insuperable problem, with fine snow penetrating the tiniest hole or gap so that a vehicle cab, for example, fills very quickly if not completely sealed. In the Advance Party's makeshift world holes and gaps abounded – and Roy's 'hutch', a workshop built from surplus materials, proved particularly vulnerable.

Thursday 1 March, 1956

A day of appalling weather. A northerly wind started this morning and by 10.30 p.m. had got quite bad with thick ground drift. The drift increased when it started to snow as well. Building work was suspended but I was able to carry on…

I've started snow-proofing the shack as drift streamed through everywhere covering everything inside…[8] *The north wind has brought warmth as well as drift, up to -8°C today. Only trouble is that snow melts into the wind-proofs so they become very damp and can then freeze like a sheet of steel at a change of temperature…*

The colder weather of a couple of days ago produced the old embrittlement troubles. When hammering a cranked claw crowbar under a packing case lid one of the claws broke off. Later, the other claw broke off…

Friday 2 March, 1956

A very good day from my work point of view as there was no wind, or only slight, and a temperature of -7°C. Snow fell all day, sometimes light, sometimes heavy. Ken said it wasn't so good on the building with drift…

To replace the four main truss plates which John lost into the sea, I have today cut up four steel base plates which were for the bonfire boilers. I cut them by oxy-acetylene and also the six holes in each…

Tremendous drifts are now spread all over the site for up to about twenty feet long and four feet high and with present light conditions it is impossible to see them. This makes it difficult driving and walking. The pups sometimes bound into one and nose-dive into it when their front feet sink in up to their chests…

---

[8] In this instance, Roy is referring to his workshop rather than the Sno-Cat crate.

Saturday 3 March, 1956
Probably our most bitter day yet with a south wind blowing all day between thirteen and twenty knots and bringing plenty of drift with it and temperatures between -21°C and -23°C...

Food wasn't sufficient tonight so Hannes had to cook another lot. I had so much that I didn't fancy a tin of Tuborg although it is Saturday night... I've had to have three of Rhino's collodion tablets for indigestion.

A terrific argument arose about expeditions with and without cooks, and scientists doing no work other than their own work...

The lack of a professional cook on this expedition obliged every man to take a turn in the kitchen. During his four-day stint the duty cook benefited from sleeping in the comparative warmth of the crate, which also allowed him to dry out his sleeping kit. In return, his duties were onerous, including the production of hearty breakfasts, lunches and dinners on Primus stoves, as well as catering for two breaks in the morning and afternoon. That wasn't all. Two paraffin stoves were used to heat metal tubs to produce water for drinking, cooking and washing. With a snow to ice ratio of just 10:1 these needed to be filled regularly – another task that fell to the cook.

Cooking was surely the most important regular job at Shackleton, but many dreaded it. Two men in particular started off very badly – the meteorologist Hannes La Grange, who shared a tent with Roy, and the doctor, Rhino Goldsmith. On one occasion La Grange made soup from watered cocoa sauce from the previous day's supper; Roy thought it 'almost drinkable after adding a large dose of Bovril'. For his part, Goldsmith could be careless, knocking over a dixie of tea and letting soup boil over. He also produced peas 'still so hard... that he tried putting them through the mincer'. Other members of the expedition proved to be excellent cooks, foremost among them being Lenton who, towards the end of March, 'gave us some very fine rissoles and a plateful of fritters, fruit and custard – a very fine and tasteful effort'.

Of course, the dogs also needed feeding – a job that would become far more manageable once they were brought up from the bottom of the snow slope.

Sunday 4 March, 1956

Terrible day again... around -24°C with 17 knot wind from the south bringing plenty of drift with it. Very chilling...

During the afternoon the twenty-one dogs were brought up. One end of the line was fixed to the rear of the Weasel and the other end to a tractor, so the line was kept tight enough to keep the dogs from getting close to each other.

The two teams were brought up separately and then Tio and Kusie and Beauty attached to sledges and the dogs loved it and went mad with delight pulling and straining with every muscle... Once up here they made a continual din and when the second team arrived it was four times as bad. They jumped, strained and leapt at their chains, pawed the snow, wagged their tails, howled, rubbed their faces in the snow and rolled on their backs in it. No doubt we shall hear them at all hours during the night...

Monday 5 March, 1956

A very good working day...

I had quite a lot of work to do digging out the stores tunnel inside and out as the drift was terrific. Then I set to and made bits of wood to fit in between the boxes and finally piled all the drift snow up the side of the tunnel wall of boxes. I went back after supper to finish it off and dig a six-foot pit part-way along the tunnel to make a lavatory.

The building group are getting near to erecting the trusses but a whole lot of square plates with a 5/8 inch bolt hole in each are missing. This is causing serious apprehension...

Tuesday 6 March, 1956

A terrible day that stopped everyone from working except me...

All the chaps in the Sno-Cat hut got busy on [clothing] repairs, etc. and then settled down to a word-making game called 'Scrabble'...

Shifting the 300 tons of stores from the sea-ice up to the base continued – but with each load weighing approximately 1 ton and with a maximum of only fifteen trips possible each day, this meant that even on a good day only 5 per cent of the total stockpile could be shifted.

The work required good weather and efficient vehicles. But Roy was already having problems with the Sno-Cat. It should have been by far the best piece of equipment on site, but it was now failing to pull loads up the hill. He also had to tend to other matters such as repairing the 'pop-pop', a small, noisy but important portable generator. In fact he was so busy that Blaiklock asked if he would like to be excused from cooking for a while. Roy dutifully responded that he would take his turn at the hated work, while no doubt welcoming the opportunity to dry his kit properly.

Thursday 8 March, 1956

A highly successful day's cooking and I shall be glad when the next three days are over.

There could have been a little more porridge. The breakfast of sausage, bacon and beans with a slice of bread made up for it. Lunch was soup of stock with bacon fat, Bovril, cabbage water and Bisto. Then corned beef, cabbage, creamed onion and dried strip potato.

Supper was curried stewed steak with raisins, sultanas and apple and with it, Pom [potato], rice and tinned Brussels sprouts. After, we had stewed dried peaches and custard. I forgot that, for lunch, I fried rounds of delicious batter.

In between time I ran the Sno-Cat for a bit and in the afternoon, re-adjusted the distributor points on Tony's Weasel as it died on him gradually. The distributor shaft bush is worn and the points were hardly opening...

The other chaps worked on the hut...

Friday 9 March, 1956

... A very successful day's cooking with many congratulations from the boys... Doing all of this cooking in Billy cans on three Primus stoves is a bit of a fatigue.

The boys have manhandled, with the aid of a Fergy, three trusses into position and it was a difficult job, but they are confident and very glad to see things going up...

No. 2 Weasel of Tony's conked out after giving no power and I found that the contact points were hardly opening due to a worn distributor shaft bush. When I'd fixed it he said it had so much power that it nearly leaped out of his hands...

Saturday 10 March, 1956

A nasty day which started very well by being sunny and calm, but the south wind came up and we had drift at fifteen knots and temperature -20°C.

I'm writing in bed at 10 a.m. not having done the washing up as my eyes are red and very painful, due it would seem, to all the Primus fumes in the Sno-Cat hut from cooking and heating. Rhino has put some Strow liquid paraffin in and sent me to bed with four tablets to take away the pain and make me sleep...

Monday 12 March, 1956

Not a bad sort of day but we had -29°C in the night... I kept waking up and squirming and my stomach muscles were quite aching when I got up.

The temperature rose during the day to about -19°C around 2 p.m. and fell to -29°C this evening. It was very unpleasant working on the Sno-Cat engine with no finger gloves...

One of the major problems for an engineer working with small engine parts in such cold conditions is to keep his hands warm enough to function. In ideal conditions, Roy wore four layers of gloves, but all too often it proved impossible to do things properly with them on. He also tried a single pair of silk gloves; these permitted greater sensitivity but they lost all insulation when they became impregnated with grease. Given the impossibility of avoiding grease, his only recourse was to work in short bursts, making the completion of every task more time consuming.

All eight trusses are up on one side of the hut floor now and it looks quite impressive. About time I organised some film and took some pictures...

Today, being sunny, Rhino hung out his 'bedding', but at -29°C I'm sure it couldn't have done much good. He also opened the tent flaps and the puppies got in and had a rare old time. Little pools everywhere, and amongst their pryings they found Tony's chocolate and ate or mutilated nine bars. Tony is our biggest chocolate addict and was very upset.

Saturday 17 March, 1956

... I got the deep pit lavatory finished and I'm very proud of it...

By mid-March all attempts at making contact with the outside world had been unsuccessful. While it was still just light enough to see at eleven o'clock in the evening, summer was undoubtedly past and it was getting colder. With no proper accommodation, no outside contact, and winter rapidly approaching, things looked very bleak. Nonetheless, the hut builders continued to do their best and Roy fought to keep the vehicles operational. Then, when he was well into stripping the Sno-Cat engine, a seven-day blizzard tore across the site.

Tuesday 20 March, 1956
... This morning was good with -13°C but after tea break (midday) we had the start of bad weather. Wind... was twenty seven knots this evening. Temperature went down to -26°C and the drift was the heaviest yet. Everyone packed up and so did I at 6 p.m. for a change. They were all playing Scrabble in the hut and after supper, I had my first game...

While we were playing Scrabble Jeff had to go out to do the meteorological observation and couldn't get the door open for drift outside. It took a long time using a shovel from the inside...

I told the boys today, after having had tinned peas for supper (with frittered Spam, etc.) the secret of the mint-flavoured peas, that they had commented on when I was cook. I had used half an inch of Mentasol chlorophyll toothpaste... Rhino especially thought it a very good idea...

Wednesday 21 March, 1956
A very nasty day. We heard the wind outside the tent this morning and didn't expect a normal 8 a.m. call for breakfast. We didn't get it either. I think it must have been about 10 a.m. when Tony called us. The wind and drift were terrible and so was the temperature. It was -33°C this morning dropping early this evening to -37°C... The wind has been about twenty six knots and the drift very heavy. Most unpleasant outside so people rarely went out...

With the stove and oil lamp my deep lavatory is the most comfortable and popular lavatory...

The Sno-Cat, with its engine innards laid bare, is thick with packed snow under the tarpaulin – I'd rather not write about it.

We played Scrabble during the morning and had some good fun... Ralph pushed off to bed in the afternoon and when we 'halloed' for supper he didn't arrive. We continued our Scrabble and then I found that we couldn't get out... It was quite impossible to push the door open more than a few inches at the top corner... Rhino, Hannes and I had to shout many times in unison for Ralph to dig us out...

An early night to bed at about 9.15 p.m. and now it is 10.35 p.m. It was quite enough just to come from the Shack to the tent a few yards, with catching of breath and nose tingling but getting down to the tent opening with swirling drift hitting straight into the face was blindingly bitter...

Thursday 22 March, 1956
A terrible day and this evening is something worse than I have ever before experienced.

During the night we had -42°C; this morning -37°C, with -42°C again during the day. Wind has been about twenty eight knots but this evening is very much stronger – about thirty five knots we think. Drift is so heavy that from the Shack I could only just see the tent tops a few yards away, the rest being a speeding milky blur.

I got to the tent alright but had an awful job trying to bend down to undo the flap. Temporary blindness was immediate from stinging drift in the face and it was impossible to breathe...

A wonderful relief to be inside and after a bit of fumbling I got the paraffin lamp alight and then the Primus stove, but methylated spirit takes a lot of lighting these days. The tent walls are violently beating and banging, isolating us from any other noises from the other tents. Having had to spend the day in the Shack my eyes are very painful from Primus fumes and I can hardly keep them open...

Ken is a bit worried about the dogs as the snow is not drifting round them for a shield and they have to put up with -42°C with no wind protection...

Friday 23 March, 1956
Another wicked day of wind and drift and this morning Hannes estimated that the temperatures in the night had probably gone down to -45°C...

After using the lavatory I was... trapped and I had to wait for Rhino to come and dig me out. We always send out someone if anyone is away for half [an] hour or so in this weather.

Ken fed the dogs and Ralph heated up the waste food with Red Heart for the puppies.[9] All are lively enough…

I made a brave effort… and went across to the Petroleum, Oil and Lubricant dump… I had time to see the ginormous drift on the north side of the skeleton main hut. It really is a monster. Starting from near the hut it mounts upwards to nearly the height of the hut and spreads away northwards for about thirty or forty yards. What, I wonder, is buried underneath? What, I wonder, is under the Sno-Cat tarpaulin – engine partly dismantled and open…

Saturday 24 March, 1956
This dreadful weather continues… The Shack door was drifted right up so we had to clamber in over a wall of food boxes under the tarpaulin of the lean-to against the Shack. Once in there the route to breakfast ran through an aperture cut in the Shack wall, about twenty-six inches by thirty inches. To get through this needed careful negotiating by our more hefty companions like Rhino and Hannes. So, breakfast at about twelve, then on to Scrabble again. Later, some of them (Ken, Ralph, Taffy and Tony) played Bridge or was it Whist?

The dogs had a tin of warmed Red Heart today as frozen seal is a bit too much for them in this weather…

Not only does the wind prevent breathing but forces some air to be swallowed in gulps… I wore my blizzard mask but the drift very soon got behind every edge and in every aperture until a layer of ice was formed inside. That which clung to the eyelashes melted and froze into big swimming masses around the eyes. With fingers in mitt-type leather gloves and duffels the only way to clear it is to take off the glove and wipe the ice and water away from the eyes. This gives a fine smooth coat of drift to the hand, and numbs the fingers, so that even back in the glove they never regain their former warmth and are dead, to later become painful in thawing out.

I had a cold night last night, mainly with cold coming up into my back and also my feet. I am not alone in this for most seem similarly to suffer. We all wake up many times in the night. The sleeping bags are all wet and frozen…

---

[9] Red Heart: a dogfood manufactured in the United States.

Sunday 25 March, 1956
The same blizzard is still going after its sixth day and we now tend to ask each other: 'I suppose it will have to stop sometime?' Perhaps that ought not to be asked until after thirty days. By that time we might as well resign ourselves to living the winter in the Sno-Cat crate – our shack. Whatever would we have done without it? Thirty-five knot wind and temperature -32°C...

I slept very badly last night with the cold, especially coming through the underside. In the end the blanket that I use around me in the iced bags I had to lie on instead, which left me cold on top. This evening I got out woollen underpants and vest, a Norwegian pullover and my woollen inner trousers. These I am wearing in bed in addition to battledress trousers, one pair of socks, one cotton vest, one string vest, one khaki flannel shirt and one woollen jersey. In the day the wind-proofs go over it all. Outside I wear a sheep-skin nose and cheek warmer in addition to a Balaclava helmet, blizzard mask and windproof hood. And other things! ...

Monday 26 March, 1956
Well, it stopped, and quite suddenly, at about 3 p.m....

I went out to the dogs at about 4 p.m. after I had noticed they were getting up, giving themselves a good shaking and rubbing their faces in the snow to clear the frozen snow from their eyes... [They] were in very good shape after their seven days of exposure to blizzard with temperatures below -40°C and winds of over forty knots. I never cease to wonder at their hardiness...

I noticed that the beating of the wind had caused the two planks supporting the Terylene tarpaulin over the Sno-Cat engine compartment to break right through. A glance under the tarpaulin told me the worst. The partly dismantled engine that I'd been working on had piled high with snow. In fact, under the tarpaulin it was one great and solid mound of snow as hard as iron. The body of the Sno-Cat was full up too...

No. 1 Weasel had snow only in the back and the uncovered engine only a thin film. No. 2 Weasel was full up and under the engine cover was a solid block of hard snow. The Ferguson batteries hadn't enough life to turn the engine but Ralph started it after turning it on the handle about thirty turns...

The drift by the hut skeleton is a small hill that can never be moved...

Tuesday 27 March, 1956

Today we surveyed the full measure of damage of the seven-day blizzard. It is pretty disheartening. Not only have seven days' work been lost, but it has set us back a few days in repairing the damage. No. 2 Weasel was absolutely choked with hard-packed snow. The engine compartment up to the cover and down to the floor was solid. Under the floor there was not an inch without hard packed snow. The exhaust pipe was partly full. The rear axle packed tightly in snow in its compartment. The heater was full right up, even the inlet and outlet pipes, and the radiator was quite blocked... I got out all that I could, which still left the engine tightly packed, and then stripped the heater. With the hot air from it, all of the snow was melted and the engine warmed by two and a half hours and ten pints of paraffin... The whole thing took about seven and a half hours...

After getting the Weasel out of its drifted hole I got on to the Sno-Cat where I nearly wept. Under the tarpaulin was a great mound of snow and every bit of the partly dismantled V8-cylinder engine was full up with hard snow...

We all feel sorry for each other...

Roy skirts over the impact on morale of these appalling events, but in his diary entry for the same date Goldsmith noted: 'Ralph gave vent to his bad mood complaining about the food and then the appalling way we are living. He attacked poor Ken about the general lack of organization. The attack left its scar and breakfast was even more gloomy than usual.'[10]

Worse – much worse – was to come.

Wednesday 28 March, 1956

A dreadful loss was discovered today. Ken and Tony went down in a Weasel to see how the path had fared in the blizzard with a view to bringing up more stores soon. Visibility wasn't too good and the sea was covered with dense frost-smoke turning into cloud and blowing away from the shore...

They noticed that the sea looked a bit near and soon discovered going along the sea-ice, that all the stores were no longer there. A

[10] Rainer Goldsmith & Anthea Arnold, *Eight Men in a Crate: The Ordeal of the Advance Party of the Trans-Antarctic Expedition, 1955-1957* (Norwich: The Erskine Press, 2007), p. 60.

small amount was left but the main part was gone and in its place was a bay of black cold water. A very large expanse of our fixed ice had broken off right through the dump and only a nice white cliff showed where it was once attached...

Among the things lost are the Ferguson tractor with digging blade, all of our coal stock, all remaining forty gallon drums of Kerosene and petrol, two Canadian sledges, all of the workshop and the balloon hut... one hundred and thirty five seals, the boat and its outboard motor... the steel bridges on loan from the War Office, the six 40' telegraph poles on loan from the GPO, the BP petrol pump, petrol drum taps and openers, all of the aero oil and hydraulic fluid, four main tractor wheels, all of the explosives and ammunition, except one mixed box, a lot of new batteries, the engine lifting tackle and various other stuff...

So now, no fires for heating or cooking and Kerosene only enough to keep one section of the hut warm and to run the generators for radio about half an hour per week. If or when we get the hut finished.

Feeding the dogs will be another headache, but we can always give them next year's corned beef and Trim, etc. Luckily the pile of dog pemmican was just inside the break...

Ken... first told me of the loss when I was making a draft damper by putting a door between my hutch and the catacombs. He first said that our morning tea was ready, and then, that the sea-ice had gone out taking nearly everything with it.

So we had an emergency meeting. Plenty of scope for the inventor. How can I run everything on petrol? There must be ways. We have two wind generators, so we should have battery power for 24v lighting. We also have two little battery-charging engines. Cooking and heating will be difficult to get over but I'm sure we will. I shall leave my subconscious to work it over and let me know when it has thought of something.

With the wind blowing all the ice out against the west current drift we might even get everything back again – if we soon get a north wind. A thousand to one – but it could just possibly happen. At the moment, with the south wind still blowing, nothing can be seen for frost-smoke from the 'warmer' sea, but the ice has gone a long, long way out.

Of course, no miracle occurred and the lost materials continued their journey north, until the ice beneath them melted in the warmer seas and they plunged down to the ocean bed. However, two days later, on Good Friday, 30 March, 1956, the expedition did experience some much-needed good fortune

Friday 30 March, 1956 (Good Friday)
... Taffy and I went down the hill in the Weasel to collect the spare hut timbers, the Ciment Fondu,[11] and the drum of paraffin a quarter way up the hill. On the way down, as it was now a beautiful clear day of -21°C and only a little wind, we were able to see what looked like RAF petrol drums and the dead seals way out on the sea-ice near the new waterline. We decided we'd bring in the dead seals. First, at the 'dump', we loaded the timber and Ciment Fondu, or at least started to, when I noticed one of the dark objects, the nearest one, only about a quarter of a mile away turn its head. Soon, after observing it for a while, we knew it was a live seal – at this time of year, when we thought all life had gone north and not a live seal had been seen for many weeks... We had no rifle or axe so we couldn't get the live seals but I decided to go out and have a look to see just what was there.

In between time Taffy shouted, 'Hell's bells, Look!' And Lo! There was a killer whale... just to our left. Then six more. Then twenty or so and they came right along near the ice edge. We were only two feet from the edge and when a couple came up to blow I clapped my hands and straight away the whole lot turned ninety degrees and put on full speed straight for us. We saw, in all directions, the big fins and shiny backs rising into the air and surging forward under the water... One after another and six at a time they came up with an echoing high-pressure blow and then plunged under again and as we watched in a trance, it suddenly seemed that we ought to be somewhere else – perhaps about fifty yards up the hill.

So we ran, just in case it really was true that, in a concerted attack, they can break up sea-ice by humping up underneath it. After running six or seven yards we felt silly and stopped to look around and found a killer whale standing up in the water looking at us. If they look to see where you've gone it is just possible that they also think up ways of how to get you for lunch. An evil intelligence was activating. We finally estimated about thirty of them toward one set end.

---

[11] A fast-drying cement suitable for use in low temperatures.

The ice was about two feet above the sea, so probably we had somewhere around ten to twelve under water. I was pretty sure that they couldn't break up that stuff, and if they tried I was equally sure that they would do a lot of harm to their outsize dorsal fins, all to no avail. But they kept charging and then slipping under at the last split second before hitting the ice, then some would come up for another look. Unnerving, very unnerving, for we had a quarter of a mile and more to go on the sea-ice in the Weasel...

We got the timber up the hill by a slightly different route due to huge sastrugi[12] and then lashed on the drum of paraffin and came back to camp. Morning tea was in progress... I couldn't wait, but got the rifle and an axe and off we went. Everything was the same and killers continued to rise up, this time to have their photographs taken... Later on they started the 'big wash' attack, probably hoping that the ice would break up and some more observers came up, but we'd got quite used to them by now...

It was with high spirits that we returned towing four Weddells... it meant about a month's ration for the dogs. I had shot my first seal, which I didn't very much like and had gutted another which I liked even less. In two of them we found seal pups, one being about fifteen inches long and the other about a foot long. We kept one heart and a lot of very large livers for our own use...

Sunday 1 April, 1956 (Easter Sunday)
Dawned bleak and cold and gradually got worse, -29°C and nineteen knots from the south... As it snowed nearly all yesterday and all today we are now getting a fair amount of drift starting. Not yet forming a blizzard, but we are all afraid of getting another week like 20 to 26 March...

Having cleaned out all of the snow from the [Sno-cat's] cylinder head, water pump, radiator, etc. with oxygen, (no compressed air cylinders here) I spent about an hour and a half straightening the fins on the radiator where the tarpaulin had flattened them with its continual whacking.

---

[12] Sastrugi are sharp and irregular ridges formed on a snow surface by wind. They sometimes reach 600mm or more in height and can be rock-hard.

I brazed the broken dip stick on the Sno-Cat and then rigged up [a] 24v light from my batteries, so today I have the first electric light in Shackleton Base...

Rhino did weighing and fat thickness tonight. I weighed 10st 6lbs in my pants... It was quite chilly to be stripped today. The other chaps have been digging all day and have discovered that a line of stores and hut parts are dead in line under the centre of the ginormous drift.

I've got my new sleeping bags at last and they are wonderfully soft and dry. So I should sleep well tonight. Jeff started cooking today and provided a magnificent sponge sandwich cake. Amazing what can be done on a Primus now.

Monday 9 April, 1956
... In the Shack, as cook, I had to remove two pullovers as I was too warm. Outside it was warm enough but the drift was unpleasant. When I say 'warm enough' I mean with -7°C as opposed to -34°C...

Tuesday 10 April, 1956
... Ralph tries every night to get contact with various stations but our power output is too low...

Despite the erection of a radio aerial mast in February, as yet the Advance Party had been unable to make contact with the outside world. This not only increased their feelings of isolation but also meant that the expedition's organisers, as well as family and friends, had no way of knowing if they were dead or alive.

Although Roy had succeeded in rigging up electric light in his workshop, the radio in the Shack worked off batteries that required recharging with the pop-pop, and artificial light was still provided by two paraffin-fuelled Tilley lamps. These worked well enough in terms of illumination, but poor ventilation meant that they polluted the atmosphere and contributed to the condensation – an incessant problem with eight men crammed into such a confined space.

They had not yet put up a mast for electricity generation but as daylight would soon give way to twilight and eventually to permanent darkness, something needed to be done. At the end of March Roy located the parts of a Lucas wind-generator, but it must be positioned high up to avoid the risk of someone being de-capitated by its six foot blades. Somewhere under the drifts a metal Dexion mast lay hidden, but where? As a temporary expedient, Roy bolted two 16' lengths of timber together, attached a strong T-piece to the base and set it in a deep snow-pit with bottle screws weighing about sixty pounds each as anchors. Unfortunately, as they hauled the home-made mast into position, a supporting ladder crashed down, hitting Lenton in the back and flattening him in the snow. He survived the experience with nothing more serious than bruises but this accident could have been disastrous as the Advance Party had no facilities for dealing with a major injury.

The following day they finished the job, enabling Roy to rig up two lights in the Shack. What a difference it made: as well as their brightness, the electric lights didn't need pre-heating, they could be switched off in bed by the duty cook, and they did not burn paraffin, thereby reducing both fumes and condensation.

Of course, having installed the generator, Roy must now add its regular lubrication to his ever-growing list of jobs. This meant furling the blade and then climbing to the top of the mast. He described the experience on 15 April:

Having arrived at the top with a can of oil, all that one must do is to twine his legs around the masthead, swing the machine into the wind, hold the propeller from turning by propping one's shoulder against it and pull out the filler plug; all this, with a can of oil in one hand which now has to be emptied into the machine's reservoir.

Before the *Theron* departed, Roy had wiped snow from a shattered windscreen and he felt sure that a piece of glass was lodged in his left index finger, which had become very painful to use. Goldsmith seemed unconvinced but as the problem persisted he agreed to undertake a minor exploratory operation.

Wednesday 18 April, 1956
... Tonight Rhino operated on my left index finger. He made me scrub it for five minutes first. Then two jabs of local anaesthetic at the base of the finger – but the one on the inside didn't work very well so I had another. Then a penicillin injection in the arm. Then 'the cutting'. He cut out a wedge-shaped piece... which included the hard core scar. Then, after another bit of cutting inwards, there was the metallic click of metal on glass and eventually it was brought out – a flat piece of glass...

I had bet Rhino ten bars of chocolate that there was a piece of glass in there... I am now in debt because he says that his fee is eleven bars...

Friday 20 April, 1956
... My finger still has a throbbing ache but it looks as if it will make a nice clean heal...

In March, after the seven-day blizzard, Roy had described a huge build-up of drift as 'a small hill that can never be moved', with many building panels buried beneath. In early April they started digging in order to find the panels and to create interlinking tunnels that would provide accommodation for the dogs during the worst of the winter. The tunnels would also serve as storage space, and even as shelter for the Advance Party in an emergency. The work of chipping, shovelling and carting icy snow was hard, laborious and sometimes futile, as on 17 April, when so much new drift penetrated the excavations of the west tunnel that it had to be abandoned.

Every member of the Advance Party took his turn at the digging save for the cook, who already had his hands full, and Roy who was kept busy dealing with all matters requiring engineering skills, as well as having to remove drift from his workshop and from inside the vehicles. Nevertheless, on 21 April he decided to help out with the main tunnelling project for a few days.

Saturday 21 April, 1956
After sorting out the carburettor trouble on the pop-pop I felt like a change so went to do some tunnelling. The east tunnel had surrendered all that had been hoped of it after going in, with few bends, for about twenty-five yards. The only thing to do was to start a new tunnel for three crates still to be found... Near the end, in the evening, I located the abandoned west tunnel at its furthest point in and joined the two. Ken and Hannes went around up top digging three-foot holes and probing with a six-foot length of half inch square tool steel. Eventually they located a box about eight feet ahead in the direction of my tunnel so that is tomorrow's objective. An ice axe has to be used on most of it, as it is so hard-packed...

Rhino isn't taking very kindly to his cooking. The porridge was hard and thick, he burnt everything at dinner. The batter wouldn't form on the pineapple rings and then the fat burst into flames. He dropped the beans all over the floor, the patent opener wouldn't open the cans and everything else happened. Then Tony knocked over some of his beer in the Scrabble lid. I'm sure tomorrow will be better...

The first roof panel went on today, but a slight hold-up occurred after the first half dozen as one has to be found, amongst ninety-nine, to go next in sequence.

Finger comfortable today in spite of being squeezed twice between a shovel handle and a hard chunk of snow.

Tuesday 24 April, 1956
Bad day of wind and drift. Tunnel work went on till teatime...

I fitted up a... roof light at the bench-end of the Shack. It lights up the generator switchboard and the radio... I also put in a light at my 'workshop' tunnel with a switch just inside the door.

Got out new pants, vest and shirt from my kitbag in the penthouse and de-snowed all of the stored kitbags. Also, got out a green scarf which Ralph and I unravelled and made into two balls of wool to make myself some gloves...

Wednesday 25 April, 1956
Nasty day again with wind, drift and low temperatures... and the sleeping bags don't get any drier. Eleven weeks in a tent today I think...

Rhino kept getting large white patches on his chin and cheek and the icicles on my moustache grew so long that they swung and touched my chin. Our eyelashes froze together where drift had settled on them and partially melted and the tip of my nose kept stinging.

Ralph and Taffy somehow managed to continue panelling on the roof but it must have been nippy up there. Jeff and Tony looked for particular selections of roof panels in the drifted dumps...

The moon is full today or tomorrow and today it didn't set at all but went right round...

Rhino took out the three stitches from my finger tonight and it looks pretty good and healing nicely.

Thursday 26 April, 1956
Writing late at 0220 hours because some of us had a bit of a drinking session for the first time. Ken, Rhino, Ralph and I... Rum punch, dreadful stuff. Have a headache...

The only surprising thing about the drinking session was that it hadn't happened sooner. The men of the Advance Party continued to live in truly appalling conditions and they were still nearly two months from midwinter. The shack provided a safe haven of sorts, but the poor ventilation meant that they suffered from carbon monoxide poisoning, the tents were far from satisfactory to sleep in, they still had no contact with the outside world, the building work progressed very slowly and the vehicles, particularly the Weasels and the Sno-Cat, caused endless problems.

Roy's comments in his diary entry for 29 April indicate how bad things really were.

Sunday 29 April, 1956

A terrible day of drift, wind and cold. The wind, southerly still, was twenty-four to seventeen knots this evening and the temperatures started at -42°C and fell to -44°C this evening but had registered on the minimum thermometer -44.6°C up to 2100 hours. During last night it went down to -43°F which was our lowest temperature up till then. Today's of course were lower and we expect -46°F to-night.

We were unable to go out and work today of course, although... Tony did some digging in a tunnel today in preparation for storing meteorological equipment...

We were feeling the effects of bad air and no ventilation in the Shack. Headaches, dizziness and sore eyes. It has driven us all to bed early.

This is not very acceptable because, after five or six hours, or even sooner, the cold causes wakefulness and discomfort and it means lying in a stiffly-frozen sleeping bag, sore, shivering and fed-up for about four hours. Perhaps the answer is codeines instead of rum...

If these conditions go on it is not going to be possible to finish off the hut. I can't imagine us sleeping in tents through the winter with -68°C and sixty knot winds. Neither can I imagine living a winter, night and day, in the Shack. One day in there is killing. We have all talked about 'if the hut is not finished', but I don't think anyone has seriously believed that it might not be...

The jokes about our predicament are enjoyed with a perverse relish. Today, as Taffy sprawled his elbows out on the table and rested his head on his arms, Ralph said, 'Hey, Taff! Don't die like that or I shall have to break your arms to get you in the coffin.'

We joke about trying to get to Belgrano, the Argentine base, seventeen miles away and begging some coal and so on.[13] Don't know if they also have accommodation for an extra eight men, and food and the dogs, etc! If we do get the hut up it will still be a long time before anyone knows of our predicament because installing the engines, generators, high power radio sets and wiring will take a long time. And we soon will have no daylight, not even the benefit of twilight.

Some daylight remained but the sun had now disappeared permanently below the horizon and wouldn't return until well into August. The weather remained a crucial factor in how much work could be completed and the wind just kept blowing. In fact, from 2 May to 10 May conditions were so bad that no regular work was done at all, apart from meteorological observations. Then, on 7 May, the party at last had cause to rejoice.

Monday 7 May, 1956
Enid's birthday. Many Happy Returns Darling. Wish I could send you a message... but at least you and the outside world know now that we are still alive...

Ralph gate-crashed Base E[14] (who were 'sending' to someone) and found that they had heard him. He jumped up waving his arms, executed a stomp dance and kept exclaiming, 'I've got him, I've got him!'

He then 'sent' and when the Morse came back he did another dance and kept saying, 'He's calling us.' We were spellbound and didn't quite know how to express our excitement. Ken hurriedly composed a message giving brief news of our plight...

No work today and it has been bad. This morning Hannes went out and recorded fifty-three knots south wind and thinks we had sixty knots earlier...

Gamel was brought into the lean-to for a hot meal as he seemed affected by the cold. All of the dogs must be feeling pretty chilly now with no exercise and this continual south wind.

---

[13] General Belgrano base was actually 24 miles from Shackleton Base.
[14] Falkland Islands Dependencies Survey (FIDS) Base 'E' at Stonington Island, off the western coast of the Antarctic Peninsula. In fact, Base E was closed at that time and contact was almost certainly established with Base Y nearby.

Tuesday 8 May, 1956

Just another nasty day with a slight difference. Temperatures this morning -43 °C then -44 °C. Minimum during the night -43 °C. Minimum during the day -45.6 °C. Wind south thirty-six to twenty-four knots. So now we've gone below -45.6 °C...

Tonight Ralph gate-crashed Port Stanley radio... who were calling bases and got acknowledged from about 2000 miles away! This was about 1910 hours GMT and they had so much traffic that we were not able to do any sending. They have a great deal for us and tomorrow will probably send blind (even if they can't hear us, that means) because we can quite likely pick them up as they are powerful enough...

Wednesday 9 May, 1956

A big day, for radio contact was fully utilized with Port Stanley. Our little 5-Watt Pye set was received strength five at 2000 miles distance. We received our telegrams and sent Ken's official preliminary message and my birthday message to Enid...

I had one from David Pratt to say that, 'the Fergusons still have temperate oils in them. Change to suit. Greetings, Pratt.' Of course the oil was changed ages ago. We ought to send a signal, 'Sorry, can only find one. Homard.' One went out with the stores when the ice broke away...

I am reading Flying Saucers Have Landed.[15] *Very interesting; I am considering the theory of levitation to fetch some coal...*

The following day they learned from the same source that Fuchs wanted to speak to them via a BBC broadcast at 5.30 p.m. This meant that Taffy must now dig out the expedition's 88 radio set, if they were to have any chance of tuning in to the correct frequency.

Friday 11 May, 1956

Today has given us fresh hope for, after a very boisterous night, the wind gradually dropped after lasting twenty-three days. Temperatures remain low though, but we can stand that with no wind... During the day we had... -47.5 °C...

---

[15] Desmond Leslie and George Adamski, *Flying Saucers Have Landed* (London: Werner Laurie, 1954), a supposedly non-fiction account of UFO sightings and alien encounters.

We were able to do a bit of work. Tony, Hannes and Jeff unblocked the tunnel. Taffy dug out the crate with the 88 set in it and then he and Ralph fixed it up.

Rhino and I dug out Dump A and re-laid it while I looked for the case with the fire extinguisher CO2 cylinders in it. Not there. I dug around my dump without success but opened up Smith's instruments box and my case of fluorescent paints. I did a bit of work in the 'workshop' but it was too cold with only a pair of woollen mitts...

Today was Ken's first cooking and he produced a very fine steamed duff.

That the search for firefighting equipment was conducted in such a desultory fashion seems surprising. The environmental conditions in Antarctica, including high winds, the desiccating effects of low humidity, and the absence of liquid water with which to firefight, all increase the threat of fire substantially. In addition, at the time of the TAE, expedition huts were manufactured almost entirely of wood; they were heated by solid fuel burners and often lit by liquid fuel lanterns; most personnel smoked tobacco; and, in the winter months, accumulations of drift snow could quickly block windows and doors. As Roy himself acknowledged, in these conditions, 'apart from our camp breaking away and drifting out a fire is the worst thing that could happen to us'.[16]

Saturday 12 May, 1956
... The 88 set works alright and tonight we had news from home... and two hours of music...

Sunday 13 May, 1956
... Temperature today has gone down to -34°C and the wind back to south rising from seventeen knots to twenty-seven knots... We were able to work today though but if the wind gets worse we won't be.

---

[16] Diary, 29 March 1956. For more information on fire risk in Antarctica, and for examples of fire-related disasters, see Stephen Haddelsey, *Icy Graves: Exploration and Death in the Antarctic* (Stroud: The History Press, 2018), pp. 27-52.

I de-snowed the Weasel engine, got the heater running and the pop-pop going. Eventually I got the Weasel running too, first time for weeks...

Verbal contact made today with Base A at Port Lockroy[17] who arranged a schedule for tomorrow... If I don't get a message tomorrow you're in for big trouble, Enid!

Monday 14 May, 1956
... No telegrams again tonight, which makes us highly suspicious, angry, disappointed and again angry...

Tuesday 15 May, 1956
Tonight we are rather more displeased than yesterday. Still no telegrams. We got a message [from Fuchs], something about:

HOW MUCH TRAFFIC CAN YOU TAKE – RELATIVES ANXIOUS TO SEND MESSAGES. HAVE YOU STILL GOT TRANSMITTERS, BEACON, ETC...?

YOU HAVE ALL BEEN ELECTED TO THE ANTARCTIC CLUB AND I AM BRINGING DOWN THE TIES...

It seems, on the face of it, that the office has asked relatives not to send messages. If so, nothing could be more stupid and infuriating...

Thursday 17 May, 1956
Good day today with little wind from the north and temperatures not too bad...

When I came in a telegram was waiting for me. I was pleased about it but it was a bit of a shock. It read...

JERSEY 17 1514: TERRIBLY SORRY TO HEAR OF YOUR LOSSES – NEWS HEADLINES HERE - HOPE YOU ARE FIT AND WELL – HAVING GRAND WHITSUN HERE AT GOREY.

MY LOVE ALWAYS, ENID.

---

[17] Base A was established on Wiencke Island, off the Antarctic Peninsula, by the top secret British military expedition, Operation Tabarin, in 1944. At the end of the war its management passed to FIDS.

I did think you might have mentioned who you were with Enid. Later, Ralph picked up another telegram for me... This one was sent from Sheerness at 1310... two hours before the one from Jersey. This I couldn't understand. Then suddenly it dawned on me that Ralph had made up the Jersey one and everyone was in on it. The name Gorey they got from the atlas... and it was just coincidence that we had stayed near there. The official telegram explained the mystery of no telegrams:

... HAVE BEEN AWAITING INSTRUCTIONS ABOUT SENDING MESSAGES.

Everyone else, except Taffy, who had a telegram from 'Audrey', highly indignant at office stopping messages coming to us. Damn silly. Messages could come as far as Port Stanley and be held there until we could get them through...
Temperature at midnight last night, -37°C...

Winter gripped ever more tightly as the days passed. Work outside was sometimes possible, sometimes not, and benign conditions could quickly change for the worse. Some days blizzards laid down more huge drifts; on others calm prevailed but it remained very cold. On 25 May the temperature fell to -49°C.

Whatever the conditions, dog-feeding and meteorological observations continued and Roy turned his attention to one of the Weasels with a burned out bearing in the rear axle. The shack provided some respite during the day but sleeping in tents remained miserable.

Saturday 26 May, 1956
Blowing cold again, so breakfast postponed to 12.30. I didn't sleep very well, feeling the cold for most of the night, in fact, shivering for long periods. I was forced to struggle with my frozen sleeping bag in order to get out and light the Primus. Normally I prefer to stay in the bag even though cold but I couldn't put up with any more shivering when the Primus was so close...
At midnight temperature was -47°C...

Prior to the expedition, Goldsmith had taken crash courses in dentistry and veterinary medicine. Doubtful about his abilities, he had advised all members of the Advance Party to have their teeth checked before departure but, according to Goldsmith, Roy had ignored this recommendation.

Monday 28 May, 1956

... While sitting up in bed sewing a loop and toggle on my inner bag in place of the zip which ripped off, I pulled out the stopping in my front tooth by breaking cotton with my teeth.

Rhino put in a zinc oxide filling and started inspecting the other teeth. While probing on the left-hand side a filling dropped out of a back tooth on the right-hand side. Absolutely amazing that it should drop out just like that and just at that time.

He had a long job getting out another piece from the same cavity and then scraping it clean. We have no drill operating so it had to be scraped. This one also got a zinc oxide filling – quite a large one...

Temperature at midnight -45 °C. Wind south thirty-six knots...

Wednesday 30 May, 1956

An interesting day in all, wind to start with which delayed getting up to a 12 o'clock breakfast. The wind showed signs of dropping and we were able to go out and do some work in the afternoon. My first job of course was to repair the wind generator... It was quite beastly up the mast in the wind and my hands got so frozen that I had to come down a couple of times. I lashed myself to the mast top so as to leave both hands free. I got it working alright but I don't think it will last more than about a month. I shall have to get another motor ready to change when I get a good chance.

The hut had drift in it up to the beams on the south side and looks hopeless but it can be got over at our leisure once all of the walls are up. The loft has large quantities in it too. Everyone was digging in the hut or for food re-stocking. I got on with Dexion assembly but it was murderous on my fingers putting in nuts and bolts....

One of Roy's vital contributions to the expedition during the first winter was his design and construction of a highly effective bread oven. With only Primus stoves for cooking, even the more accomplished chefs found it an onerous and tricky job to provide a varied diet for eight healthy appetites. There could be no question of installing the Aga in the crate, and besides, the Aga's coal had all been lost to the sea in March. No oven meant no baking, and once the supplies of bread from the ship had been exhausted the men were reduced to eating biscuits instead.

In fact, Roy wasn't the first to attempt baking. Meteorologist Peter Jeffries produced a sponge cake using a biscuit tin on a Primus at the beginning of April 1956 and the next day he followed this with a jam roly-poly. A week later, Roy made scones the same way, but he realised that something more sophisticated was needed. On 5 May, using old tins, he built a double-shelled oven with fibreglass insulation. It worked much better, though he still burnt his cake. After modification he baked bread successfully; the bottom was burnt, but the rest proved perfectly edible. Later on, in early July, he started on a new and improved oven using a five gallon oil drum. As before he formed two skins with fibre glass insulation, riveting the inner skin for extra strength. He also had a stroke of genius when he discovered that the insertion of a steel cone at the base diverted heat to the sides and stopped baked goods getting burned on the underside. From the very outset, this remarkable invention added significantly to the explorers' meagre comforts.

Saturday 2 June, 1956
Better day in the kitchen and a good one outside. Made a big effort to make bread and my two loaves came out excellently. The bottoms were burnt but that is a fault in the homemade oven. The burnt bit wasn't thick and was easily scraped off.

Ralph and Taffy fitted three panels in the west gable end. Jeff dug out the snow from inside the north-east corner of the hut ready for the panelling...

Fat thickness and weighing tonight. I have gained two pounds making me ten stone, nine pounds (virtually unclothed).

Sunday 3 June, 1956
... Washed my arms and face tonight.

Monday 4 June, 1956
Another good day of only light winds... First thing, I started the pop-pop and filled up as many cells in the battery banks as I had distilled water for and then went across to the hut for some digging. About one third of it has snow drifted up inside to the ceiling beams and the rest has solid snow varying between one foot and six feet in depth. There is an awful lot of digging but we can leave it all inside except the parts of the hut that we must use...

Tuesday 5 June, 1956
... Woke up to hear a strong wind blowing and we weren't called till 9.45 a.m. The North wind got stronger through the day and has, tonight, reached a terrific force... It has been difficult to walk against the wind and it had to be done sideways. Walking with the wind would have you running along out of control if great care wasn't exercised...

Rhino was dragging a panel crate lid (eight feet long) on a piece of cord when the wind caught it, whipped it into the air and the cord snapped. The lid flew away into the darkness and Rhino was unable to find it.

Wednesday 6 June, 1956
The wind in the night increased in strength and the tent pounded and boomed with the flapping canvas. The force of the wind caused strong draughts up through the snow under our beds and even blew out matches when I tried to light the lamp. The violence of the pounding inner tent wall had pushed all of the things off of the cook box. When I got outside at about one o'clock I found that one tent pole on my side had collapsed under the strain and the other one, also on my side, at the head, had bent like a bow.

The violence of the wind has continued all day and during the afternoon the wind generator mast snapped at its base and a guy-rope wire broke. The propeller was smashed but there is nothing that I can do with it at present. I've had to rig up the 24v JAP McFarlane generator. It wouldn't run well outside in the wind and cold but gave no trouble just inside the lean-to. It uses engine oil pretty fast though and it is a nuisance having a fuel tank that holds only three pints.

Getting about outside has been more difficult than yesterday and an angle of about 45° has to be attained in order to balance against the wind pressure. Drums and J/cans of oil on my 'workshop' flat roof got blown off and a very large sheet of plywood used as a door to one of the tunnels has simply disappeared.

The Shack creaks at one end of the roof but we are well fixed-in, in hard long banks of drift snow up to the roof...

The temperature today at 1200 hours was -11°C and wind... seventy-five knots...

Until the wind generator could be re-erected, power had to be supplied through batteries that required constant charging. To remove the need for this tiresome task, Roy began work on constructing the much stronger Dexion mast. Unfortunately he couldn't find the 266 nuts and bolts that he needed and, assuming that these had been lost in March, he decided to cut his own. He had made 180 when, on opening the Dexion packages, he found the missing nuts and bolts. In his diary, he recorded his amazement at this discovery – but it seems natural to wonder whether, at the time, he expressed his feelings rather more forcefully.

The mast under construction was too large to fit inside his little 'hutch' workshop, so it lay in the open. Then, during the very stormy conditions on 6 June, it blew away. He searched all around on foot but found nothing.

Thursday 7 June, 1956
An improvement in weather but other things are not so good…

When I got to my tent last night I found that both tent poles on my side had broken and the whole side sagged in and the top bent over. For a while I was undecided whether to sleep in the Shack or not. Finally I thought I'd try the tent for the night. What a crush getting in under the bent-in tent wall. There was just room for me to lie there, but very close to the inner edge of the bed. The tent-wall flapped on me all night and twice after turning onto my left side I awoke in a panic with loss of breath where my head was buried in the head of the sleeping bag and the folds of the tent. I have to do it again tonight as I've made no alternative arrangements yet. I don't think that the tent will blow away though…

I had hoped to go out with the Weasel and look for the Dexion and after working on the engine, heater and batteries for four or five hours, I found that the fan and pulley had broken away from the water pump. So I had to abandon everything as soon as I'd got the engine running. The heater air intake pipe was tight with snow and so was the engine compartment. The starter was frozen up and when that came free the engine started easily. Can't do much about the fan pulley without a workshop as the radiator has to be removed from the front, outside the vehicle…

Friday 8 June, 1956
Lovely warm day for outside work. I decided to get on with the Sno-Cat… De-snowed the engine and ran it but it was misfiring… No. 2 plug had its end battered in. Will have to try to probe inside the plug hole for a foreign body…

People have been digging and searching for panels. The next panel to go on the north wall has disappeared, believed blown away. Meteorological office and radio room entirely clear of snow and the loft at the end (east) complete...

The Shack is running with melting ice and the floor has to be continuously mopped up. Even the snow on the tarpaulin roof of the lean-to is melting with the warm air going out of the Shack hatch.

Temperature at midday GMT was -15˚C...

Saturday 9 June, 1956

... We feel that we must have had gusts of over one hundred knots to do all the damage that was done. At times it was practically impossible to stay on our feet. Sometimes, in struggling against the wind, we were actually forced backwards a pace or two before finding a firm foothold to brace against...

I'm trying to write, all hunched-up, with a broken tent pole pressing onto my back. Tomorrow I really must put up a spare tent...

Sunday 10 June, 1956

... Tonight I'm going to sleep in the Shack on the form next to the wall. Taffy, as cook, will sleep on the table and Ralph on the other form.

It has been a nasty day. When I came to breakfast at 10 a.m. it was nearly calm but in half an hour or so the north wind was bringing in a blizzard... Brought the pop-pop to the hut and have given three hours charge to the Shack batteries...

Bringing over the pop-pop was a dreadful job in complete darkness and blizzard. It weighs about one hundred pounds and I staggered along, half-faced away from the wind and drift, stumbling over sastrugi and buckling up as I dropped over the uneven surface into the hollow places. I bumped into one of Taffy's new aerial posts before I knew where I was but even then I walked away from the Shack entrance. When I did get to the opening I could hardly hold the blessed motor as I slithered down a bank of snow to the inside. Thank goodness it has run without a fault, for three hours, before running out of petrol.

Everyone has been digging inside the hut today...

Tuesday 12 June, 1956

Tony, as cook today, slept in the Shack last night and we both woke up with dizzy headaches, Ralph little affected. I shall tonight sleep in the lean-to...

South wind and drift have been bad today and the temperatures lower than recently...

During this afternoon and evening I've been working up a four hundred word telegram to David Pratt on the vehicles. I had to tell him I think a piston is broken in the Sno-Cat... and asked for a number of Weasel spares not previously available...

Delighted with Enid's telegram to say that I'd been officially adopted by the London Boys' School instead of a husky.[18] *Shall have to send 'Woof, woof' to Enid to pass on to them...*

Wednesday 13 June, 1956

A day suitable for working but cooler than the last few days. Although we had some north wind it didn't bring such 'warm' wind.

I decided to take a chance at changing our tent... [The new one] looks a pleasure to get into after our other old torn tent with broken tapes and poles and heavy lumps of ice stuck all the way around the bottom of the walls.

I thought I'd better get on with the wind generator so cut several lengths of Don 8 field telephone wire to increase the number of lines in each guy to six. When I took stock of this tangled mass of steel wire I decided to find something else. I cut up some lengths of three-eighths of an inch diameter steel cable and fixed bulldog grips on them ready to put up. I now have to find a way of fixing it all to the top of the mast.

The others have gone on digging in the hut, bringing panels to store and fitting one in the hut side and one in the gable east. Bundles of tongued-and-grooved board were brought in for more flooring to go on. Rhino and Ken have been digging out the tunnel for dog recesses and have places now for seven...

Saturday 16 June, 1956

... A telegram from Bunny [to Blaiklock]:

---

[18] Schools across the UK had been invited to 'adopt' a husky as part of the expedition's fund-raising initiatives.

IN VIEW OF YOUR HARD TIME AT SHACKLETON PLEASE
CONFIRM HOMARD AND YOU ARE STILL WILLING TO
REMAIN FOR SECOND YEAR. WOULD LENTON STAY AS
EXTRA MECHANIC (?) AND WIRELESS OPERATOR FOR
CROSSING?

PLEASE GIVE YOUR VIEWS REGARDING SUITABILITY FOR
CROSSING [OF] WILLIAMS, LA GRANGE AND IF WE FIND IT
NECESSARY STEWART OR JEFFRIES. WOULD LATTER WANT
TO STAY IF ASKED?

The bracketed question mark after the word 'mechanic' was added
by Roy, who doubted Ralph Lenton's qualifications to serve as a
mechanic when the expedition needed a well-trained and experienced vehicle engineer. Lenton had an entirely different set of
skills. In terms of staying on, Roy had joined the expedition for the
long-haul, but he would have to obtain Enid's agreement. He
decided to send roses.

Another potentially significant telegram arrived the same day:

PHOTOS (AIR) FROM CLAYDON[19] SEEM TO SHOW SNOW-
COVERED CREVASSES, THE LONGEST POINTING TOWARDS
SNO-CAT CRATE. RESTRICT VEHICLE MOVEMENTS SOUTH
OF CAMP. CONSIDER ALARM UNNECESSARY.

Crevasses are deep cracks, sometimes very large, in glaciers or ice
fields, caused by the movement of the ice sheets and often
concealed by the gradual accumulation of drift snow. They can pose
a grave danger to polar explorers, and in December 1956 the
expedition would learn that a member of the American IGY team
had been killed when his Weasel fell into a crevasse 100 feet deep.

If the interpretation of the aerial photography was correct,
vehicles moving around the base could disturb a crevasse cap,
risking the destruction of a vehicle and the death of the operator.
However, the news produced no particular anxiety at Shackleton,
perhaps because the absence of any accidents to date bred
complacency, and perhaps because crevasses constituted just one
more danger to add to an already lengthy list. Although no disasters

---

[19] Squadron Leader John Claydon, senior pilot with the New Zealand
contingent of the expedition. He had accompanied the Advance Party on
the *Theron*.

occurred at Shackleton, in 1957 the expedition's geophysicist, Geoff Pratt, confirmed that the base was completely afloat, rising and falling with the tides, and three decades later, in 1986, the ice shelf did calve, and the entire base was lost to the Weddell Sea.

On Sunday 17 June the repaired wind generator was re-erected, just in time for Midwinter's Day. This latter date is the most significant in the Antarctic calendar, marking the turning point towards summer and the return of the sun. The Advance Party sent Midwinter greetings to HM Queen Elizabeth and then set about celebrating properly.

Thursday 21 June, 1956 – Midwinter's Day
I'm writing this 'tomorrow' for it's not to be expected that I would feel like diary writing on top of Midwinter celebrations. Now that I think of it, I don't feel like it today either.

Breakfast yesterday was with some quite excellent cured Red Gate side of bacon... at 11 a.m. and then I went to do a little light work in my hutch...

We, most of us, gathered in the Shack, about 2 p.m. and drank beer... and we had our lunch at 4 p.m.

Ralph made a very nice gin and vermouth with a cherry each. He also did all of the cooking for Midwinter feeding. For lunch we had turtle soup, ham and sprouts, etc. and then strawberry shortcake, and then thick double cream and chocolate sponge. He'd also made a lot of beautiful bread rolls. We opened up little gifts, pulled our crackers and handed round gifts from the Scott Polar Research Institute and Hal Lister.

Alan Tritton[20] had given a Fortnum & Mason case of food. Hal[21] had sent a lot of musical instruments, masks, bubble liquid and a toy train. This track just fitted on the table around the Dundee cake. On the cake was mounted a Scott Polar Research Institute gift – a most entrancing round-about of three angels who swing round ringing two bells as they go by... [They also] sent a lot of fine musical instruments and there was a good deal of noise... There was also plenty to drink...

---

[20] Alan Tritton served as base leader and meteorologist at the Falkland Islands Dependencies Survey's Signy Island base from 1952-54.
[21] Hal Lister, glaciologist during the main expedition.

The party went on very happily into the small hours. Throughout the day it had remained calm and not too cold and at about 1 a.m. Roy – 'somewhat the worse for wear' according to Rhino Goldsmith[22] – decided to take a solitary, moonlit walk down to the sea – something he'd wanted to do for a while.

Once alone, his main concern was that he might confront an aggressive leopard seal:

I took the rifle and some ammunition and set off, stumbling in patches of soft deep snow. I went down the hill and straight across the sea ice to the old edge. Every dark mound of ice and sastrugi looked like a seal. I hoped I might find one but I was quite afraid that I might be attacked by an angry or hungry sea leopard. It took all of the pleasure out of the walk.

In the moon's ghost light of misty silver nothing was clear or real and everything waiting and menacing. At the ice edge there had built up a ridge of broken pressure ice. In some places it was only a foot or two but in others ten feet high of ice boulders all neatly stacked. I stood there and looked around...

Coming across the sea-ice I had thought what little time I should have to fire a second shot at an attacking sea leopard if my first missed a vital spot. Carrying [a bullet] in my heavy glove in addition to the rifle would not have been the best and quickest method for a re-load so I warmed up the base of the cartridge in my hand and carried it with its rim between my teeth. I took care not to dribble on it and wiped it occasionally.

In that still fantasy of hazy-silver, objects of light and shadow came and faded again... I knew that, if anything really moved, I should see it quite distinctly, but an ominous noise coming from just along the pressure-ice bank caused my senses to be alert. It sounded like something groaning and pushing its hidden way through the broken ice in a narrow channel... where the new sea ice meets our old ice.

Quietly I crept forward with rifle ready although I wouldn't have shot anything still in the sea. Movement in the ice made me think of a seal breaking through but as I watched, the blocks of ice 'crunch, crunched' and groaned and split, then rose up and toppled over. With hissing and creaking, more would collapse in a crunch and

[22] Goldsmith & Arnold, *Eight Men in a Crate: The Ordeal of the Advance Party of the Trans-Antarctic Expedition, 1955-1957*, pp. 87-8.

MARVELLOUS!

become slowly spouted upwards like the opening petals of a flower and then fall away to lie quietly out of the battle ...

I walked along to the edge to where our dump had floated away, without seeing any life... I came back along the base of the hill... After walking a long way along the bottom I knew it was still too early to turn up the hill but I decided to do so just in case I'd missed the turn and because this was such a smooth slope up. Everything about me... looked entirely different from the old days down there before the sun went...

Now and again a post would quietly show itself and fade again, but I had the shadow of a hill to guide me, so I got safely into the camp at 3.30 a.m. ...

Everyone had gone to bed when I got into camp and I got to sleep at 4.30 a.m. Breakfast next morning was at 11 a.m. and I forced myself to get up for it ...

3

HOPE DEFERRED

The Midwinter's Day celebrations had constituted a welcome contrast with the rest of the year so far, but they provided small consolation for all the difficulties endured.

Of course, the vehicles loomed largest in Roy's personal nightmare. After the loss of a tractor to the sea, the Advance Party was left with one Sno-Cat, two Weasels and one Ferguson. Of these, the Sno-Cat should have been the best by far. Originally designed for laying telephone lines in the Arctic, this large and sophisticated machine weighed more than three tons and was over six metres long. Its greatest innovation was the four tracked pontoons that could turn in opposite directions front and rear, allowing the vehicle to turn on its own axis and providing excellent traction. Its eight cylinder engine could tow up to five tons on sledges plus an internal load of up to one ton. Unfortunately, for all the brilliance of its design, the Sno-Cat's performance had been far from trouble-free, and the manifold problems that had manifested themselves by Midwinter gave considerable cause for concern – particularly as the Sno-Cats were expected to be the expedition's mainstay during its gruelling trans-continental journey of 2000 miles, much of it across previously unexplored terrain.

The problems had begun early, with the steering and clutch malfunctioning. Then, in March, Roy had decided that he must strip the cylinder heads and valve timing case – a distinctly unappealing prospect in the prevailing conditions. He worked under a tarpaulin to keep the drifting snow at bay and had got as far as stripping the radiator, the water pump, and one of the cylinder heads when, with everything exposed, the seven-day blizzard had struck, leaving the engine encased in a block of frozen snow as hard as iron. Having chipped away the snow he continued the job so that by early April the engine was working again, but on the 13th it had developed a curious rattling noise. When, in early June, he had discovered that one of the sparkplugs had a damaged end he realised that there must be a loose foreign body in the cylinder. He probed No. 2 plug hole with a piece of wire, but instead of hitting the top of the cylinder, the wire had passed right through. There could be only one explanation: the Sno-Cat had a broken piston, and that had necessitated another major repair.

Of the other vehicles, the two Weasels didn't have traction comparable to that of the Sno-Cat, and their six cylinder engines could haul only two tons or so, but they should still have been useful. The problem lay in the vehicles' reliability – as Roy knew only too well from his time in Greenland with the BNGE. Moreover, the Weasels acquired for the TAE were second-hand and in poor condition.

The first problem relating to the Weasels had come when Roy discovered that the rear springs of No. 1 had only eight leaves instead of twelve, meaning that they would be wholly unsuitable for rough terrain and must be replaced. Then, on 18 February, No.1 had seized up altogether and he had found a 'differential pinion bearing well mashed-up'. This had meant that, barely three weeks after landing, he already had one vehicle completely out of action.

On 7 June he had wanted to get No. 2 Weasel going so he could search for the parts of the Dexion mast that had blown away in the recent gales. He had spent four or five hours working on the machine only to find that the fan and pulley had broken away completely from the water pump. This meant that Weasel No. 2 also required substantial repairs that could be undertaken only in a proper workshop.

By Midwinter, only one vehicle remained functional: the surviving Ferguson. Despite being designed for agricultural work rather than for operations in the Antarctic, the tractor had proved reliable enough, but its poor traction limited its use significantly. In fact, at this stage, the Advance Party had no vehicle that could safely descend the snow slope to the sea and get back up again.

It was not in the least an encouraging picture. Thank goodness Midwinter's Day in the Sno-Cat crate had turned out to be such a success.

Friday 22 June 1956
Supposed to be a working day but nobody felt much like it…

Two days later, the Advance Party received, via the London office, a telegram from no less a personage than its royal patron, the Queen, responding to their own Midwinter greetings:

I SEND MY SINCERE THANKS TO THE ADVANCE PARTY OF THE TRANSANTARCTIC EXPEDITION FOR THEIR LOYAL GREETINGS. PLEASE EXPRESS TO EACH OF THEM MY GOOD WISHES. I SHALL BE FOLLOWING THEIR EXPLOITS WITH GREAT INTEREST

ELIZABETH R

Monday 25 June, 1956
... I spent the evening writing a one penny per word telegram of two hundred and seventeen words to [the] headmaster of Latymer Upper School, Hammersmith. Tried to give a general picture of what we are [doing] and hope to do and our present circumstances...

Temperature at 1200 hours -35˚C...

Tuesday 26 June, 1956
... I received message from David Pratt... He ended with 'Wilco Roses'. This means he is sending twelve deep red roses to Enid via Interflora for me...

Thursday 28 June, 1956
First of my four days of cooking finished. Very wearying cooking on Primuses and trying to make a variety.

In addition snow blocks have to be brought in for melting, and cake and bread baked in our tin 'oven' that sits on a Primus...

Now that's a full day's work, hard going all day without a break. The washing up of pans, plates, cups, knives, forks, etc., is no joke and of course milk powder has to be mixed for eight and for four meals a day including with porridge with breakfast.

All of the food has to be thawed out or re-hydrated; also, the water-heating stove, Tilly heater and three Primuses have to be filled. A large square tin has to be taken outside and emptied of washing-up water – no taps and plug holes here. A very big square tin box has to be taken one hundred yards or more for emptying of tins, packets and rubbish of all sorts in darkness and the clothing, personal gear, mukluks[23] etc. of eight men line four walls and ceiling of the crate. When all eight bodies are here as well, it seems, when reflected upon, as though a miracle is being wrought to overcome difficulties we could never have imagined.

This Sno-Cat crate, with two radio sets, electric lighting, eight 6v batteries, my home-made oven, my home-made electric mixer, an eating and writing table, two forms, a kitchen bench, a work bench and vice, a snow-melting stove and a twenty-five gallon tub, a larder, electric shaving with my 12v/230v Remington that I had in Greenland, and the roof being one big festoonery for drying clothing and the four-day-cook's bedding, is our refuge.

Once a month, the inner and outer sleeping bag of each man can rid itself up on the ceiling of the ice cementation through its fabrics and linings. And, for four nights a warm atmosphere makes sleep sound and very pleasant to look forward to, even if the table is hard.

At 10.30 p.m. I'm just having my first cigarette. I've thought about a ten-minute sit-down all day...

Three telegrams today. One from David Pratt about Weasel tracks and two from Enid. Her first on 26th 'agreeing' to my staying on and then a lot of warnings to be careful and the second sent on 27th to say that the roses had arrived but soft soap a bit late...

Friday 6 July, 1956
... Ken has interpolated (from five dates of sun positions received) that our last day of seeing the sun here was 24th April before disappearing below the horizon. We will probably see it [again] on 18th August...

The building work continued whenever possible, though bad weather inevitably interfered and drifting snow remained a constant problem. The dogs were gradually moved into the tunnels as room became available and by 4 July, all were in shelter. This made a real difference in relative terms: on 1 July, for example, the dogs' accommodation registered -20°C compared to -39°C outside.

---

[23] Mukluks: a soft, flexible footwear of Inuit origin. Although usually made of sealskin, those used by the TAE were probably made of either sheepskin with a leather sole or canvas with a rubber sole.

There is no doubt that the cold and hard physical labour made the men hungry. The Advance Party discovered at the end of June that in just five months they had already eaten an eighteen-month supply of spaghetti and baked beans. Later in July, they calculated that they had eaten 500lbs (227 kilos) of sugar over and above their ration and a year's bacon in barely six months.

Sunday 8 July, 1956
... I decided to do something about the No. 1 Weasel with the burnt-out bearing in the rear axle...

I collected up all of the bits that I had removed a long time back and dried them out and then started on track removal. I have managed to block up all of the springs on the left-hand track.

That was quite a job on my own, levering down on a six foot crowbar and inserting a steel block under each bogie arm. After levering down it was necessary to keep my weight on it by clamping the end of the crowbar with my feet and ankles. This was some balancing feat...

Finished The Postman Always Rings Twice...

Monday 9 July, 1956
Bad sleep last night from 5 a.m. onwards. Very cold underneath so I knew what to expect when I rolled back my bed this morning. The sheepskin is hard with ice in the middle and the blanket on top of that is thick with frost through three thicknesses...

After sorting out the Weasel parts this morning I started gathering tins for a new oven...

Temperature at 1200 hours -29°C...

Thursday 19 July, 1956
'Orrible day again continuing blizzard through the night from yesterday. The only time I went out was to go with Rhino to feed the puppies in the tunnel. We used our blizzard masks which are satisfactory in bad drift and high wind for short periods.

Ralph carried on with the hut interior and was part-time assisted by Jeff. There was little for him to do but keep the wood fire going, but when he broke up a piece of wood that Ralph had cut for a job he got the sack...

Temperature at 1200 hours -37°C...

Monday 23 July, 1956

... There was a beautiful glowing dawn today and Hannes took some black and white silhouettes. It seemed so promising that I decided to work on the Weasel with the u/s back axle. I enlisted Taffy and we got on quite well.

Right-hand springs blocked up, tracks removed, final drives removed and the axle assembly ready to be lifted out: trouble is it is so heavy that I don't know if I can get enough manpower to lift it out.

Ken and Rhino have been digging for... stove boxes. One box of Aga parts is missing...

Temperature at... 1200 hours -29°C...

Tuesday 24 July, 1956

... Mr Wordie[24] gave a talk to IGY [on the BBC] but it wasn't very clear. We heard about Magga Dan[25] *going to do trials off Greenland and coming to England in September...*

Temperature at 1200 hours -22°C, wind... twenty-one knots...

Wednesday 25 July, 1956

Blizzard today which developed during the night from the light wind of yesterday and the night before. It has been going on all night and all today with no sign of abatement. It's not as bad as we can get and do get, but the drift, high wind and temperature make outside work far too uncomfortable.

Ralph and Taffy have worked in the hut putting up beading. Some are a little perturbed at not being 'in' on the interior work preparing for our moving in. Ralph seems to have no work to allocate to those who want it.

I brought over my sleeping bags, sheepskin and blankets this morning to sleep in the Shack ready to make breakfast tomorrow. My sheepskin is solid with frost and the six thicknesses of blanket between it and the sleeping bag are thick with frost... They will dry out during the four days while I am cook in the Shack...

Temperature at 1200 hours -31°C, wind... forty-five knots...

---

[24] James Wordie, geologist and chief of the scientific staff on Sir Ernest Shackleton's Imperial Trans-Antarctic Expedition of 1914-17. He became Vivian Fuchs's mentor and a champion of the TAE.
[25] Under the command of Captain Hans Christian Petersen, MV *Magga Dan* was to replace the *Theron* as the main support vessel of the TAE.

Although not expected to contribute significantly to the construction of the hut, Roy was responsible for some specific aspects such as the assembly and installation of the Aga stove. He had attended a course to this end in the United Kingdom and with part of the hut at last near to completion, he must now remember what he had learned so many months ago.

Monday 30 July, 1956

... I went to the hut to look at the Aga parts taken in there. Spread all over the place, against walls, on the floor, in a corner, and against the partition were dozens of parts. One glance told me that I couldn't remember what ought to be there so I got my notes and had a look through them and the Aga instruction book...

I found everything there apart from the stuff in the missing box [lost in March]... I decided to bring in all of the parts of one oven to the Shack so I picked up the largest and heaviest part... which weighed about three quarters of a hundredweight. In the other hand I had a light iron frame. Carrying the heavy part on my shoulder I made my way through the snow in the unlighted part of the hut and fell over outside. Several times, in complete dark, I stumbled over mounds of snow in the high wind and drift. I fell over again and got the oven part back on my shoulder after finding it in the snow. Two paces further I hit a mound of snow and fell down the little bank. My hands hit the snow to take my fall and then the stove piece came down, corner-ways, on my left hand. It seemed to me that the hand was smashed so I carried the parts back under my right arm.

Rhino was in when I got to the Shack and when I took off my leather glove and duffle, my woollen yellow glove was scarlet with blood. Rhino was interested immediately. A large swelling was already there between the first two fingers and a puncture was letting out blood which, Rhino said, was due to a ruptured vein. No bones were obviously broken but I don't know. The pain was as much as I could bear and I had no appetite for anything at supper. I had a hot sweet cup of tea for shock. For a couple of hours, till two Codeins and a large whisky got to work I didn't know what to do with myself. Now, at 11 p.m. the bruise has spread down the first two fingers to the first joint and a patch of blood has come through the thick dressing and bandage. Rhino will change the dressing before I go to bed...

Tonight we've got our next three months' chocolate ration of four two-ounce bars. This time we have Bourneville and Dairy Milk. Unfortunately the 'whole nut' and 'fruit and nut' weren't found so next time we'll have to have those two types together...

Temperature at 1200 hours -39°C, wind... twenty knots...

Tuesday 31 July, 1956
A very cold day, most unsuitable for being outside. The temperature didn't quite get down to -51°C...

I went out this morning to the hut to bring in the rest of one oven and the tin of oven cement and after that stayed in the hut to rest my hand. Rhino changed the dressing this morning instead of last night. My hand is double size and the puncture still bleeds and looks rather gory...

Thursday 2 August, 1956
Continued cold all night but started slow rise today. Very surprised to sleep very soundly last night but probably due to whisky and wearing of a down jacket. This, in spite of -53°C...

Saturday 4 August, 1956
I'm glad today is finished for it has been tough going. The welding of the Aga cast iron oven frame has been done but plenty of work now still remains in shaping the weld to the original dimensions. Taffy and I worked together, with Taffy doing most of the hard work due to my bashed hand...

With the fumes of the welding and the pop-pop I ended up suffering rather from carbon monoxide...

Another argument about changing the clocks to get daylight hours and a minor (ought to have been a major) altercation about work on the hut.

Temperature at... 1200 hours -31°C.

It is hardly surprising that, after six months of sleeping in tents in the biting cold, tempers had begun to fray – and Lenton's obvious reluctance to employ those he deemed to be amateurs in the hut's construction obviously rankled with many. And yet, almost miraculously, a major – and potentially very damaging – dispute was avoided. Perhaps, in the circumstances, all eight men realised that they could ill afford to quarrel too seriously.

Monday 6 August, 1956
Cold last night but, until about 7 a.m. I slept well – after that I was too chilled to sleep other than fitfully...

I had... a dig around the dumps for the missing Aga box but there's no hope of finding it – especially when using an ice axe with only one hand. I've decided to make the parts...

Temperature at... 1200 hours -46 °C.

Tuesday 7 August, 1956
'Orrible day with a hefty northerly blizzard blowing... No-one has been able to do anything much...

Last night Ken and Rhino slept on wooden plywood bunks with sleeping bags in the hut but were very cold. Tonight they will try again with wood-wool for mattresses. They can hardly bring out their bedding in this weather anyway...

I have finished volume 2 of Somerset Maugham's The World Over*...*

Wednesday 8 August, 1956
The wind was still blowing very strongly this morning so I decided to stay in bed till lunchtime.

Hannes woke up at 8 a.m. with my alarm and brushed the rime off my bed before pumping the Primus. If one lights the Primus before the other is ready to get up then we brush the white coating of frost off the other's sleeping bag so that the Primus warmth won't let it melt into the material.

It was pretty awful last night getting to my tent for I got blown off my course and couldn't see for the drift. The wind was strong enough to blow me off my feet twice. The wind had undone the tent flap tapes with the continual pounding and the circular flap was blowing flat along the face of the tent. It took several minutes to pull it back to the opening so that I could get through. Inside, the violent flapping of the canvas reminded me exactly of the heavy vicious bursting of anti-aircraft guns and shells in thick concentration. My tent wall was forcing right in on my small bed space so that the wall pushed against my sleeping bag. As the wall is thick with ice and quickly gathers a layer of thick frost, it is not very nice to lay against as the bedding freezes to it...

Getting about outside is a difficult, uncomfortable and time-absorbing business. It took me ages to get to the hut and I kept falling over in the dark while the wind and drift made it impossible to look up, or in the direction that I wanted to go. Although only three yards from the hut, I didn't see it until I fell down a drift bank into a scattered pile of timber...

I have written a telegram to Enid to say that the two [air] letters have arrived and asked her to make the contents more brief and less full stops...

Saturday 11 August, 1956
No call this morning and it wasn't difficult to guess why. The wind blew hard all night and the temperature was still going down when I went to bed. Rather broken night's sleep with cold but made it up in short spells till 11.30 a.m. when I got up.

Drift, coming to the Shack, was as thick and bad as it has ever been... an incredible amount going up inside the windproof waist, sleeves, gloves and hood... I was full of drift and fingers chilled while all of the bones in my head ached with cold...

Tuesday 14 August, 1956
Improvement in some ways for the wind had dropped a lot and the morning was clear and bright with a suggestion over the sea that the sun wasn't far below the horizon. Daylight was perfect. I wanted to get on with the Weasel so asked Taffy to have a go at the wind generator. However he didn't stay long up the mast...

In the Weasel I removed the water pump and have fitted the new one, so tomorrow I should be able to fit the generator, dash panel and engine side cover. Pity that the batteries are in such a low state or I could have run the engine this evening...

Telegram from Enid getting at me about economising suggestion on telegrams...

Temperature at... 1200 -42°C...

Wednesday 15 August, 1956
Cold and windy and quite disappointing as we had hoped for the southerly to die down and a warm spell to arrive. Instead, the temperature... went down steadily all day to -45°C...

There was a further sign of the nearness of the sun's return for a little 'twink' of brilliant glow showed on the horizon above the apparent position of the sun below...

This evening I was able to make the last Aga rod...

Thursday 16 August, 1956
... Taffy and I struggled with the ovens and got them out of the Shack hatch, through the lean-to, up four food boxes and three snow steps and onto a man-haul sledge. This was all dragged round the south side of the hut over the drifts which have smoothed out and then round as near as we could get to the east door. Here, door to said hut not having been found, I had to un-nail one large sheet of plywood and, down a steep snow slope, we man-handled the ovens into the hut ...

Wind about forty-three knots and has been strong all day but temperature is only -26°C instead of nearly -46°C last night. So I hope for a warm night's sleep ...

Sunday 19 August, 1956
... Dead calm, warm – well, warm to us – and the pressure steady ...

Armed with a roaring blow-lamp I got into the Weasel and found the starter still well jammed so I attacked the pinion end with the flame. Great amounts of ice inside ran out as water and after an hour of many persuasions the Weasel not only awoke to roaring life but was also pleased to pull the Maudheim[26] out with a right-angle pull.

This cheering feat was viewed with – I am quite sure – a good deal of satisfaction by two digging teams ... All stopped work and stared at a Weasel actually moving ...

Temperature at ... 1200 hours -17°C, [wind] ... at six knots ...

Monday 20 August, 1956
... The missing door has been found, and also the 'dining table' ... There are still many boxes of stores missing, including chimneys, two stoves and Aga parts ...

Thursday 23 August, 1956
The sun at last ... It didn't rise very far and cloud hung low over the horizon so the glow was not for very long. The daylight lasted till 4.30 p.m. though ...

---

[26] A 14-foot Norwegian sledge designed specifically for towing by motorised vehicles and first used at the Maudheim base of the Norwegian/British/Swedish Antarctic Expedition of 1949-52.

Ken has written a monthly press report on the sun's return after four months. At the end he says, 'Some are even considering changing clothes and washing'...

Friday 24 August, 1956
... Slept badly last night with the cold but tonight it is colder...

Digging going on in the hut and Ralph brought in a piece of average-type snow block and weighed it. From this it was deduced that there were about one hundred and twenty tons of snow in the hut and that about thirty tons now remain in the two western bays, without the large amounts still in the loft...

Temperature at... 1200 hours -37°C... Temperature at 2400 hours -45°C, wind 180° at twenty-seven knots.

Sunday 26 August, 1956
... Cold, heavy drift and south wind... I slept again only about five hours and then had very broken sleep, through cold, till 9 a.m.... The inner surfaces of my sleeping bags and blanket were stiff with frost as well as the outside and around my head the blanket for covering me in was thickly white with deep frost...

A large filling in the back upper right tooth has been loose for some days and today it came out leaving only two walls of the shell of what was once a tooth. Rhino has temporarily filled in what's left but if it doesn't last I'll have it out.

Tonight I sleep in the Shack so I should have a good sleep. I suppose it will be just my luck to have four fine working days lost to me [due to cooking duties]...

Temperature at... 1200 hours -43°C [wind] thirty knots...

Monday 27 August, 1956
First day of cooking done. Seems I've done nothing but cook all my life. Successful day, though I feel very sorry to lose a day of light wind and no drift even though 'tis southerly...

Ralph reckons about five tons of snow were moved today from the hut...

Tonight I went up the mast because the generator wasn't charging and found an eighth of an inch coating of ice and rime on the propeller while the leading edge had a quarter of an inch thick line of ice on it. Although not fully cleaned, it made about 4 amps difference.

Ken and Rhino, now used to the hut, have struck their tent. I expect we'll all be inside the hut soon.

Temperature at... 1200 hours -31°C... [wind] at five knots...

Thursday 30 August, 1956

Last (and also successful) day's cooking done. Ken takes over tomorrow and sleeps in the Shack tonight.

Beautiful bright day with sun brilliant but temperatures still down with a south wind. I took my sleeping bag to the hut this morning to save having to move from the tent later. I feel that it is going to be a little chilly in that little room in the hut. It is the one inside the hut from Ken and Rhino's which is against the wall and has a window. Next door are two more rooms in the same way, the wall room bunks having been booked by Hannes and Jeff. In the inner room, similar to mine, will be Taffy and Ralph...

Temperature at... 1200 hours -42°C...

Friday 31 August, 1956

... Slept last night on Ken's bed in the hut. Very comfortable on two Dunlopillos, but chillier getting up than in a tent.

Tonight new twenty-four hour meteorological programme starts. Hannes sits in the newly furnished Meteorological office in the north-east corner of the hut...

Saturday 1 September, 1956

Dreadful day so we all stayed in the Shack. I did go to my 'workshop' to get a few small tools to repair the anemometer again. During Hannes's all-night meteorological duty he broke off the repaired cup by flicking it with his finger. This was particularly unfortunate in view of the very high north wind today...

Tonight, with the wind dropped a bit, the speed is fifty knots so it must have been up in the seventies this morning. It seemed to be the strongest that I have been out in so far because it was more difficult to walk and to stop being blown along. At times the wind would just manage to unbalance me and then I was forced southwards at a run until I could check myself. All moving was done with back or side to the wind in order to breathe and escape the heavy driving drift...

I had a lovely warm night on the comfortable Dunlopillo in the hut... The temperature in the hut is lagging well behind compared with the outside temperature but this will be compensated for when the outside temperature goes down I hope...

Sunday 2 September, 1956
Uggish day, similar [to] yesterday. High wind, snow and drift, but temperature quite well up. With the temperature and the salt in the drift it was very sticky and blew inside the clothing at every possible opening...

This morning I heard the dogs wailing in the tunnel so, after lunch, I visited them. The space for some is very reduced now, and drift had piled through the ventilator to almost shut off Bouncer at the end of one tunnel. I dug a lot away and was able to crawl through. Next to him was a wall of snow with a hole in it just big enough for Captain to look through so I dug away enough of that for him to feel not quite so shut in. All of this manoeuvring was done wriggling around on stomach and all fours. It was very warm in the tunnel and I was sweating in my windproof...

Temperature at... 1200 hours -10°C... [wind] at forty-five knots...

Monday 3 September. 1956
Same weather today with heavy drift and snow and wind as strong as ever.

Last night we had fat thickness and weighing. [My] weight much the same at ten stone six pounds. Some interesting exhibits were displayed from rotting underwear to scaling leathery skin, from long twisted toenails to large rolls of matted wool. Jeff, picking up his clothing, found a dull coloured vest and exclaimed: 'Crikey! Am I still wearing that?' The dirty vests are discoloured mostly around the neck down to a rust colour...

I've set up my bedding on my own bunk because Ken comes off cooking today while Tony takes over...

Ken hopes to move out those dogs with least room and put them on the span tomorrow.

The Shack has been dripping very badly these three days but, strangely, the floor has remained a thick layer of large knobs of ice instead of a slushy great puddle at the work-bench end as it usually does in this temperature.

Temperature at... 1200 hours -7°C... [wind] at sixty-two knots...

Tuesday 4 September, 1956

Thank Heaven for a decent day... [The wind] has dropped all day and the temperature has remained high so it has been very good for outside work.

Taffy was good enough to de-snow the Weasel, which was just about full up, while I rolled an empty paraffin drum over to my 'workshop'. I cut out a piece with oxy-acetylene for the Cairn stove chimney and have since been trying to shape it into a chimney but, gosh, it is tough stuff.

Gave the Weasel a bit of a run round while Ken and Rhino brought all seventeen dogs out of the main dungeon (for I can hardly call it a tunnel now) and put them on a span to east of the north drift. They were terribly excited and deliriously happy as they pranced about on the chains barking...

Rhino de-snowed the Fergy and had it on a short run.

Temperature at... 1200 hours -8°C... [wind] fifty knots [but by] 2300 hours... calm...

Wednesday 5 September, 1956

Very fine day but a bit chilly with a light southerly. Some cloud but the sun was shining for most of its few allotted hours...

Mirages abounded for most of the day all around us. Icebergs, including a massive tabular, were inverted in the air with the top of the real 'berg stretched with grey web to connect with the mirage above. Far distant snow wastes were also inverted into the air and to south and south-west were prominent white lumps, one like a snowball and another a small group of white lumps. The hill running in from Vahsel Bay was very clear today showing its rock outcrops and the sweeping slides of ice down its steep side.

I've welded together the chimney that I made for the Cairn stove so we hope we'll soon have a wood fire in the hut. Now I'm trying to make air ducts for the Aga. The paraffin drum sheet is much too tough to make two inch diameter pipes from so I'm making them of flour tins.

News from Bunny says Endeavour[27] *sailed 23rd August very spick and span, no deck cargo except twelve embarrassed huskies.*

---

[27] Previously the FIDS supply vessel, MV *John Biscoe*, the *Endeavour* had been purchased for use by Hillary's Ross Sea party and renamed. Her departure on 23 August was to New Zealand for loading.

Magga Dan *trials due to be completed 28th September. Expedition stand at Schoolboys' Exhibition, Olympia, very popular...*

The sledge trial run was done this morning with Ken and Rhino and a couple of boxes of sledge rations. Only five dogs went out to start with... Poor little Mary was found dead in the puppies' tunnel this morning.

Friday 7 September, 1956
Rotten night in the hut. I got to bed about midnight but Ken and Rhino, in the next bunk, separated from mine by only a blanket in the doorway, kept talking till about 1.30 a.m. After that, I found my back was feeling too cold to be able to get to sleep. So, until 3.30 a.m., I lay tense and shivering, at which time, I was very sick...

Haven't felt very well all day... Rhino says, get to bed with a hot water bottle or, if I stay up, have only milk. I can't go to bed – too cold and too much to do – but I don't seem to have got much done. Checked all the taps, dies and drills to see if we need more...

All telegrams and letters away satisfactorily today...

Temperature at... 1200 hours -32°C... [wind] at forty-three knots...

Monday 10 September, 1956
Worked on the Aga for most of the day... Handling hundredweight castings at -26°C was a bit much.

When all was assembled there came the delightful job of filling the whole stove with 2½ hundredweight of this [diatomaceous] earth... [28] *Now I look as though I work in a cement factory and the floor is covered with it. Before laying the half hundredweight of Stillite[29] on top I'm leaving it to settle down. As a last minute job I've had to make two back-plate stiffeners from a BP paraffin drum. The auxiliary air ducts and the nine rods that I made are all just right...*

All roof and ridge panels now on and only two wall panels to go – apart from the missing ones...

---

[28] Diatomaceous earth: a naturally occurring, soft, siliceous sedimentary rock. When powdered, it is used as thermal insulation.
[29] Stillite: an insulating mineral wool.

Thursday 13 September, 1956
Very good day of some success. Northerly wind all day a bit strong at times but temperature not too bad. The drift is always the worst feature of a northerly.

Visited all of the dogs and tackled the Weasel starter problem. There came from somewhere a spark of determination and out came the propeller shaft and gearbox and about half a hundred-weight of ice that I had to chip out with a crow bar. It stretched from the engine to the back axle and was ten inches deep in the hull. A nasty job removing bolts holding the starter under the engine and then I enlisted Ken as 'crowbarer' to lever up the rear end of the engine while I hauled up the starter motor past the exhaust manifold. This really was a struggle as the heat shield got stuck. I've stripped the starter down and titivated it and now it is OK. It was full of ice, dirt and oil and the commutators were dirty and pitted. Unfortunately there is almost nothing of the carbon brushes left but it will have to do till the ship comes. Tomorrow I have the nasty cold finger job of assembling the propeller shaft, gear box, starter motor, etc. again.

Wonderful surprise when six [air] letters arrived tonight, one from Enid. A nice letter and good to hear that she is making another recording this month and hopes to get Mum to say a few words. Asks me not to worry about New Zealand expense...[30] and goes on to say that she hopes to get part-time job in the evenings. Must put a stop to that!

Temperature at... 1200 hours -26°C... [wind] twenty-one knots.

Friday 14 September, 1956
Good for work today but spoilt when south wind came along tonight and put a stop to my latest repairs. Fixed the starter back in today and gearbox and propeller shaft... Without finishing off further I soon found a towing job offered me. A most monstrous seal had been laid clear by Ken in a pit three or four feet down and wanted dragging out. I dragged it (by Weasel, that is) around to the dog lines while Ken sat on its back. All of the dogs and puppies are out now on four spans to get used to being next to their prospective team mates...

---

[30] Enid planned to travel to New Zealand in order to welcome Roy on the expedition's return.

Dull all day starting at -21°C with a light north-east wind. Later it was practically calm but the trend was toward south again.

During the seal hauling I found that the radiator was leaking rather badly at the top just as our BNGE Weasels did. I've started to remove it to put in a new spare...

Sunday 16 September, 1956
Ups and downs today but the weather has been good to us. Got the radiator fitted but engine wouldn't start and starter wouldn't work properly, then a heater pipe broke and all the anti-freeze ran out near the pump so I couldn't do anything to put it right with the dynamo in the way.

I removed the propeller shaft and gearbox and, again, the starter motor. Took brushes from spare Sno-Cat 24V starter motor and filed them to fit... Eventually, all ready for test at 11 p.m....

Temperatures at... 1200 hours -19°C...

Monday 17 September, 1956
Success at last I hope. I fitted starter, gearbox and propeller shaft, battery box, flooring, etc. and repaired broken rubber pipe. Did five mile test run to the sea-ice and all went well except that the ignition wants retarding slightly...

Wednesday 19 September, 1956
... Jeff starts cooking tomorrow and will sleep on the Shack table tonight but, after breakfast, meals will be in the hut, for it is 'moving-in' day tomorrow...

Temperatures at... 1200 hours -39°C... [wind] at fifteen knots...

For 225 nights, from 7 February until 20 September, the Advance Party had camped out in the most appalling conditions – in the process, becoming the first expedition to spend an entire winter under canvas at such high latitudes. During this period, each man enjoyed a temporary respite only when he moved into the Shack to take his turn as duty cook. A few hardy souls, including Roy, Blaik-lock and Goldsmith, had chosen to relocate to the main hut before the official moving-in day on 20 September, but as the hut was still unheated and sleeping areas could not be warmed up quickly with a Primus stove, as a tent could, in reality they had prioritised novelty over comfort.

Why had the hut construction taken so long? There is no doubt that the serious delay in the *Theron*'s arrival was a significant factor. Ten of the eighteen men who had travelled south in order to shift stores and erect the frame of the hut were obliged to leave with the stores still on the sea ice and not a single bolt in place.

Then there were question marks over the practicality of the hut itself. The design needed to be sizeable, providing accommodation for sixteen men and all the facilities for daily living as well as communications and scientific work, and it had to withstand the weather and the weight of accumulated snow. However, it also needed to be capable of quick construction, and this is where it failed. The Advance Party found the components heavy to handle, the design complex and the plans difficult to follow. Moreover, many of the wooden beams had warped, so that pre-drilled holes did not align. Of course, these problems were greatly exacerbated by having to undertake the build during an Antarctic winter with frequent gales, mountains of drift snow, and bitter cold.

When the construction work started in mid-February the Advance Party hoped to have proper shelter before the onset of winter, but the work was painfully slow from the outset. Then the seven-day blizzard left side panels under huge drifts, making it extremely difficult to find the right ones. In early April, Roy noted, the hut 'still looked only a skeleton'.

Each side of the hut required forty-five panels that individually weighed about 150lbs (68kgs) and care had to be taken because panels for the sides, the roof and the gable-ends were of different shapes and sizes. There were also concerns about four main truss plates that had been accidentally dropped into the sea during unloading, but Roy managed to make replacements from steel base-plates intended for bonfire boilers.

The sun disappeared below the horizon towards the end of April and the work soon required artificial light. Further heavy drifting in May meant 'a shortage of panels for the roof... as the wrong ones were dug out, and the right ones haven't yet been found'. By the beginning of June, more severe drifting left the hut half-full with some 80 tons of frozen snow; at the eastern end the drift reached the rafters. In addition to the natural obstacles, Lenton seemed reluctant to accept help, perhaps believing that the amateur carpenters would only hinder progress. And yet, in spite of everything, the work continued, however slowly, and, in mid-July, Roy observed that the east, south and west walls were complete, along with half the north wall.

Was there a better alternative? The committee tasked with equipping the Ross Sea element of the expedition thought so. Instead of purchasing a traditional hut of the type erected at Shackleton, they chose an innovative new design that relied upon large insulated panels that bolted together. Crucially, all of the panels were interchangeable, removing at a stroke the requirement to find a specific crate of parts before progress could be made. Hillary and his team chose a site at Pram Point on Ross Island on 9 January 1957; they had laid the mess hut foundations by 13 January, and by the evening of the very next day Hillary could say that we 'had effective shelter for the first time'. They completed construction of the last of the main huts little more than three weeks later.

Of course, there were disadvantages to the New Zealanders' design, chief among which was the cost. A FIDS-type hut might be purchased for around £9000. In stark contrast, the accommodation for the Ross Sea Party cost an eye-watering £36,000 – but the Ross Sea Committee believed that the ease and speed of construction justified the outlay. Given the problems they had encountered at Shackleton, Roy and his companions would probably have agreed.

Thursday 20 September, 1956
Writing this on Friday as yesterday was a busy one and yet, in a way, a holiday. We moved into the hut and there were constant comings and goings between the Shack and the hut with man-haul sledge loads of boxes of food, clothing, personal gear, cooking equipment, etc. ...

In the evening we had beer and brandy but it didn't develop into a party. It probably would have if the hut was properly inhabitable with heating and other refinements as intended. But going to cold cabins and the thought of having to get out in the night were restrictions. Neither is there electric lighting yet. With mains power we could have had other inducements to party spirit such as radio and gramophone. I fixed up my box with its shelf (now brought from the Shack) in a corner above my bed and supported with a strut from the full-length shelf. In this are lots of books etc. ...

Ralph and I were the last to bed and we decided to have a kipper so I put a tin on a Primus. It swelled out with constant pops and snaps and... the tin blew up with a crack like a two-pounder gun.

Kipper or bits of kipper were hanging from the window frame [and] a large amount was firmly flattened against a goodly area of the ceiling, while plenty was scattered over the floor, table and chairs. The array of tins on the shelf had taken on a brown, mottled effect, while one and a half kippers, together with separation paper, had landed almost in the same spot from whence they had arisen to wrap themselves around the Primus. The whole place has taken on a most nauseating kipper smell and Taffy found a piece in his tea for breakfast.

Temperature at... 1200 hours -37°C.

Friday 21 September, 1956

Didn't feel like getting up for breakfast as it was 2 a.m. when I got to bed this morning. Stayed in till 11.30 a.m. and it was very warm and comfortable. Such a bad day that nothing can be done outside in high wind and drift...

For the two nights in my cabin my sleeping bag has been very warm and the two Dunlopillos make it very comfortable. I no longer have the Terylene blanket inside the bags but, instead, the bags inside the blanket. Now all of the frost collects on the blanket leaving the bag frost-free. Perspiration has always been our worst problem...

Temperature at... 1200 hours -35°C... [wind] thirty-seven knots...

Sunday 23 September, 1956

... All day, with spasmodic assistance of Rhino, Hannes and Ralph, I've been digging out the Freelite wind generator cables to the Shack... I will run cable from halfway down the mast to the ridge of the hut at the west end...

Ken's been repairing a tent for his trip with Rhino to Vahsel Bay to seek seals... I hope later for a Weasel trip to Vahsel Bay to collect any seals that Ken gets...

Jeff's finished [as] cook and I start tomorrow morning – curse it...

Monday 24 September, 1956

... Ken and Rhino making haste to get everything ready for the sledge trip. Thawing out and repairing the tent, making red marker flags, assembling cooking gear, food, medical supplies, spare clothing, etc....

Tuesday 25 September, 1956

... Ken and Rhino left at about 11.30 a.m. I took time off to see the dogs being harnessed and not much trouble occurred. This is the first time that eight have been together at once and there was a bit of difficulty getting away. Several false starts and several fights but eventually they disappeared over the hill to the sea-ice ...

I slipped a loaf of bread into the kitbag for the sledge before they left. Unheard of on a sledging trip so they were in for a surprise ... The loaf surprise never materialized for at about 5.15 p.m., as tea was nearing its end, Ken and Rhino walked in well coated with frost and ice.

Things had gone very wrong. First, the small food depot laid some days ago a couple of miles along the sea ice was not found and in an effort to locate it, they turned back after three miles and came about two miles towards base again, along the top. Then they did two miles out along the bottom, still without recognising the depot. Moltke Nunatak[31] and an iceberg that had been their sighting marks were not visible due to drift so they had to come back three miles to base, making ten miles in all.

During this time the sledge had overturned a few times but the bad tumble came going down the hill for the second time. Ken was on the brake when the sledge overturned and neither dogs, sledge nor Ken could stop, so the whole lot went down sideways ending up with a broken brake ... The compass box had got broken in one of the falls too so altogether it was not a successful run. Rhino had lost a piece of windproof trouser leg on a screw and Ken hurt his leg when the sledge went over it ...

Thursday 27 September, 1956

Last day of cooking finished and Taffy takes over tomorrow. Bad day of strong southerly and low temperatures but ... very bright day, and with no clouds, it is now remaining twilight during the night.

The third box of library books was opened yesterday so, now, everyone is reading polar books, while Jeff has brought out a lot of Illustrated London News *and* Esquires ...

---

[31] Nunatak: an isolated peak of rock projecting above a surface of inland ice or snow. The Moltke Nunataks were surveyed and mapped by Wilhelm Filchner's German Antarctic Expedition, 1911-12.

Everyone is thinking about, or writing, air letters before 5th October [deadline]. I have written one to Enid.

Temperature at... 1200 hours -38˚C... [wind] at thirty-nine knots...

Saturday 29 September, 1956

I'm worn out but satisfied. Took down the wind generator assembly bit by bit and hauled up a complete new set. Was pretty good till after lunch when the northerly got stronger and stronger. Carried on after tea in a very nasty wind and drift but now have only to fix the propeller. My fingers were killing me but I wanted to get all done that was possible in case we have a southerly tomorrow.

Ken and Rhino went off again this morning to try again for Vahsel Bay. All quiet except that Caesar got hold of Guy's eye and wouldn't let go. Ken and I were really thumping him...

They came up on the hand-cranked radio at 8.15 p.m. tonight and had done seven miles...

I got my ears in the South wind yesterday while filling the petrol cans. Today the right one is a bit painful and burning. My left hand that stopped the Aga oven about three months ago is still swollen and the middle finger, when bent or gripping tightly, hurts the top knuckle.

Temperature at... 1200 hours -26˚C... [wind] at nine knots...

Sunday 30 September, 1956

Had a bit of a party last night for [my] wedding anniversary, mainly Ralph, Taffy, Hannes and I. I got out the Midwinter musical instruments and Ralph fixed up his one-string bass on a tea chest. Also had the radio going. I fried cured bacon and made toast with the Tilley heater. Went to bed at about 2 a.m. Found some old broken cigars and South American cigarettes which Ralph made into a cigar laced with rum wrapped up in toilet paper and banded with adhesive tape. I didn't smoke much of that! ...

Brought over the wind generator switch-panel from the Shack and fixed it in the attic. Also put up a light for the radio. The wind generator is now working and the cable runs through the loft. Next is to put 24v lighting in.

Temperature at head level has been +16˚C in the living room this evening and the thermometer near floor level, for the first time, registered just above freezing...

Sledge team didn't hear us at 6.15 but they sent three times that they haven't moved all day due to conditions...

Temperature at... 1200 hours -22°C... [wind] at twenty-two knots...

Monday 1 October, 1956
... South wind and thick drift increasing through the day...

Nothing much going on. Stationery, typewriter etc. unpacked and I did some successful patching on the Singer sewing machine.

Last night the recreation box was opened up making available football, chess, draughts, dice, darts, etc.... Nothing from sledge today...

Wednesday 3 October, 1956
A goodly day and much accomplished. I wanted to help dig out the last bay of the hut at the generator room end but first had to bring in the Weasel batteries to charge... Ralph, Taffy and I shovelled out a series of steps to get the snow over the north drift. I chopped snow with an axe and shovelled it to the opening and up to the snow just outside. From there it was shovelled to a small platform halfway up the drift and, at that stage, shovelled onto the top and as far out as possible. We did very well. Taffy says he thinks more was shifted today than on any other day...

Nothing from the sledge again...

Tonight Hannes is busy making a kite. A never-ending stream of odd things have been, are being, or are to be made for a variety of strange ideas. We are working on a two-day cooking roster now while Ken and Rhino are away. Tony has done his two days and Ralph goes on tomorrow. Ralph rushed up a quick kite from slips of bamboo and a sheet of brown paper stuck with Sellotape and has been out twice. Final adjustments to be made. Hannes is on the floor with his, muttering at it...

Monday 8 October, 1956
... At 1.45 p.m. the sledgers arrived, well-covered with frost and ice...

Rhino and Ken saw the first bird of the season – an Antarctic petrel. There were quite a few seals, one with a new-born calf and some others about to give birth. They found one very young Weddell about three feet long which was dead. This they brought back. They killed only one, feeling satisfied with the knowledge that seals were there. The soles of their leather moccasins have worn very thinly and holes have appeared so they are not strong enough for sledging. They did a total of nearly eighty miles. It is about thirty miles to the first seals that they saw…

Wednesday 10 October, 1956
… Rhino, Taffy and I were able to dig out the 13cwt case with generator and switch board in it and the Weasel dragged it out of its six feet deep hole and up a ramp that we had dug. Having got it up we came in to tea and then I pushed it back in the hole again with the front of the Weasel… to allow Ralph to photograph the operation with the cine camera. Various shots and sequences were taken though the light was not very good…

If Ralph can get his clearing-up done in the generator end of the hut tomorrow I hope to get the generator to slide down a ramp into the doorway which Ralph finished putting in today…

Friday 12 October, 1956
A fine day of progress. I feel that nothing can stop us now… We got the first generator into the hut this afternoon by sliding it down planks through the hut door while checking it with the Weasel in reverse gear…

Ken took time off from cooking to take the Ferguson down to the cliff edge but saw no seals. He made some very nice cornflake chocolate crunchy things today, and, first time for ages, we had seal liver, from the recently shot seal…

Wednesday 17 October, 1956
Shackleton doesn't look the same anymore. Three masts have been erected today. We've had very little wind so it was just the day for masts. First up was one of Taffy's radio masts… With two sections its height is 52'… Next up was Jeff's meteorological mast… I climbed to the top while they finished off the guys and let down the tackle-block. Quite a good view from the top…

Thursday 18 October, 1956
At about 9.15 a.m. the wind started to go round towards north and we've had a northerly with snow all day… Taffy got his third mast up this morning but the last one is held up for weather…

At the generator end I've been preparing cables for the main switchboard and, of course, digging up electrical spares, boxes for sockets etc.

Heard on the news tonight that an American Neptune aircraft crashed killing four men in the Antarctic while bringing supplies to their expedition...

Friday 19 October, 1956
North wind blowing all night and day and it has dropped a great load of snow all over the place... We've had it comparatively warm of course but all this soft sticky snow will make transport difficulties...

Ken and I gradually built up a support of timber till the generator was level with the mountings and then we rolled it on exhaust pipes into position where it came down quite in place over the mounting bolt holes.

We put up Taffy's fourth mast this evening and also brought in his great heavy transmitter which is now at the eastern end of our living room...

Saturday 20 October, 1956
Haven't got much done today, only bits of this and that... Awful lot of deep sticky snow everywhere. It will probably never go now, so conditions will no doubt be as bad as when the ship was here last February. Northerlies and soft snow are probably a summer condition...

Sunday 21 October, 1956
... I took most of the day just to wire all of the fuse boards and their switches together ready for mounting on a panel... Tomorrow I start two days cooking so it will have to wait now...

Tuesday 23 October, 1956
Have got today's cooking well in hand so I'm writing this before preparing supper (dinner). It is a rotten day outside. Started with a light north-east wind and then went north and has been coming from there in a big way all day bringing plenty of snow and drift with it.

Another good loaf today puts us one-in-hand after making two yesterday. Made two cakes yesterday and made two more today from yesterday's preparation so we're two cakes in-hand. I've also made a Christmas pudding (nearly). As it is still boiling I don't know how it will turn out but it has got seven tablespoons of good brandy in it. I've made a sprig of holly from a piece of cigarette tin for decoration. The berries are painted with red fluorescent paint but the green hasn't been brought over from the Shack so the leaves will be shiny, icy, silver…

The Christmas pudding was warmly praised and although a large one, the spare portion soon went in second helpings – Rhino having four helpings…

Wednesday 24 October, 1956
Bit more progress today with generators wired up and switch boxes and fuse boards fixed and connected together. I bolted down second generator this morning…

Northerly blizzard continues in full force and has wrecked poor old Jeff's meteorological mast. The anchor guy… snapped and the tower crashed crumpling the base end and the top end. The anemometer on the wooden spar at the top has a damaged cup and the spar is snapped. Jeff is, very naturally, upset after so much work on it. At present he is on his two days of cooking.

I went outside after tea with Rhino who fed the dogs. It was exceptionally difficult to walk against the wind and keeping a foot-grip while very slowly moving forward doubled up…

Temperature to… 1200 hours -10°C… [wind] at forty-three knots…

Thursday 25 October, 1956
A red letter in the annals of Shackleton but even greater for me in my personal triumph. What twaddle. Truth is, that, after all these months, I've got the first generator running – and producing power… I feel much better than if it were my birthday…

4

SUMMER AT LAST

The next day, 26 October, would be the first upon which the sun remained above the horizon for the whole twenty-four hours. Except when obscured by cloud, it would now be visible continuously until mid-February. Against the odds, the Advance Party had survived the winter.

Roy had maintained his diary assiduously throughout the difficult months of darkness, focusing almost exclusively on the positives and on his plans for overcoming the myriad challenges facing him personally, and the expedition as a whole. Nonetheless, it had been a brutal experience that tested all the men keenly.

Individuals reacted differently to the harsh conditions. In his diary, Goldsmith noted how one man had a 'damping effect' while another became 'more and more gloomy'. He described Roy as 'cheerful but very conservative in his tastes and although extremely hard working [he] tended to accuse others of not pulling their weight'. In another entry, he observed that Roy had a tendency to stick 'like a puppy to a slipper to the wrong end of the stick'.[32] Roy may have been argumentative and outspoken but he didn't harbour resentment in the privacy of his diary. Goldsmith knew, for instance, that Roy held him responsible for failing to identify more quickly the carbon monoxide poisoning from which they all suffered for weeks in the shack, but Roy's diary only mentions the problem, without apportioning blame. In terms of the wider organisation of the expedition, only later, during the strain of the crossing itself, does he become overtly critical.

------

[32] Rainer Goldsmith, diary, 7 May, 1956. Quoted in Haddelsey, *Shackleton's Dream: Fuchs, Hillary and the Crossing of Antarctica* (Stroud: The History Press, 2012), p. 67. For more details regarding inter-personnel conflicts during the Advance Party, see Haddelsey, pp. 60-74.

Throughout the winter, the temperature went up and down depending upon the wind direction but it always remained well below freezing and the men slept regularly in bedding thick with frost. On 25 July, for example, Roy recorded that his sheepskin, his sleeping bag and the six layers of blanket were all solid with ice particles.

On 1 August the temperature fell to -53°C. Not surprisingly, the men dreaded going to bed and they dare not drink much alcohol for fear of having to get up in the night. When they did opt for a tot of warming whiskey before retiring they found it had to be thawed out first. All things are relative, of course, and when the temperature rose to -34°C by noon on 3 August, Roy described the day as 'much warmer'. Indeed, back on 7 July when the temperature rose to about -12°C, he had enthused '... oh boy, it was warm...'

Clothing presented another problem. Although, in his diary, Roy never really complained about its quality or suitability, he recorded on 18 August how holes in his wind-proofs had allowed vast amounts of drift to gather inside. Years later, when asked if the clothing provided was adequate, he replied: 'No, it wasn't, but we just put up with it...' He added, 'If you are over-active and work hard for a long time you start sweating and the clothing absorbs the moisture and then you really are freezing because you've got freezing wet clothing, so you never work hard enough to make yourself sweat... The clothing you get these days is far superior...'[33] An additional problem for Roy – and for anyone recruited to work on the vehicles – was the effect of grease. Grease prevents fabric from breathing and body moisture therefore becomes trapped. As a result, the clothing loses its insulation and the wearer becomes more prone to frostbite.

But, despite everything, the men were alive, well, and living in the hut; and it would not be too long before *Magga Dan* arrived, bringing the rest of the expedition and the longed-for mail and new supplies. With the return of light and improving weather, they could also undertake excursions from the base: to search for seals, to begin preliminary short-range surveys to find possible routes for the Crossing Party, and to lay a supply depot some 50 miles along the most probable route identified.

---

[33] Roy Homard, interviewed by Duncan Knight, 8 February, 2014. The recording and transcript are held by REME Museum.

Friday 26 October, 1956

... Rhino and Hannes took dog team Erik, Nanouk, Kernek, Peso, Nutarak, Whitenose, Caesar and Guy to collect yesterday's seal; also the rifle was taken. This was fortunate as two more seals had come up through their holes in the slushy ice so they were bagged as well. We got down with the Weasel as they brought the first seal in and we all helped bring in the second one. This all took a long time as the journey to them meant going a long way round the pressure ice and a long way back on the other side of it to the newer ice which was mostly pretty rotten. We left the third seal till after lunch... I had already gutted the third one and was sorry to find it had a pup pretty near ready for birth. Back at base we found that it weighed forty-seven and a half pounds without all the additional birth business. It was about four and a half feet long and was also a female. I and Rhino photographed it and then skinned it. I've just finished washing it in six changes of water. That was at midnight and it is now a quarter past. Another hope of an early night gone. The skin is quite beautiful underneath, it being yellowy in colour with white markings. The back is dark grey...

From the young seal we've taken the liver and kidneys and a chunk of the back for little chops. Hannes has been presented with the eyes which he says are 'lovely fried'.

Beautiful day, especially while we were seal collecting; very little northerly or north-east wind and a warm sun. We wore no gloves or wind-proofs and I ended up in my long underpants as I was so hot. That is how I drove back...

For the last couple of days the hut roof has been dripping from the ridge due to the warmer air and the sun's warmth being absorbed by the black roof...

Saturday 27 October, 1956

Rather a lazy day of odd jobs. However, the generator job is all buttoned up except for exhausts up through the roof...

Ralph carries on building the partition for the bathroom next to the generator room...

I spent a long time this afternoon on the 'Singer' patching my wind-proofs. Even the patches are, in many places, patched...

Sunday 28 October, 1956

Nothing very great today...

Tonight we are talking straight to Halley Bay on the main set but we can't receive them very well on the main receiver so whoever is talking has to dash up the ladder into the loft to listen on the small set and then back down again to speak...

Ken and I have been preparing for our trip to Vahsel Bay to-morrow. Ken filled seven petrol cans and dug out a Canadian and a Maudheim trailer sledge and has also prepared all of the sledging and camping gear. Hannes is coming as Tony is not very keen.

Temperature at... 1200 hours -13°C... [wind] at sixteen knots...

Monday 29 and Tuesday 30 October, 1956

... On Monday morning the finishing preparations for the journey took most of the morning... We started just after midday in very fine clear sunny weather with a light southerly.

The first three miles were torturous. Sastrugi, as hard as iron and deeply rutted, interspersed with mounds of ancient broken sea-ice, gave the Weasel a hard time. Like a rowing boat in a rough sea, it pitched and tossed, sometimes thudding down nose first as it rode over a large bump. This made progress slow and our route very winding. We came to Ken's small depot of dog and man food and a can of paraffin all marked by a red flag. That was only three miles out, but it was the worst three miles...

The dogs soon got used to the idea of following the Weasel and, after each rest they leapt to their feet yelping as soon as the Weasel engine started. I stopped every four miles to rest the dogs for ten minutes. We arrived at the pressure ridge running into Vahsel Bay at about 8.15 p.m. having done about twenty-nine and a half miles. We had a good scout round the pressure ice of a tide crack a good way out from the cliff. The crack appears to be continually moving and keeping fairly open...

We found several seals with young pups and one emperor penguin. I used up about one and a half magazines of cine on all this. Each magazine holds fifty feet. It was used all too quickly and I could have done with half-a-dozen magazines on the pressure formations and the seals and penguin.

It was still beautifully sunny and ideal for photography. One mother was enticing her baby into the water – a very lengthy business. She had had the baby about fifteen yards from the crack over the other side of an old mound of pressure ice and, with continual calling in a sort of drawn out bark, answered by the pup with a bleat like a sheep, she gradually got the young one over the pressure to the water's edge. Still calling and nuzzling the young-ster she slipped into the water, then stuck her head up calling for the pup to follow. He lay on the bank looking into the water answering back for five minutes and at last with a note of obstinacy wriggled and humped himself away and lay against the old pressure. The next morning, however, he and his mother were both in the water...

It was about 11 p.m. when we got down to supper. Ken and Hannes had rigged up their tent and Ken boiled up the Pemmican and made cocoa. They settled down in the tent and I in the Weasel. It seemed to me too much to erect another tent for one night. It was a bit cramped with radio and Smith's heater, so, diagonally, my head was in one back corner and my feet propped up on the back of the driving seat or curled up behind it next to the radio. I slept alright too – until the darned dogs woke me at 3.30 a.m. ...

The next morning, Tuesday, was the most sickening I have ever been involved in for it meant killing four mother Weddell seals and their four young ones. No others, single, were about and the dogs were nearly out of food due to our losses in March... I was very glad when this horrible job was over and we got back to the tent where Ken made a cup of tea...

We moved at about 2.45 p.m. with all of the sledging gear inside the Weasel and a tent lashed to the Weasel roof while Ken took a tent, his sleeping bag and the petrol and oil cans. Hannes travelled all the way there and back standing up through the roof-hatch like a tank commander. I don't think he has got much skin left on his hips after that rough journey. After three miles I couldn't get out of top gear as second had seized up – an old fault of Greenland days. In the end I was able to come back on bottom and top gears...

We had a fry-up of sausages, bacon and fried bread and I had a glass of whisky. Dead tired, we were very glad to get to bed and fade out.

Thursday 1 November, 1956
Removed gearbox from Weasel and found several damaged parts all of which I replaced by improvisation except some scoured roller bearings...

Ken and Rhino have chopped up all of the seals that we brought back and we should now have enough to last to the end of the year.

No doubt we have a good chance of getting a few near at hand during that time.

Tomorrow Ken and Rhino hope to get away on a sledge journey south to investigate a route through the one place where we hope to get through, thirty-five miles from here, where a crevassed area restricts our direction. A depot will be shuttled out to fifty miles eventually. Pity we haven't got two vehicles operating or we could use those after the recce. Perhaps I can get on with the Sno-Cat engine soon but it might now have to be done outside as the Sno-Cat crate is drifted up level with the roof.

Tonight we've had fat thickness and weighing and my weight has dropped to 10 stone 3 pounds. Must be result of our recent sealing expedition.

Friday 2 November, 1956
Quiet day due to strong northerly and heavy drift outside… The gearbox was made ready and I took it to the Weasel and fitted it… Tonight I have read that delightful and simple tale by Ernest Hemingway called The Old Man and the Sea…

Saturday 3 November, 1956
… I topped up the Weasel sump and rear axle… and had a test run to the hill edge… The Weasel gearbox works well.

Ken and Rhino went off about 1 p.m. today without any trouble. At 1930 hours Taffy contacted them and they were about eight miles south [en route to lay a fifty-mile depot for the Crossing Party]…

Tuesday 6 November, 1956
… I started the job of putting full tracks on the Ferguson. The skis were removed, wheels put on and the two parts of the tracks connected. Unfortunately I haven't got the large front wheels for full tracks so they hang slack.

We had another contact with the BBC this afternoon but mostly conditions were poor… Mrs Honnywill[34] spoke and gave us the latest news including the surprise that Enid is to be hostess and give a speech at Latymer High School at a Christmas Party. The

---

[34] Eleanor Honnywill worked in the TAE offices in London and would accompany Fuchs to the British Antarctic Survey on his appointment as director. She later became the second Lady Fuchs.

school is sending me a Christmas parcel I gather. Poor Enid must be so nervous I think...

Wednesday 7 November, 1956

... Not very brilliant outside, wind north-east at twenty-five knots and a little ground drift but temperature is -13°C. Getting a bit better than it was earlier.

Ralph and Taffy have got a part of the middle section of the hut clear now having cleared snow from the loft, beams, trusses, etc. and knocked down the heavy clusters of frost crystals. The south side then had its floor swept clean and Ralph is busy making partition frames...

Yesterday... [the sledge party] did fourteen miles in poor visibility and increasing wind. Today they were forced to stop with northerly gale...

Thursday 8 November, 1956

... We heard from Ken and Rhino tonight, who last night and early this morning did a further seven miles south to lay the start of the depot and since then have done fourteen miles on the return trip. They hope to be in base in a couple of days if the weather is alright...

Ralph and Taffy have finished the partition frame next to the engine room and have erected it and Jeff has been assisting with nailing up hardboard for the ceiling of this part which will be the Medical Room.

Sunday 11 November, 1956

Still blowing northerly with snow and drift. I had a look up the meteorological mast at the wind-direction instrument and re-fixed the connections... It was a bit unnerving in thirty to forty knots remembering that the mast had been blown down once... [35]

While I was on top of the meteorological mast after lunch I saw, through the drift, the sledge approaching from the west about three quarters of a mile away. I told Taffy, who, at present, is cook, so that he could start preparing something for them, then I went out to meet them. They were a bit snowed-up from sledging into the wind and drift but the dogs were pulling very strongly. Altogether

---

[35] See diary entry for 24 October 1956.

they've clocked one hundred and one miles. I helped to put the dogs on the span and Rhino fed them some seal meat...

Still high temperatures, around -7°C, but five lower than yesterday.

Monday 12 November, 1956
Started on the Sno-Cat engine but, of course, it has to be done the hard way. I had hoped that the sump might come off without lifting the engine but it comes down as far as the steering platform, but does not clear the crankshaft. Now I hope to be able to raise the front (only) of the engine to get enough clearance.

Other things like exhaust pipes and starter have had to be removed and tomorrow I shall have to remove the hydraulic reservoir, pipes and so on, to remove the right-hand cylinder head...

Temperature was just high enough to work most of the time bare-handed, though it wasn't very comfortable...

Tuesday 13 November, 1956
Big day at home and it all seems to have been successful. We heard on our Antarctic programme an account of the Queen's inspection of the Expedition members and Magga Dan *at Butler's Wharf, Tower Bridge, and were immensely impressed by Mrs Honnywill's vivid description of it all... [She said] 'the Queen had a special word with Enid Homard who was the only wife whose husband is to be away for the two years'. (I think that is a correct quote of Eleanor). That interests me immensely and dearly long to know what they said...*

Thursday 15 November, 1956
What a big day at home. We heard the programme from the BBC about Magga Dan *leaving Butler's Wharf...*

Donald Milner did a lot of recording and a BBC commentator, Raymond Baxter, was there as well and the programme was presented by him. Donald and Raymond aren't very clued-up. One phrase by Raymond, 'The Expedition has started' set up a bitter howl of protest. Referring to the round hull, necessary to ride up on the ice, Donald said he expects the ship to roll in the rough seas of the Weddell Sea! – the Weddell Sea, being practically solid pack. We heard the programme at the same time as Light Programme listeners to 'Preparations for the Pole'. I suppose Enid managed to get time off to see the ship leave but I shall be very sorry if she didn't. Somehow I have an uneasy feeling that she may not have...

As the southerly continues with drift and low temperatures there is nothing I can do outside...

Saturday 17 November, 1956
Didn't write yesterday's diary as I didn't come in from work till 0215 hours. I worked on the Sno-Cat but didn't get far, though not for the want of trying...

Tried Taffy's aerial mast tackle but not powerful enough to lift the engine so I unreeved the large blocks used for erecting meteorological mast. This had about one hundred yards of two inch rope in it and it was rather tangled. I used a much shorter piece. Had to remove engine mounting bolts and rear mounting bolts to the gearbox and many other bits but, due to a northerly working up this morning, I had to pack up at lunch time...

The broken piston has been caused by the exhaust valve head snapping off. The cylinder head is damaged too...

Tuesday 20 and Wednesday 21 November, 1956
Started work on the Sno-Cat in morning in continued northerly. Turned out that I had picked the right day, for it gradually turned into a dead calm so I worked on to 1.15 a.m.

Replaced broken piston with new one and got cylinder head back on, amongst other things. Very pleased with day's progress. It really is the most difficult thing to work on without proper facilities...

Thursday 22 November, 1956
... Yesterday a telegram from Bunny said Magga Dan *bouncy, twelve knots. I think they were in Madeira last night and today. One from Eleanor Honnywill said Advance Party will always have special place in hearts of all at 64 Victoria Street.*[36] *Jolly sweet of her.*

---

[36] London headquarters of the TAE.

Ralph's been 'felting' on the roof for a couple of days and is now working again on indoor partitions. Hannes, who took over cooking from Ralph, has finished today, and tomorrow I'm on for two days.

Friday 23 November, 1956

First day of cooking done. I thought this morning that it was going to be a fairly calm day. That would have annoyed me because I could have done the Sno-Cat tappets. The southerly has continued however...

I have been forced to do some washing. First lot of socks and underpants finished and second lot of socks and vest soaking ready for tomorrow...

Saturday 24 November, 1956

Cooking finished and tomorrow Taffy takes over...

I have done my second lot of washing and am now doing a khaki shirt. I have changed into clean pants and new battle-dress trousers. Tomorrow, when my vest is dry, I'll change into that too. Next day, the clean shirt.

Rhino used the 1250w electric toaster today for the first time and it worked very well. It can be used only during the few hours of daily radio schedules when the generator is running.

Sunday 25 November, 1956

Rotten day. Not too cold, but no good for the Sno-Cat...

Started digging for Canadian trailer covers but not successful. Petted dogs instead. Their welcome much more rewarding...

Changed into clean vest and shirt this morning together with clean socks. Feels good, but a long soak in a hot bath would go very well. Tonight Taffy shaved with an ordinary razor! Then he washed his hair with a preparation Rhino has in his stocks. I washed my hair in it too but it was pretty painful as I have so many knocks and cuts on my head from working under the Sno-Cat...

I left a chunk of Rich Dough mixture to Taffy which was to save him having to make anything for tea. He made some jam buns and left them to one side before letting them rise. They started opening slightly at the top so he commenced to pinch them together. Unfortunately the tray slipped off the top of the Aga and the whole lot plopped into the can of swill water. A pathetic look of desperation came over his face. Quite pitiful. He transferred them to the dogs' can after fishing them from the bottom. Later, one, which had been overlooked, floated to the top. It has spread out like a big knobbly jelly fish...

Monday 26 November, 1956
... The boxes containing the gramophone and those containing the records have been found so, soon, we'll be having a little home music...

Tuesday 27 November, 1956
Another advancement with the Sno-Cat engine after a whole day of it, ending at a quarter to midnight. I cleaned, re-cleaned and changed the plugs, re-set the tappets, ignition and so on and at last have got it nearly right. At least, it is about as good as it was when we were first using it. Now the starter solenoid is shorting with melted snow in it and the clutch is noisy...

This morning Ken set off with one sledge and a little later, Rhino and Jeff set off [to cache more supplies at the fifty-mile depot]. Set off, ha! Team wouldn't go south for a long time but kept turning left and trying to turn right round to where they came from. Poor old Rhino must have been exhausted when at long last the team got the idea correctly. They were the second team and haven't much experience. Also, Beauty was with the team and he, two years old and from Whipsnade, has never before been in harness. Apparently he was shivering with fright...[37]

Thursday 29 November, 1956
Lovely day, with temperatures rising to -3°C...

Worked on Sno-Cat all day and went for a run to the sea-ice. Quite successful but not entirely satisfied with exhaust note at idling and the slower speeds. It accelerates like stink, and from standstill almost, it picked up on the hill in third gear.

Unfortunately the clutch needs looking at again. It really should be worked on with the engine removed but that is impossible...

---

[37] As well as dogs from Greenland, the expedition possessed four born at Whipsnade Zoo. Three of these were found to be unsuitable for work in the Antarctic because of their thin coats, and were destroyed. See Fuchs and Hillary, *The Crossing of Antarctica* (London: Cassell, 1958), p. 34.

Friday 30 November, 1956

*'Orrible day outside so I took advantage to start a letter to Enid.
Last night I stamped sixty envelopes with the special overprinted
Trans-Antarctic Expedition set of 6d, 3d, 2½d and 1d. Ralph did a
couple of hundred for dealers...*[38]

*I dug up one of the boxes of HMV reproducers, brought it into
the living room and opened a box of records. Having assembled the
thing, I brought it in and we had a short session including a few
records for the three sledgers. As it is a bad day we didn't expect
them to transmit (which they didn't) so we don't know if they heard
us...*

*When we awoke this morning it sounded as though we were at
the beginning of a tropical rain storm. There was a steady, concentrated, heavy pit-pat of water-drops all over the floor of the hut
outside our bunk rooms. When I looked, I saw the whole floor
covered with water. Snow, brought by our strong north-easterly
wind was sticking to the roof and melting, where it was able to run
down between the roof panels where roof-felting has not yet been
fixed. Not surprising, for our maximum temperature today has been
-1.4°C. Another 2.5°C rise and we are at danger point. If we go
above freezing we'll have an awful mess outside.*

*Remarkable that, in a few months, we have had about 50°C
change in temperature. The warm spell is showing up flaws in the
ice. The route to the hill is now glaringly crossed by a crevasse
about twenty feet wide running diagonally in from the hill edge to
the left of the track. It shows as a sunken gully whose edges are
showing cracks. However, I am sure it is well-filled except for its
edges and constitutes no danger...*

Sunday 2 December, 1956

*Beautiful day with an all-time high in temperature. Started this
morning with a light southerly, which became almost dead-calm
which, with sun out, gave us 1°C. I was able to work in shirt
sleeves, wearing no hat or gloves. Unfortunately, the southerly got
slowly brisker, till this evening it is around fifteen knots.*

*When I went out after lunch I saw that Ken, Rhino and Jeff had
arrived and had nearly finished putting the dogs on the span. They*

---

[38] Establishing a post office is a recognised way of asserting a territorial
claim. The sale of franked mail was also a means of raising money for the
expedition.

have got quite a tan except where their glasses have been worn...
Today they did the last seventeen miles, arriving about 2 p.m. ...

I have been working on the Sno-Cat all day to repair the clutch which doesn't disengage properly...

Monday 3 December, 1956
Yesterday's southerly turned into a northerly...

We've had a rotten day on the Sno-Cat trying to take things off before we can get at the gear box. Having spent the whole day at it we were able to move the gearbox back about an inch where it came up against a nut on the steering box. The nuts securing this are all obscured by brackets and plates apparently all welded on afterwards. Tomorrow perhaps...

Tuesday 4 December, 1956
Another tough day on the Sno-Cat but it ended with a triumphant note. I couldn't get any assistance but managed to remove the gearbox on my own. I got it out and lowered it only sufficiently far to just be able to see some of the clutch parts. At last I was able to remove the release bearing and forks. The release bearing was loose and not attached by its spring. This had allowed it to revolve and receive uneven pressure from the forks, so one fork got bent and so did the shaft.

A priority signal has gone to David Pratt explaining and asking if he can get [a] new fork shaft in Montevideo as I don't have a spare here. Since then I have been able to straighten the fork to within .003" and have got the shaft just about straight. Also, with the aid of Ken, I've got the heavy gearbox back in again and bolted up. For this I am truly thankful and greatly relieved. There still remains a day or two of work before I can try it...

Wednesday 5 December, 1956
Well, the Sno-Cat has been running again. It was a very fine day, slightly spoiled by getting a little cooler towards evening. For most of the day it was warm enough, in spite of a slight southerly, to work quite comfortably with bare hands. This enabled me to get all the propeller shafts and steering assembled very quickly. I had a try out before tea and the clutch worked well. After tea I took it down to the sea-ice. (No seals, pack-ice right up against us). It pulled well but I still don't quite like the exhaust beat...

Ralph and Taff have been very busy felting joints in the roof to stop the flood of melting snow. In glorious sunshine Ralph has a red scalp and neck and Jeff has had to plaster his nose with zinc ointment. Looks like a circus clown...

Friday 7 December, 1956
... Ken and Rhino set off today with the sledge before lunch [to reconnoitre the vehicle route as far as the Theron Mountains]. The usual bit of trouble for the first half mile or so trying to prevent the dogs going to the right... and then they disappeared over the edge of the low part just south of us.

Saturday 8 December, 1956
... Magga Dan and Taffy were in fairly good contact. Bunny says, 'Good work Roy, David trying to get parts for clutch in Monte.' This was in answer to my message that Taffy sent yesterday to say that I'd repaired the clutch. They arrive in Montevideo 0600 hours Sunday. They hope to reach Halley Bay 26th December and expect seven days unloading and building the Otter aeroplane.[39] They hope to reach us end of the first week in January.

Ken and Rhino tonight were camping forty miles south, seven miles from the depot.

Sunday 9 December, 1956
First day of cook. I used steaks from the unborn seal that we got a few weeks back down on the sea-ice – very tender. I made the first jellies and blancmange today after Tony had dug up fresh stores...

Contact good with Halley Bay... Heard from them that the Americans expect to be down this way in about twelve days... with Antarctic man Finn Ronne in charge. Ken met him once at Marguerite Bay. We hope to attract a landing...[40]

---

[39] The de Havilland Canada DHC-3 Otter: a single-engine, high-wing, propeller-driven, short take-off and landing aircraft. This machine would be used for the planned trans-continental flight during the austral summer of 1957-58.

[40] As part of the United States' contribution to the IGY, Antarctic veteran Captain Finn Ronne (1899-1980) had been placed in command of an expedition to establish a base on the Weddell Sea coast. Supported by USS *Wyandot* and the icebreaker USS *Staten Island*, Ronne built Ellsworth Station, at Gould Bay. It was commissioned on 11 February 1957.

Monday 10 December, 1956
Cooking finished. Beautiful outside all day with a ten to twelve knot southerly...

Sledge party did sixteen and a half miles yesterday, and fourteen and a half miles today. This should make them about seventy-eight miles south... They passed over some very large well-filled crevasses on the way. They want to know from Bunny if they should carry on south or head towards Theron Range.[41] *I should say keep going south for shortest route.*

Tuesday 11 December, 1956
Pleasant change today but it would have been excellent for vehicle work outside... I had to stay in to do the one hundred hours running check on the two [generator] engines...

Bunny wants Ken to head east for the mountains. Don't think Bunny knows how far these are from Ken. According to Ken's map (that he made), they might be around one hundred and fifty miles east of him.

Magga Dan *hopes to reach South Georgia on 17th December.*

Thursday 13 December, 1956
Beautiful day with wind light from south then north and back to south again...

I opened up the Boyles 'X-Ray' prospectors' diamond drill (adapted for ice-drilling)... and later today, got it into a hole that I've dug for it next to the Shack...

All of this digging I did wearing only boots, socks, underpants and trousers... Inside the Shack the roof, lamp, insulation, etc., are dripping with jewel-like crystals of ice. Other dripping – that of water leaking through the roof is not so delightful...

Ralph has given me a haircut tonight. (Tony also had haircut). Over a year's growth shorn from the back of my head and neck. This, and the naked digging, all brought on by a new maximum of +3 °C...

---

[41] The Theron Range had been first spotted by Fuchs and John Lewis during a reconnaissance flight on 6 February 1956. Blaiklock and Goldsmith would become the first men to set foot on its slopes.

Friday 14 December, 1956

... The dogs are covered with seal blubber oil and they smell. Worse is the condition of their coats; matted and filthy dirty, they look almost like skeletons and their colours have become variations of muddy brown. I hope the fur fluffs out again before they get cold weather or they won't keep their body warmth...

Ralph... scrubbed the living room floor. It looks cleaner but I'm hanged if I can see that it is more important than all the other work still to be done. In fact, I can't see that it is important at all...

Sledge today heard us but a lot of noise made it difficult for us to hear them. They have gone four days to the east on 094° and are about thirty-five miles from Theron Range...

Sunday 16 December, 1956

Busy most of this sunny day on the drilling room and got the roof nearly finished...

After supper Ralph and I went down the road to the hill-edge with the huge 'Shackleton' sign on a Maudheim sledge. We fitted legs and supports and erected it a little way down the slope...

Tonight we contacted Wyandot *but for a long time they wouldn't answer. They did at last, after asking Washington if they knew who was calling them. They didn't know of course, and they couldn't hear us. After their first call to us asking who we were there was about ten minutes of silence. Then they asked us to give ice conditions in their area of 61 degrees South 16 degrees West but we said we could only tell them our own local conditions at 78° south 35° west. This rather shook them I suppose for a first-class fast operator came on. Ralph sent a message to the Commander-in-Chief welcoming them to the south and hoping they have an easy passage through the ice. Also offered assistance of local weather and ice conditions. Answer from Captain McDonald[42] thanked us for nice welcome, etc. We now have two daily schedules with them. Now we feel that we have a better chance of them dropping in here. Personally, I'm looking forward to meeting a dentist...*

Monday 17 December, 1956

... I topped up the eight batteries in the generator room with melted snow from a two gallon polythene acid jar. The rest of the day I

---

[42] Captain Edwin A. McDonald, captain of the icebreaker, USS *Staten Island.*

spent on the drilling room [for ice core sampling], finishing off the roof and roof walls... I haven't got the drills and rods out yet or made the base for the drill so can't do any drilling yet...

Magga Dan *at Grytviken at King Edward Point. Aeroplanes have wings on now and one is standing on the wharf for testing tomorrow. They didn't hear us or BBC.*

Sledge position 79° 16 minutes south 28° 50 minutes west, travelling fifteen miles per day from 0300-0900 hours. Mountains very close and very few large well-filled chasms over the last sixty miles. Course 094°. Plan to look at range of mountains to south, then return to base...

Tuesday 18 December, 1956
... Ralph has dug up the seeds for our hydroponic effort. He has got a tea-tray of radish seeds, two of cress and one of mustard on water soaked cotton wool. We'll get the special earth out for the radishes before they start growing.

I think that, tomorrow, even if the weather is still warm and fine, I must spend the evening writing telegrams for Christmas and letters for the boat...

Friday 21 December, 1956
Collected up Maudheim and Canadian sledge load of burnable rubbish and took it up to the hill edge where I built two beacons ready for lighting – one for Wyandot *and one for* Magga Dan. *Although the wind was southerly I was able to strip to the waist on the hill...*

Wyandot *loud and clear tonight but later got interference. Ralph had a natter with Howell[43] and asked if they had a dentist for me. He said that Captain McDonald would be glad to give assistance of their dentist so Ralph will send him a signal...*

Wyandot *and* Staten Island *both in mushy ice, finding it difficult. This was the stuff that* Theron *found so hopeless...*

Although Roy doesn't mention it, 21 December was also the day the Ross Sea Party set sail from New Zealand to fulfil their important role in supporting the expedition, laying depots and route-surveying. Accompanying them were five scientists – New Zealand's contribution to the IGY, with the entire team – both TAE

---

[43] Radio operator aboard the USS *Wyandot*.

and IGY – funded by the New Zealand government and through public subscriptions. In order to achieve obvious economies, these men would co-locate with Hillary's team on Ross Island – a strategy at odds with that of the Weddell Sea contingent, who were located some 200 miles from the Royal Society's IGY party at Halley Bay.

Saturday 22 December, 1956
Oh boy, how thankful we are this day. At lunch-time Ralph and I were considering going straight off to, and straight back from, Vahsel Bay as very little seal meat was left. Only enough for one feed. And tonight we know that we don't have to worry over Christmas nor over New Year for our prayers were suddenly answered...

We've had a northerly all day and since yesterday, the pack has been hard and tight up against our permanent sea-ice, so no chance of seals coming up. Even when the ice goes out it leaves such a very high and wide barrier of pressure ice stuck to our fixed sea-ice that seals couldn't possibly get out of the water. So we dumped off some rubbish (Taffy was with us) and laid seven large radiosonde boxes in a pile on the hill edge.[44] *Then Ralph took the glasses down the hill a bit and I followed so as to turn on a space on the hill. Right away to west, about a mile or more along the sea-ice, we could see a seal and possibly a second one so we decided to try to get through.*

For the first time, I took the Weasel off our fixed sea-ice where the disastrous breakaway had occurred and went onto the new ice... We found three Weddell bulls half a mile further, near the hill edge, where they had come up through holes they'd made in a tide crack...

With the three seals on a rope we started back... A crevasse opened up as the back end of the tracks went over it. I gave it a bit more throttle and looked back. The trailer plunged into the hole and out again and I gave more throttle to keep the seal ropes tight

---

[44] Radiosonde: a battery-powered telemetry instrument carried into the atmosphere by a weather balloon. It measures various atmospheric parameters and transmits them by radio to a ground receiver. The stores lost in March 1956 included the chemicals required to make the balloon gases, thereby seriously reducing the work that could be undertaken by Peter Jeffries, the meteorologist responsible for the radiosonde.

and they leapt in and out of the hole like porpoises. I stopped and we had a look. It was only about two feet six inches wide but went down about twenty feet, perhaps more, to what appeared to be slushy sea and ice. Anyway it was a straight-forward run back and we got to the hut just before 8 p.m. after leaving at about 5.30 p.m.

I had my trials this morning when I was making a Christmas tree. Ralph had made a fine one in wood about three feet six inches high covered in green crêpe paper with the edges snicked. He's hung lights, crackers, toys, musical instruments, etc. on it and it looks grand. So I thought I'd make one too. Mine was welded of course. Made of welding rods and covered with wire-wool soaked in green and brown paint it was beginning to look alright when, just as I was bending part of its trunk straight, it broke at a weld. I removed the painted wire-wool from around that part and started to weld. The length of flame kept catching light to some branches and not only does the paint burn but so does the wire-wool – with a very pretty scintillating effect. These outbreaks I kept blowing out and squeezing in my hand, but when a blob of molten metal fell onto a branch the whole lot started. It was quite a beautiful sight I suppose but I was too busy with a fire extinguisher to notice then...

Sledgers have done sixteen and a half miles and are about three days (fifty miles) from depot. Dogs tired and hungry. Should be in here about six days hence...

Sunday 23 December, 1956

... Tonight started making fishing game for Christmas. I have three small horseshoe magnets for ends of miniature fishing rods and have cut out lots of different fish in cardboard which are painted with fluorescent paint. A steel wire ring in the head will allow the magnet to catch a fish... My Christmas tree looks a treat and surprisingly real. It just needs a few decorations but it is not on show yet.

Two telegrams today, one from Enid and one from her Mum and Dad. Port Stanley are handling two hundred to three hundred telegrams a day now and are already up in the three thousand mark for December...

Monday 24 December, 1956

Christmas Eve but not much chance of getting much spirit. Among six of us only a small percentage are keen for real party-going fun.

However, Ralph has put up the decoration lights and cut up crêpe paper for decorations. He has also made curtains from 'Bungalow check' red and white material. All the various liquor bottles are lined up on the radio table using the large Ferguson flag as a tablecloth. I've taken a few time exposures in colour but don't feel over-confident. I've made the fishing game so hope that it will help for half an hour. Ralph found about two pounds of mixed nuts that he had collected bit by bit from Theron, *so he has put them out. Quite a welcome surprise.*

Heard the Christmas 'Goon Show' dedicated to the Forces, Trans-Antarctic Expedition and IGY at Halley Bay. Taffy Williams was mentioned, also Magga Dan, *Bunny, and Ken 'Bloodlock'...*

Tonight we have had a very fine rain. Rain of all things! Very, very light, but Tony and Hannes are confident about it. I could just feel it on my face and hands, but couldn't see it. It has been cloudy all day with a fresh northerly...

Tuesday 25 December, 1956

Fairly quiet day. Not much drinking and some of the six drinking very little or not at all.

Had seal steaks for lunch – nothing special though; and sort of buffet this evening. This morning we heard the Commonwealth programme but not too clearly... The Queen's Christmas message came through alright though. Our 'Calling the Antarctic' programme was clear enough fortunately and I was particularly pleased to hear Mum's voice. Enid's was very clear, but with the excitement a lot is missed so I hope that we receive tomorrow's repeat clearly...

Tony brought out a box of preserved ginger and a box of preserved fruit. This all helped very much as we have no Christmas goods of any sort, apart from the large stock of tinned Christmas puddings for general use... Ralph, Taffy and Hannes played with the fishing game, but most of the fun came from throwing back huge lumps of metal rubbish just as someone had let in a line.

We have a tray of cress in use today and the seeds have come up thickly, strongly and of a healthy dark green colour. What a very nice 'fresh' flavour it has...

Thursday 27 December, 1956

Nasty outside, with strong southerly and lots of drift. It has come into the hut at several cracks, but especially past the diesel exhaust pipes, so I've got quite a lot inside the engine room.

I spent the morning sorting out my kit and preparing my trunk with things to go home on Magga Dan *and in the afternoon, Rhino had a look at my top left tooth and after fixing up the drill and digging out a box of drills and tools, we got to work. A head-rest was fixed to a plank on the table and I lay down horizontally. The old filling was removed by drilling and a probing thing and a temporary filling put in.*

At 9 a.m. the sledgers arrived – quite a surprise. They have done forty-eight miles in the last two days, doing the last twenty-four miles in six hours. The strong southerly helped very much. They had had a good long journey [but] of little use to the Crossing. They had covered about three hundred and fifty miles and had reached a point at the foot of the Theron Range about one hundred and twenty miles east of our position... Ken estimates that they were about one thousand feet high here and the mountains rose perhaps a further three thousand feet. There was no way up the almost sheer slope, and ice falls and avalanches were possible dangers.

They were in the vicinity for only one day, and that night, as they slept in the tent under the mountainside, Ken and Rhino heard an exploding roar that carried on its roar loud and long. Ken looked out and saw a tremendous avalanche about to gather speed on its two thousand feet fall. It was coming straight down at them and Ken shouted, 'Christ – it's coming! Come on Rhino!'

Rhino was out of bed in a flash and they both ran from the tent across the snow. After running about twenty yards they stopped to get an appreciation of the situation. By the time that it was nearly over they could see that it wouldn't reach the tent and they were very thankful for that as they weren't really dressed for standing outside. Rhino wore only pants, shirt and no socks, while Ken wore only socks, pyjama trousers and shirt. Rhino's feet were extremely cold and uncomfortable, but the general state of comfort for both wasn't enviable. The settling noises of the avalanche went on long after, and everything including our two sledgers was covered with a fine snow-dust which hung thickly everywhere in the air...

Saturday 29 December, 1956
... Wyandot and Staten Island *sent their helicopter over to Halley Bay this afternoon... We have an ETA here from them of about 2-3 p.m. (local). We'll have a short party then they fly on to catch up with ships. Don't know if they expect to see Belgrano just down the 'road'...*

Taffy said the flywheel was loose on one of the generators – and it was. He had heard it rattle when he started it. I've stripped it down and found two bolts out of six sheared, and all of the six sets of rubber bushes broken up... Looks as though damage occurs during running when they are cold. I shall have to make some other sort of rubber bushes from old parts of Weasel tracks...

Sunday 30 December and Monday 31 December, 1956
Writing this on 31st December, so will probably forget some details. I finished off the [generator] engine today but it took most of the day to do it...

Wyandot *and* Staten Island *weren't heard at all so we still expected them at about 2 p.m., but we couldn't understand the silence. Everyone was prepared and cleaned up, but I carried on with the engine till about 4 p.m. Then I had a wash, but still silence. I went back to the engine and finished the job at about 9 p.m. In the evening signals between us and the ships were very weak and had, apparently, been affected by temporary fade-out conditions. They estimated that they would be here in about three hours' time, at 11.30 p.m. (local). However, at 11.30 p.m. they extended the estimate to 2.30 a.m. (local). So, disgustedly, we tried to make up our minds about what to do – stay up or go to bed. Rhino went, only to lie in bed reading. Jeff went straight away. We all wandered off to bed except Ken and Ralph who fell asleep in chairs...*

Ralph called me at a quarter to three. Ken, Ralph and I went down in the Weasel to light the bonfire that we'd put the finishing touches to, during the day. The ships had asked for smoke and they were able to see it. They picked us up on radar seventeen and a half miles away. The ships loomed up as large black blobs to east in our open water and soon they were level and the first helicopter took off from Staten Island *about 3.30 a.m. (local). Soon the second was up after the first one had brought Captain McDonald and a large box of apples, oranges and lemons. The second brought Captain Finn Ronne and nine Red-Cross Christmas parcels each containing a writing set, Biro-type pen and plastic key case. McDonald went with Ken to the dogs. He had a whisky and a cup of coffee, but Finn Ronne only had coffee…*

We went to bed at about 7.30 a.m. (local) and started getting up at between 2 and 3 p.m. today, 31st December. As I'm cook I had to get up at 2 p.m. to make a 'brunch'…

Tonight the wind has come up and now has reached gale force from north-east. News tonight mentioned Magga Dan *reverses. Having met heavy ice she has had to go north to find a way round…*

Telegram received yesterday from Enid about Christmas tele-grams and Christmas broadcast. Asks if party was successful? Well, guess we hardly had a party.

In contrast with the somewhat riotous party that marked the arrival of Midwinter's Day, Christmas at Shackleton had been little more than a damp squib. And yet, given the progress made over the course of the previous six months, the Advance Party had good cause to celebrate. Perhaps the lack of party spirit resulted from exhaustion – both mental and physical. Perhaps, too, the hilarity of Midwinter's Day had been a product, in part at least, of a need to release pent up emotion in circumstances which, at that point in the expedition, remained little short of dire.

Since Midwinter Roy had made a lot of progress but it had been slow going. In July, for instance, all his efforts to resuscitate No. 1 Weasel had come to nothing when he discovered that it required a whole new differential. Since he didn't possess a spare, the vehicle was, to all intents and purposes, 'dead'. He turned his attention to repairing No. 2 Weasel with its malfunctioning water pump. This was no easy job in the open and with the vehicle encased in snow, but he persevered and identified the trouble as a broken boss on the pulley assembly. It took weeks to remedy the fault, with his efforts interrupted by bitterly cold weather, cooking duties and the need to work on the Aga stove, but on 19 August he had noted with justifiable pride how his colleagues had 'stared at a Weasel actually moving'. Even then, the starter remained troublesome, a gasket leaked, a door had been blown off and drift-proofing was sorely needed. Later, the radiator failed, and Roy was obliged to send to London a list of the many spares needed for this and other vehicles.

Once functional, No. 2 Weasel managed to haul and tow, hoist masts and recover the Ferguson tractor whenever it got stuck, but at the very end of October, during a two-day trip to Vahsel Bay to hunt for seals, the second gear seized up: a fault common to Weasels, just like the leaking radiators. Roy managed to repair the gearbox but the constant failures didn't augur well for the trans-continental journey.

As for the Tucker Sno-Cat, Roy had considered it impossible to tackle such a big job until the summer arrived, but even with plenty of daylight he found it 'the most difficult thing to work on without proper facilities'. Nonetheless, he managed to dismantle the engine, repair the damaged cylinder head and install a new, albeit sea-water corroded, piston. To remedy the noisy clutch, the heavy Chrysler V8 engine really needed to be removed; that was impossible, so Roy decided to improvise, as his diary entry for 2 December explains:

I have been working on the Sno-Cat all day to repair the clutch which doesn't disengage properly. It means removing the gearbox, but all day I've been trying to remove other parts which have things in their way, to remove some other parts which are in the way of other parts which are preventing the removal of other parts etc., etc., which are preventing me getting at the gearbox which must be removed to look at the clutch. Curse Tucker.

In the end, without assistance, he succeeded in lowering the gearbox sufficiently to see the clutch. He discovered a loose release bearing and other parts damaged, so he sent a signal to David Pratt, who was already at sea, asking him to try and get the parts in Montevideo. Meanwhile, with a bit of judicious straightening-out, he managed to get the Sno-Cat running again and the clutch working well. Pratt later hit the nail on the head when he described the Sno-Cat repairs as 'pretty bloody'.

For its part, the Ferguson tractor remained as mechanically reliable as ever, but its tendency to get bogged down substantially reduced its effectiveness – so much so that Roy eventually dismissed it as being of little use beyond carting 'away the snow in its shovel'.

On the bright side, Pratt's imminent arrival would enable Roy to share the burden of the engineering work. However, Pratt would be bringing yet more vehicles and Roy must have wondered whether they would prove any more reliable than the four that he had nursed through an Antarctic winter. After all, if the burden doubled in size, the ability to share it between two engineers would amount to very little.

Tuesday 1 January, 1957
New Year's Eve and New Year's Day had not the slightest effect on us. Everyone went to bed early and no-one thought to tune into BBC reports on London celebrations. The only day that received a celebration was last Midwinter in the Sno-Cat crate...

Friday 4 January, 1957
Big day at Halley Bay, for both ships have arrived. Tottan *possibly about midday and* Magga Dan *at 6.30 p.m. ...*

Sunday 6 January, 1957
... Surprisingly enough Bunny hasn't sent any message to us since their arrival at Halley Bay. Until we know when they expect to be here, or what is happening, we won't be able to decide what to do about our proposed depot trip. For the past two days Halley Bay hasn't been on the air at all to us...

Monday 7 January, 1957
... Still nothing heard from Halley Bay...

Wednesday 9 January, 1957
Dull day again which started off with a little sunshine. Wind still light though. Did some maintenance on the Sno-Cat which took most of the day. I changed oil in both axles and transfer case then greased all of the track rollers. Greasing track rollers – sounds simple enough [but] there are two hundred and ninety-six rollers, each with a grease nipple. Half of them are on the inside, under-neath the vehicle. It took fifteen pounds of grease and thirty-two re-fills in the grease gun.

My wind-proofs were pretty greasy before, but, after this, they were slimy. Dozens of patches are on the trousers and lately more and more rips have got longer and longer, so I did some machining and have washed the wind-proofs in petrol. I did this outside, but, to dry them, I hung them over the engines for the warm air to get at them in the loft. Now the whole hut reeks of petrol, especially the radio room at the other end from the generators...

Still nothing from Halley Bay...

Thursday 10 January, 1957
... After lunch I started on the Weasel rear spring. I dug a 5' pit and drive the Weasel over it, slacked tracks off, removed rear bogie assemblies and let down the spring after jacking up rear of Weasel...

Ken seems to have told Bunny how we felt about not hearing from them for five days. Bunny had some very transparent excuses...

The unloading [at Halley Bay] has just about been finished now and the aircraft has been flying. It is hoped that it will arrive here the day after tomorrow and the ship will leave at the same time. All of the ex-Halley Bay people will be coming down...[45]

Friday 11 January, 1957
Slightly strong southerly with plenty of ice crystals in the air. These made a very strange and beautiful pattern which I have never seen before. Looking towards the sun in a bright blue sky I saw a glittering 'Cupid's Bow' type of rainbow above the sun with the ice crystals sparkling through it. Below the sun was an arc of light shining from the crystals with a large round glare in the centre.

After lunch I made a fuss of the dogs and then turned to the Weasel. By 10 p.m. I had got the main spring back on and the bogies re-assembled to it, so now I only have to re-adjust the tracks...

The Otter leaves Halley Bay at about 11.00 a.m. tomorrow and should be here at about 1.30 p.m. (local). The ship will leave about noon... We expect Bunny, George Lowe and Donald Milner[46] *with John Lewis as pilot. They will be homing in on our beacon...*

Tony put out a tin of creamy toffees last night and with my first chew, out came the large stopping from the top right-hand rear tooth which Rhino had so recently repaired. Today he had to dig out a deep splinter from my right index finger.

---

[45] The nine members of the Royal Society's IGY Advance Party, along with their leader, Surgeon-Lieutenant Commander David Dalgleish RN, had completed their tour of duty and were returning to the UK on board the *Magga Dan*.

[46] The BBC correspondent had accompanied the expedition to conduct interviews with its members. He would return to the UK with the *Magga Dan*.

Linoleum is going down all over the place now and this alone makes the place look more finished...

Saturday 12 January, 1957
What a big day for Shackleton! The Otter arrived at about 2 p.m....

It took two loads with the Canadian trailer to bring in all of the mail bags, parcels, etc. after greeting Bunny, John Lewis and Donald Milner. We settled down right away to sort out and read the mail and I even did without lunch.

A little note from Eleanor [Honnywill] told me that Enid had packed a lot of mail in the box in the Sno-Cat crate [on board Magga Dan] but I still had forty-two letters...

Having read Enid's fifteen letters I realise how she must have felt all last year and how much I need her and how inadequate my own letter (one) to her will be. But of course, all my diaries are written as though to her even if not written in the first person, so it is the same as a very long newsletter. So, you will understand, won't you darling? ...

Sunday 13, Monday 14 and Tuesday 15 January, 1957
Don't expect ever to catch up with my diary and I get a very depressed feeling in my stomach when I think of all the letters that I ought to answer. I won't be able to. I have about eighty letters now, not including those in parcels in the large wooden box. The large wooden box was absolutely wonderful apart from the fact that petrol had got into it and made some things taste a bit. Probably happened when one Sno-Cat was unloaded from its crate at Halley Bay and filled up there. However, what a magnificent collection of gifts. There never was such a welcome, great big parcel. I got it off the ship yesterday (Monday) and haven't looked at everything, not even read any of the letters. Anyway, it will pass.

First, Magga Dan. With radio contact we knew that she was progressing very well and when she could be just made-out towards Vahsel Bay they said that they would be here in about two hours, which would be about 4.30 p.m. (local) I think. Anyway, it seemed to turn up much quicker than that. I had a job to convince everyone that she was only a very short way off and at last I drove Bunny and some others down to meet Magga Dan as she nosed along the ice edge below us.

We stopped near to where the ship was turning her nose into the ice edge and watched while she nudged in and out and sideways starting to make a little dock for herself. We took lots of photo-graphs but, after about half an hour felt that it was time we went aboard out of the wind. David Stratton put a ladder down and Rhino climbed aboard when the ship came to a halt after biting a bit more out of the edge. After a few more chews Ken and I went towards the ladder but got shouted away by Captain Petersen from the crow's nest, from whence he operated the ship.

We all felt that this was a bit much and after a further twenty minutes, drifted back to the Sno-Cat except Bunny and Tony and possibly someone else, having decided to come back to base. As we were about to move off Bunny waved us back and after a few minutes of indecision, we went back, but not at all sure that the Captain wouldn't make us wait. What a gallant reception after our cheerless, lonely year!

We had dinner on board and then drinks in various cabins and in the lounge before leaving for base. As we had to be up for 6 a.m. we couldn't stay late and I got to bed about 12.30 a.m. Next morning we were up and I still felt the effects of the night before. Unloading started, but not in a very big way as Sno-Cat crates had to be dismantled and lowered over onto the ice before hatches could be cleared for opening. Since then we've been bringing up hundreds of barrels of petrol.

The Weasel had shed its fan belt yesterday evening so, after last loads, I got on with the repair job and then brought up my last load. I got in at 11 p.m. and to bed at 1.20 a.m. Normal finishing time is 8 p.m. I got up at 6 a.m. though, and today has been a big load-hauling day.

So far we have brought up about three hundred and fifty drums, the Sno-Cat crates and many tons of RAF and vehicle stores. Two Sno-Cat crates have been erected... one for RAF stores and one for Engineering...

David Pratt's three 'Pratty-Pusses' (i.e. Sno-Cats) are all over-heating and he and I are investigating...

5

ALL TOGETHER

The whole expedition was together at last. Soon the scientific programme would expand beyond all recognition and preparations for
the crossing begin in earnest. But first, hundreds of tons of mail,
petrol, coal, scientific equipment, spare parts, man and dog food,
clothing, and six vehicles, including three Sno-Cats, two Weasels,
and a Canadian Muskeg tractor, must be brought up from the
cavernous holds of *Magga Dan* and hauled or driven to the safety
of the base. The second priority would be to complete the hut.
Fortunately, to undertake this work, Fuchs now had at his disposal
not only his full complement of expedition personnel, but also the
ten men of the homeward bound IGY Advance Party, and the ship's
crew.

After such a lengthy period of isolation, this influx came as a
shock to some, with Goldsmith observing that: 'As soon as the ship
came in the hut and the base lost all its intimacy. All that had so
long been ours exclusively suddenly became transformed and was
no longer home; intruders first slowly then with ever increasing
pace took over and moved in'.[47] Of course, the doctor's sense of
dislocation was exacerbated by the knowledge that he, along with
Stewart and Jeffries, stood on the brink of departure, Goldsmith and
Stewart heading for the UK on board *Magga Dan*, and Jeffries to
take up the role of meteorologist at Halley Bay.

If Roy shared Goldsmith's mixed feelings regarding the arrival of
the full expedition team, he didn't say as much; perhaps his years of
army life had inured him to change, and to the sudden arrival and
hasty departure of personnel. What he must surely have felt,
however, was that he and his seven companions of the Advance
Party had achieved something quite extraordinary, indeed un-

---

[47] Goldsmith, diary, 29 January 1957. Quoted in Haddelsey, *Shackleton's Dream*, p. 91.

precedented. Moreover, despite occasional discord and mutual antagonism, they had achieved it by working together. For many, it would remain a pivotal episode in their careers, and the friendships forged at that bleak spot in Vahsel Bay would last for the rest of their lives.

Of the five members of the Advance Party remaining at Shackleton, four – Roy, Blaiklock, La Grange, and Lenton – would take part in the land crossing. They would be joined by eight of the new arrivals, first and foremost among whom was the expedition leader and geologist Bunny Fuchs. Also taking part would be David Stratton (deputy leader and senior surveyor), Geoffrey Pratt (a geophysicist on secondment from British Petroleum – and no relation to David Pratt), Jon Stephenson (an Australian geologist), Dr Allan Rogers (medical officer and physiologist), David Pratt (senior engineer), George Lowe (photographer and cameraman), and Hal Lister (glaciologist and, like Roy, a veteran of the British North Greenland Expedition).

The fifth member of the Advance Party, Taffy Williams, would participate in the planned trans-continental flight, along with Squadron Leader John Lewis, Flight Lieutenant Gordon Haslop of the Royal New Zealand Air Force, and Flight Sergeant Peter Weston, the aircraft mechanic. They would have at their disposal two aircraft: the de Havilland Otter, which, as well as the trans-Antarctic flight, would be used for depot-laying, and a two-seater Auster T7, intended primarily for reconnaissance work.

Wednesday 16 January, 1957

Still haven't read the letters that came in the large box – not even three or four of Enid's. I worry every time I think of all the people who wrote because I'm sure I shall never have time to write to them...

Not as much seemed to be hauled today mainly because of breakdowns. The Sno-Cats are overheating still and one packed up on top of the ice-shelf while bringing up a double load. Carburettor trouble often crops up and it seems to be vapour-lock due to the heat of the engine...

One Weasel has been offloaded (as well as the three Sno-Cats already working). It looks to be in good shape, having been over-

hauled by FVRDE.[48] *A very nice cab of aluminium... and inside, plywood. Outside it is a dark red with aluminium and chrome fittings. Looks like a fire float. These two are M29C which are the amphibious type. I have found fault with the steering adjustment and clutch so tomorrow will go through the adjustment...*

Large dumps are spreading out in long lines east-west of the hut and the petrol dump lines are very impressive in length though not complete. They run north-south...

Thursday 17 January, 1957
... All of the food, pemmican, miscellaneous stores, etc. and replacement workshop are up and now the coal is making an impressive dump. After that (twenty-five tons) comes the remainder of the fuel and the job's complete. We hope that the ship will be able to go sealing then...

Friday 18 and Saturday 19 January, 1957
Didn't get my diary done yesterday due to my birthday, of course...

The forward hold had been cleared, so, after dinner, (5.30) nothing much was to happen till the change over to the other hold had been accomplished. So I brought a gang up who work in, on and around the hut. Chimneys are going up like mushrooms and big black stoves have rapidly spread in growth throughout the hut. Lights are now in the living room. Four are on the trusses and two will be wall lights.

I took the bottle of Haig from the goodies box and went with the others to the ship. There were three, with Allan [Rogers] driving his Sno-Cat, making the fourth. On Magga Dan *I ordered two dozen Tuborgs and another bottle of whisky but the Chief Steward, who contracts on tender to do and supply catering, wouldn't sell by the bottle – only the glass.*

Nearly everyone turned up, filling the lounge, and even Captain Petersen had a whisky. David Dalgleish and a few others were in the 'Espedisionchef's' room so I and Bunny went back there for a while. Afterwards I went to the lounge again and soon everyone had left except David Pratt, Gordon [Haslop] and me who were alone, while the night watch came through at set times to wind his clock on a key hung on the aft wall of the lounge.

---

[48] The Ministry of Defence's Fighting Vehicles Research and Development Establishment at Chertsey, in Surrey.

David Pratt and I took the few remaining cans of Tuborg to his cabin and, as we were about to leave, Jon Stephenson (Steve) shot up in bed, pushed his curtain aside and thrust out his hand to shake ours and said, 'Ah, hello, have a good time!' We said we would, but had no idea what he meant. He immediately settled into sleep again...

One more thing about today. The Aga is working...

Saturday 19 and Sunday 20 January, 1957

... [Jon Stephenson] explained handshake. He had dreamt that he was on Magga Dan *which was sinking and while still in the nightmare wished us a good time – meaning on the crossing. He wasn't coming as he was sinking...*

The Otter, with Gordon, Bunny, David Stratton, Ken and George [Lowe] went up at 11 a.m. today and had a look at the mountains south of us. They run rather north-east to south-east, cutting our route to the Pole. They thought that there were some places where we could get the vehicles across but are going to have a look east, rather where Ken and Rhino went. They found some nunataks about two hundred and forty miles in where our depot could be made and 'Base 300' established...[49]

Monday 21 January, 1957

This is all getting to be a bit too much for me. Pottering around in the evening, then letter writing and then diary always sees me late in bed. Two a.m. last night after ten letters...

After lunch I took a bag of washing to Magga Dan *and used the washing machine and rotary drier. This did a fine job and an hour later I was on my way up again with nearly-dry clothes. It took one and three quarter packets of Persil and could have done with more! Ugh! ...*

David Pratt rigged a great rubbery balloon thing over the Weasel. The rubberised fabric is like a Nissen hut and is supported by a frame work of twelve-inch diameter rubber tubes which is all inflated by a fan with nozzle running off 12v Weasel battery. Quite a fine job but can't be pegged down in snow. Under normal ground

---

[49] Fuchs's plans included the establishment of a forward base roughly 300 miles inland from Shackleton. This three-man base would become a staging post for the Crossing Party and a laboratory for meteorology and glaciology.

conditions it is said to stand up to sixty miles per hour gales. The 'give' in its structure slightly flattens with the wind and the flat surface pressure helps to keep it down. It can just house a vehicle...

Tuesday 22 January, 1957

... I've had Dave 'Doom' Limbert (IGY meteorological man returning home) helping me with the derelict Weasel today. We've made good progress, having removed the dud differential assembly and put in a new one...

Have written six more letters tonight.

Wednesday 23 January, 1957

... Dave Limbert has been helping me again today and we've got on pretty well. Unfortunately I'm now held up for the fan shroud that the ship's engineers are making. I could have the Weasel running in a day.

We are doing a few tape recordings today which Donald Milner will bring back for relatives. I hope to do mine after I finish this. I've done a few letters tonight making my present total twenty-eight...

All of the fires are going. The Aga is doing beautifully and the fired boiler for the bathroom is producing hot water...

We've got a bit of extra kit today. Among the new stuff, David Pratt and I get two suits of heavy windproof for vehicle work.

Friday 25 January, 1957

Have spent most of the day pretty successfully on the manufacture of a fan shroud for one of the Weasels. The ship couldn't make one, so I've started with the ends of some petrol drums...

Tomorrow morning we shall be writing letters and in the evening we have a party up here for us, Halley Bay boys and ship's officers. On Sunday Magga Dan *leaves us I expect.*

The boys got twenty-six seals... Half a dozen of the boys went through the ice while Donald Milner was leading. He got across alright but the remainder all dropped through. A very chilling ducking but they all managed to scramble back onto the ice and get back to the ship for dry clothes.

David Pratt and I did recording on vehicles with Donald Milner tonight.

Saturday 26 January, 1957

Didn't get any further with the Weasel fan shroud as I found myself as 'gash-hand' for the cook. The duty entails keeping fires alight, bringing in coal and kerosene, sweeping up, serving, washing up, getting supplies in, emptying the dirty water bin and rubbish box, filling the two 80 gallon water tanks with snow and so on. As all the fires had gone out in the night, in spite of someone being up, I had the task of getting them all going again...

Gordon took the Otter out with Bunny, Ken and George, but over the mountains where Bunny wanted to finalise the situation for a way over the mountains, they came into thick cloud, so nothing more is known...

The party was pretty good. Lots of champagne was drunk to start the evening off and then it was anything, including four or five different beers, until 1.30 a.m. I had a load in the Sno-Cat going back [to the ship] and, unknown to me, two on the sledge – Donald Milner and Peter Jeffries. David Pratt had the Muskeg with blokes hanging on all over it. The bo'sun, a cross between a trunk of an oak tree and a bear, kept jumping off and running beside the vehicle then jumping on again. He cut his forehead but wasn't worried. He is always to be seen wearing a sort of large Turkish fur fez hat. Ken had it this morning, and, I'm told the bo'sun was last seen happily going away with two tins of baccy.

David Pratt was ahead of me and showed signs of challenging me to try to pass. On the flat at the bottom of the hill I was able to and they tried to re-pass me but I kept them pretty well blocked out.

We decided to have one for the road with somebody. Captain Petersen settled that by saying that he would have a court trial of two drivers in his cabin and everyone was to come along as witnesses. We had quite a little party there on Aquavit and Tuborg. David Pratt and I got back at 0245 hours, then I started making up the fires, so I suppose it was about 0345 hours when I got to bed.

Sunday 27 January, 1957

Lazy day today. Didn't wake up till about 9 a.m. and stayed in bed till midday reading. Then when I got up, feeling groggy, I learned that there is a party on board tonight...

Monday 28 January, 1957

Next day – not feeling so good. The party was very fine, held in the dining room. Plenty to drink and eat and everyone had an

*enjoyable time judging by the noise. I think I left at about 2 a.m....
Apparently everyone, except Hal, (cook) and I (asleep) went down
to see* Magga Dan *sail at 8.20. I didn't wake up till about 11 a.m.
(I'm very glad to say!). Gordon slept on the ship so he was forced
to see it off...*

Tuesday 29 January, 1957

*... Nearly finished the [Weasel] fan shroud today. It's had its first
fitting, needs only a couple of adjustments...*

*Quite fine day but bit chilly with light southerly. Bunny, Ken and
Gordon went up in [the] Otter from about 1245 to 1915, looking
for route round glacier in mountains. That looked fairly OK but
great amount of crevasses for long distance on ice-cap in waves.
Not sure yet if this will perhaps have to do...*

Wednesday 30 and Thursday 31 January, 1957

*... In the evening I had my bath, starting the roster. It is about [a]
three-quarter length enamelled iron bath with no means of
draining. It was quite dirty so I had to clean it first. The hot water
came from a tank in the adjoining workroom, the water being
heated by a separate Bonfire boiler. Eventually I decided I had too
much water so put back three bucketsful. When I sat in it with my
legs out straight the water didn't cover my thighs, though it was
quite a good temperature at any rate.*

*Before [I had] any chance to settle down to a quiet bath, a
steady stream of blokes came and went, either to wash in the wash
basin, talk with someone having a wash, ask me what the bath was
like, or to look for someone and so on. There was a constant
draught. At one stage, two were talking with the door open while
one washed his hands in the bath water – I was forced to make a
very loud remark about the door. To empty the bath, the water is
bailed out with a bucket into a metal water butt. Gash hands have
the job of emptying it...*

*Today, has gone pretty well. Drift and fairly strong wind have
kept people busy clearing the doorway, but inside the air shelter
I've been free of the wind and have got a good step onward.
Radiator and shroud fitted and cooling system filled. All dash
connections, etc., fitted up and several repairs made and the engine
ran for an hour keeping within the temperature limit...*

*After tea today David Pratt gave me a hand to fit the L/H track.
This took about 1¾ hours as the vehicle had been sitting on the*

track since about last August, I think. Tomorrow we'll do the R/H one…

For five days now we've had frost smoke on the sea and clearly the weather is past its best…

Having settled in and undertaken a series of route-finding flights, Fuchs turned his attention to establishing the inland meteorological and glaciological observatory, where a small hut would be built to accommodate three men through the coming winter. After careful reconnaissance by air he selected a site on the far side of the Shackleton Range, roughly 270 miles from Shackleton Base. The base would be established entirely by air, and supplying its needs before winter would require a good many flights, which began in early February.

Fuchs chose Hal Lister, Jon Stephenson and Ken Blaiklock to spend the winter at the forward base, with Lister as leader.[50] During his time with the BNGE, Lister had wintered at a remote station called 'North Ice' and, under his influence, the TAE's forward base quickly shed its official name of 'Depot 300' and became known, instead, as 'South Ice'.

Sunday 3 February, 1957
Big day of preparation for the first depot flight. For my part I rounded up four cases of MacFarlane battery generators and spares. I uncrated two generators and two spare engines with a lot of other spares. One generator I set up ready to show the chaps who are going to Depot 300. This was explained to them and then the wind generator…

I learn tonight that Captain McDonald is arriving tomorrow morning by air.

Monday 4 February 1957
Last night several of us swept out the hut and scrubbed the floor with a broom and soda. A squeegee and floor cloth finished the lino off nicely. Didn't get to bed until about 2 a.m.

---

[50] Given that Blaiklock had served as leader of the Advance Party, Lister's selection as leader at South Ice might seem odd. However, Blaiklock fully supported the selection, believing that a scientific station should be headed by a scientist. See Haddelsey, *Shackleton's Dream*, p. 95.

There was a bit of a mistake about when the Americans were expected. In the meantime we went to see our Otter off with John Lewis driving. Passengers were Ken, Hal, George and Jon Stephenson... I got a couple of shots of the boys ducking in the slip-stream and drift as the plane moved off to turn around and go down wind for start point. Take-off into the wind is in line with the petrol drums and it looks as though he's actually taking off among them...

[The Americans] arrived here about 12 o'clock I think... Lunch was at 2 p.m. – very nice, roast mutton and fruit and cream sweet. Hannes was cook in a bit of a 'diz' but very ably assisted by Ralph.

The wind went east and then north so our friends had to leave in a hurry. With northerlies come clouds and possibly snow. I got their autographs on a sheet of expedition paper before they left. The landing was superb. The young pilot went over us once and then came in on a turn and swooped straight in to a landing and up to the Auster by the RAF shack.

After things had settled down I got back to making a long vertical exhaust pipe for Depot 300's MacFarlane pop-pop... I had to saw up various pipes and threaded connections and now they have an eight feet extension in two vertical sections and a curved screwed pipe adapted over the little silencer. David Stratton looked in near the end so I gave him a half hour lesson in welding...

Tuesday 5 February, 1957

Built a little Dexion mast today for the wind generator at Depot 300. It looks so nice, I don't want to part with it... I've almost finished tonight, 11 p.m. and have only to make guy ropes for it...

Almost a whiteout this morning so the Otter didn't go up. John Lewis took it up at about 3 p.m. with Ralph as passenger and to check the radio. They got back about 10.40 p.m. and had had a good flight with weather better than here. We still have a northerly but only light, while at Depot 300 the wind is easterly with temperature -23°C. Our temperature is -6°C...[51]

---

[51] Differences in weather at Shackleton Base and South Ice would lead to considerable frustration during the construction of the forward base, with Lister and his companions often wondering why no deliveries were made on days which, locally, seemed ideal for flying.

Wednesday 6 February, 1957
Very pleasant day with light northerly then calm and then very light southerly...

I'd heard Bunny wasn't very fond of music and tonight we found out – during our first playing of the reproducer since the new chaps arrived. Chaps were listening while pottering in their rooms and Bunny put it off thinking no-one was listening. It's not necessary to sit on the instrument to listen to it, Ralph explained.

Bunny feels that we should have a record evening. Hardly possible, I feel, while we are working to 10 p.m. and 11 p.m. and even later. Mostly lately some of us have come in after 11 p.m. Probably be better when Bunny's office is made...

Friday 8 February, 1957
... John Lewis and Allan went to Depot 300 with fourth load this morning...

Monday 11 February, 1957
Spent the whole day inside giving No. 1 generator its 500 hour de-coke and check...

Gordon went with Geoff to Depot 300 today, fifth flight, leaving about 1.30 p.m.... At Depot 300 they have used all the building parts so far sent up and have dug a trench and chamber for the generator. The hut is being erected in a pit about 5ft deep to make less drift.

Bunny's birthday today and he's having a bath to celebrate.

Tuesday 12 February, 1957
We expected [the] Americans about 9 a.m. but they were banging on the east door of the hut at ten to five a.m.... David Stratton got up and made coffee for the two who had arrived and they also had a rum. They had this, took the mail, wrote their names on the wall, signed my sheet and went again. They were just young airmen, while in the large helicopter were two more who didn't come in...

After lunch Allan had a go at my teeth. He only did the top L/H one which pains with cold and heat and this took from 3 p.m. to 6.45 p.m. and included inspection and two injections. The injections kept wearing off – I could have done with three. He took out the filling Rhino had twice done and found it OK... After filling the lot with a temporary stoppage the trouble was still there – and has been since about October and also after all repair operations.

Poor old Allan, with a heavy physiological programme, thinks it will take a month to put my teeth right...

Wednesday 13 February, 1957
... Tonight is my bath-night and I had a good long soak. Used bath water is now poured in bowlfuls through a hole in the floor and has sunk a shaft about 25' deep...

Friday 15 February, 1957
... Today 'gash hand' with Bunny. Had to dig drift off the shelter and blow it up... [I] have run a power line from generator room to distribution box for washing machine. Later, power line will come off the same box for hut workshop and office. Had to leave switch box wiring till generator was off. Hope to be first to use the washing machine in the morning...

Hut gets too warm now so living room fire has been allowed to go out. Generator room very warm and I work in my vest. Water dripping through the roof at that end...

David Pratt and Ralph have worked on the bath to make a drain hole. This is now finished and a polythene bottle connects the hole to the opening through the floor. Gordon made a plug for it today and attached a heavy dog chain to it. He's also made a clothes drying rack for himself to draw up into the roof with pulleys...

Saturday 16 February, 1957
... This morning I finished off the power line for the washing machine and got a few 'whites' in together with some of David Stratton's. The water was only lukewarm so I let it run for ten minutes instead of only four. All came out very well. Trouble is, it has to have 6¾ gallons in it and that's a lot of water to make hot from snow...

Wednesday 20 February, 1957
... I had the left-hand top tooth out sometime after supper. A couple of stiff rums and two codeines later have put me right...

Thursday 21 February, 1957
Gash hand today and chopping up seal for dog feeding. Got a little time after tea to work on the Weasel track and connect it up with the assistance of David Stratton.

Light southerly today but good for work outside. Due to poor weather here the Otter didn't return… first thing this morning, but came in this afternoon at about quarter to one. We had high mist and the plane flew over twice above it. Third time he came over just visible in the mist and went out to sea a good way, turned and came in low under the mist and all was well…

John Lewis and Allan went off with 10th load this afternoon in mist and have been advised to stay. Soon be my turn to go up with the wind generator and mast…

Sunday 24 February, 1957

Should have flown today but north-easterly brought snow all day. This I forecast last night and bet a bar of chocolate with David Stratton and Taffy…

Loaded the Otter ready for my flight and we had a dickens of a job with the two mast sections. The first in, the base section, must have taken an hour to get in. South Ice… had -40°C last night…

Gordon and Ken arrived from South Ice about 3.30 a.m. after a spot of excitement. On the way back they were going through cloud while nearing Base, but they were about 5 miles off course. Through the cloud their speed was 120 m.p.h. when suddenly came a 'bump' on the skis as they touched the (invisible) hills running in from Vahsel Bay. Gordon immediately climbed but it was all over in a split second and the 'bump' was only a light one. Rather solid cloud![52]

Tuesday 26 February 1957

… Writing this in bed in South Ice at 0015 (Shackleton time). Early reports from South Ice not good, but 1030 one was fairly reasonable, but it was 10 past 12 when we took off. John Lewis had been de-icing the wings. I was rather disappointed in the large number of crevasses that appeared shortly after take-off and the extent of them. On the whole it is pretty much a crevassed area all the way to near South Ice. They vary very much in type, direction, regularity, closeness, lengths, widths, shapes and everything else…

---

[52] The snow-covered hills struck by the Otter on the night of 23/24 February were subsequently named the 'Touchdown Hills'. See Fuchs and Hillary, *The Crossing of Antarctica*, p. 111-112.

Wednesday 27 February, 1957
... Gordon came in at South Ice earlier than anticipated... We took off [for Shackleton] at about 3.15 p.m....

Thursday 28 February, 1957
... David Pratt and I dug out the drilling machine chamber which Geoff has started on. A lot of drift had got in, burying the machine. The big push at the moment is on ice drilling. There are also two different sets of hand drilling apparatus. They were doing some hand drilling when I arrived at South Ice yesterday... [53]

Sunday 3 March, 1957
Half-hearted sort of day. Had a little too much rum last night...
We've fiddled around a bit with the ice drill but are having to raise the machine in order to get the long coring tool down...
Sixteenth Flight. Plane took off today with Hal and David Stratton for South Ice and then took Jon Stephenson out to the rocks that he's been so keen to get to. I don't know the story yet.
We all assisted in putting up the first two trusses (to meet at the top) at the west end of the workshop foundations and expanded metal (XPM) floor. Another one tomorrow morning...

With South Ice established, Jon Stephenson had requested permission to undertake a brief geological survey at the Whichaway Nunataks, nearly thirty miles to the north of the forward base. Fuchs had agreed, believing that the excursion would bolster morale prior to the long lonely winter. Accordingly, Stephenson and Blaiklock were flown out on 3 March with a 6-foot Nansen sledge, a radio receiver and fuel and rations for ten days – though they anticipated being collected by the Otter within twenty-four hours. These plans would go seriously awry.

Mon. 4 March, 1957
In bed early tonight – 2115 hours.
Ice drilling all day and packed up at 30ft partly due to feeling a bit worn out after heaving the rods up and down all day (it's

---

[53] Ice drilling and the subsequent analysis of ice cores constituted a major element of the glaciological work undertaken during the TAE. Core-drilling was also undertaken during the IGY, with one team drawing a 400 metre core. The TAE's achievements were more modest.

quicker than withdrawing by machine)... no successful cores obtained...

Clear this morning with light southerly, but soon got heavily clouded over and snow fell for most of the day from the South, so no flying...

Tuesday 5 March, 1957
Gash hand today...

During lunch David Pratt noticed a flickering glow up in the loft and dashed down the room and climbed up the loft ladder with a CO_2 extinguisher. I shot through to the hut workshop thinking to go up that ladder, but met the fire down below. The wall between the engine room and the hut workshop was alight with very active fierce flames and the ceiling above was also well alight.

For a moment I wondered where the nearest fire extinguishers were, when I remembered the water in an old paraffin drum. A bucket on the floor behind me grabbed at my hand and leapt into the water drum. One swish put out the whole of the wall fire and the second swish put out the ceiling fire and at the same instant David Pratt stuck the CO_2 nozzle through the trap door above the fire and squirted. We couldn't see for thick white dust and I had to yell out 'hold it' several times as I beat a retreat.

I've never seen such a transformation. Everything was white and much still is. It spread right through the hut and up along the loft and the whole place looked like an old-established flour mill or cement factory...

The cause of the fire was that the bonfire boiler for the bath has its chimney about a foot from the wall and the chimney had got very hot, especially near where it joins the stove. This happened because the grate door had been left open and the fire allowed to burn fiercely with so much draught. The heat from the chimney caught fire to Peter's windproof hung up to dry behind the chimney and against the wall and so the wall caught light from about 3ft off the floor and all the way up to the beams and floor of the loft...

Wednesday 6 March, 1957
... Weather this morning bad at South Ice with high drift though only 14 knots. 1530 weather OK but later radio conditions faded and weather not known so Bunny decided to go with Gordon about 6 p.m. In the meantime South Ice came through to say weather bad so Otter had to return - got in about 1945 hours...

Thursday 7 March, 1957

... Dug out some empty oxygen and acetylene bottles and toyed with an idea of making a fire siren powered by oxygen but don't quite know how they are constructed.

Plane still didn't go due to drift at South Ice, -37°C and 23 knots. Here it has been clear with light southerly which turned northerly this afternoon...

Friday 8 March, 1957

Mild day with light northerly and snow while South Ice had -40°C and 34 knots in the night. Today they had -37°C and 24 knots. Later visibility was down to only being able to see a hand in front of one's face and tonight visibility increased to 50yds. Jon at Whichaways is probably getting a bit short of food and fuel so he must be visited soon...

Roy's understatement reveals that he hadn't yet fully appreciated the seriousness of the situation for the two men marooned at the Whichaways. Fuchs had warned them that, so late in the season, the weather might close in at any time. Now his prophecy had become reality with the Otter grounded by high winds and poor visibility. On the third day, Blaiklock had decided to go onto half rations and to conserve fuel. In spite of his frost-nipped cheeks and nose, however, Stephenson was still enjoying himself. In fact, he later admitted to feeling delighted 'that my Antarctic adventure had really begun!'[54] Back at Shackleton, Fuchs was feeling altogether less exuberant: 'I am now becoming slightly concerned about Ken Blaiklock and Jon Stephenson who are still out at the Whichaway Nunataks', he recorded in his diary on 9 March, after poor weather had forced him to abort his third attempt at collecting them.

Meanwhile, based upon his experience with the British North Greenland Expedition, Roy had begun work on providing recovery eyes and ropes to the vehicles. He knew how important it was to have ample means of rescuing vehicles from crevasses.

Saturday 9 March, 1957

... Today I've completed No. 1 Weasel tow eye and recovery eyes on the vehicle's sides and this took me up to supper time...

---

[54] Stephenson, *Crevasse Roulette*, p. 48

This morning David Stratton said they have four days' food left at Whichaway after tonight. Bunny's thinking of relaying to them – via South Ice – instructions to start back on the 27 mile walk and South Ice to send up flares or rockets at a set hour...

Sunday 10 March, 1957

Northerly all day with snow. Makes it miserable working outside. Wind only light so snow doesn't get swept away but builds up deeply around the hut and covers the trap-door which has to be dug out half a dozen times a day. Same with my little workshop...

Workshop building goes on with Ralph and Gordon, but flying is out. Perhaps Ken and Jon have already started to walk back. They have no transmitter – only a receiver.

Monday 11 March, 1957

Gash hand today and with very little assistance...

Dug down through soft snow to cut hard snow for the kitchen, brought up three drums of kerosene and filled the jerry cans, cleaned up, swept up, mopped up, washed up, etc. Hannes gave me a hand to empty the water butt and cut up a seal. Cutting the seal into 10 rounds and feeding the dogs took one and a half hours not including digging out the seal...

Gordon took off with Bunny at about midday although South Ice had high drift. Main object was to try to find Ken and Jon and drop supplies to them. They circled around and about Whichaways but saw no tent – only tracks. After searching, they went on to South Ice, but saw no sign of them on the way and most of the way was drift. After offloading and refuelling at South Ice they came back to Whichaways but still saw no sign of the two. They hope to go again tomorrow...

Tuesday 12 March, 1957

Snow and high winds here and high winds and drift at South Ice. John Lewis and Bunny were up at 7 a.m. when a previously arranged schedule with South Ice was on. Things seemed roughly good enough for flying and they hoped to get away about 9.30 a.m. Unfortunately things got worse here and at South Ice, so the day has been lost. We all wonder where Ken and Jon are and how they are. They have, it is reckoned one day's food left...

Wednesday 13 March, 1957

First day of cooking over. Quite successful and didn't take much getting into the run of things again. Aga [is a] great difference from primus stove cooking...

Rotten day outside, south strong wind and snow with very poor visibility. South Ice: strong winds and thick drift with very poor visibility and temperatures down in -40s...

We are all concerned over Ken and Jon. They must be having a wretched time. If they went on half-rations a couple of days ago they may have a little to last another two days I suppose. No hope of doing any good with the aircraft in this weather as it's worse than the last search flight weather. Bunny hopes to try again tomorrow...

Friday 15 March, 1957

... It was decided to fly at the break of dawn, so half a dozen were up at 3 a.m. – John, Bunny, Geoff, Peter, Taffy and David Pratt. I got up too and had a cup of tea. At 3.45 a.m. the plane was off and 5 mins later the sun started to shine over the horizon, but I was back in bed. At about 8.20 a.m. Taff came in to say the plane had found the tent and was going to land. Next, we heard Ken and Jon had been picked up and were on their way to South Ice with a touch of frostbite.

The plane had circled Whichaways and landed, finding a note there. It then flew to South Ice, circled and started back for Whichaways on a different route. About 10 miles from South Ice they saw the tent. Ken and Jon heard the plane the second time and turned the Primus down to listen, then dashed out and saw the plane a little way off going across their trail and they thought they had been missed, till the plane suddenly turned towards them.

They had had a pretty wretched time with freezing sleeping bags and too cold to sleep and had only a third of a block of Pemmican left but sufficient fuel. Last night they had to put up with -49°C and on Wednesday night, in biting wind and cold, when they pitched camp, Jon couldn't undo the knot in the tent door so took off his new leather gloves and duffles.[55] Fumbling with the frozen knot his fingers started to freeze so he rapidly tried to stuff his right hand

---

[55] Duffles were large mitts routinely worn inside heavy leather mitts for outside activity when dexterity was not essential. Fingered woollen or leather gloves were often worn inside the duffels.

back in the glove but it was too stiff and he suffered considerable fingertip frostbite... several tips are affected and the middle one has a swollen tip like a large round white blister to the length of the nail. His cheeks and nose are red and raw and most of the skin is dead and peeling. Ken has been more fortunate.

They have both been brought back, while Geoff stays at South Ice in place of David S. They got in here at about 1315 hours.

Great rejoicing and fillip to morale... Gordon's dragged out a huge bottle of Remy Martin Cognac to drink health of survivors. Also bottle of whisky, soda syphon and ice on table. Also always plenty of rum for those who can take it...

Monday 18 March, 1957
Working on generator No. 2 all day... Start made by Ken to dig out old tunnels for dogs. Tunnels being deepened and rubbish removed to one end of each tunnel.

Thursday 21 March, 1957
... Bunny recounts story of a private showing of an Expedition film at Buckingham Palace. He sat between Queen Elizabeth and Prince Charles. Prince Charles kept asking questions and then information was given about stores loaded on Theron. So many tons of this, that and the other and a portrait of the Queen. Prince Charles turned to Bunny and said, 'What do you want a portrait of her for?' Bunny thought fast and gave the appropriate answer. 'She gave it to us and she's our patron and we like it.' This explanation was accepted...[56]

Saturday 23 March, 1957
Delightful news today...

While I was performing a gash duty – chopping wood to re-light a fire – Taffy came along and said, 'May I congratulate you?' 'Sure,' I said, 'What for?' and we shook hands. 'Come with me and I'll show you,' said Taffy. We went to the radio room and he handed me Enid's telegram to say Mr Egan (RSM at University of London Officers' Training Unit) had seen, in regimental orders, my promotion to WO1.[57] *Well, what a delightful shock! Luckily, on a*

---

[56] Born on 14 November 1948, Prince Charles would have been seven or eight years old at the time of this incident.
[57] WO1: Warrant Officer Class 1.

Saturday night too, when we have a 'lights' extension to midnight instead of 11 p.m. Naturally a little party is developing...

Monday 25 March, 1957
... Otter took off with Gordon and Taffy around midday in clear visibility all the way. Last trip of the season. They got back about 1910 hours...

Tunnel digging in the north drift going on in a big way, ready for the dogs...

The completion of this last flight of the season marked the start of a winter of total isolation for Lister, Blaiklock and Stephenson. Already, their new home lay so deeply buried that only its aluminium roof panels and chimneys showed above the surface. For the next seven months this tiny building, measuring just 16ft by 16ft, would be the centre of their universe. With the TAE's aircraft grounded for the winter, with no dogs or tractors of their own, and no proven surface route in any direction, in a winter emergency such as an accident or illness, they would be beyond help.

Thursday 28 March, 1957
Temperatures -33°C...

David Pratt towed Otter into hole dug in snow for winter housing today – protection from wind...

Saturday 30 March, 1957
... I got my old Weasel running with slight difficulty and towed... the lavatory drum out on a sledge half a mile east...

Five more dogs in the tunnels today – Caesar, Bouncer, Joe, Whitenose and Nutarak. They absolutely love going in. As soon as they get to the entrance they go straight down and into the depths. Once in a recess and with chain on the collar their joy is complete.

Saturday 6 April, 1957
Good day for outside work and very interesting winds. Started south, then west, then north, then south, then west and then north again, but all quite light.

Filled seven jerry-cans [with paraffin] this morning (gash hands always give this a miss) then David Pratt and I decided to do something about a pump to bring it straight into the generator room. (He'd carried six of the jerry-cans in for me).

David got on with his Sno-Cat while I dug up the little semi-rotary pump and fixed it up on the south wall inside the engine room… I'm looking forward to trying it out. It'll save a whole lot of hard work carrying cans up the hill, lifting drums onto the stand and standing outside in all weathers through the winter…

Tonight I dug up a case of rum for Ralph to make a cocktail. Although a week or two ago the cases were only a few inches under the surface they are now two feet under…

Monday 8 April, 1957

Completely unproductive day. Sorted out a large box of vehicle bulbs in the generator room while Allan got dental equipment sorted out and I spent most of the day on the table having two teeth drilled…

Sunday 14 April, 1957

Last night developed into a bit of a party in the kitchen for John Lewis, Gordon, Allan and me. John brought out a tin of mussels which we thoroughly enjoyed with vinegar. I got to bed at nearly 2 a.m. …

Rotten day, I think around -31°C, and 24 knots. Plenty of drift built up – now level with the eaves of the hut and sastrugi has been deeply cut in all the snow that has been falling for weeks.

British summertime started yesterday in UK. Here, we just get a few hours of sun to the north, while South Ice lost the sun about a week ago…

Monday 15 April, 1957

… This evening Scott Base was on. Ed wanted to know what would happen if we found it not possible to complete the crossing this coming summer? We couldn't try again next year because of fuel and supplies, so it would probably be three years later. Bunny told them it was the 64,000 dollar question…

Taffy heard American Pole Station (Paul Siple) calling on 'Ham' band and getting no answers, so he tried, and got them. A good chin-wag ensued and Bunny spoke to them and now there is a regular schedule arranged. They have a large station there with several underground buildings 1000ft long connected by a tunnel. Only 18 personnel there so they have a large room each.

Generally they get 10-12 knots from 0° meridian, but have had it up to 25 knots... They are expecting temperatures down to -79°C to -84°C...

Collins, publishers, want Bunny to produce his book by June '58!

Wednesday 17 April, 1957

... David Pratt and I got down to clothing repairs, though all I did was sort out two kit bags and patch some socks...

Bunny started writing his book and has also finished off dog tunnels and all dogs are now inside...

Thursday 18 April, 1957

Today would have been my fifth day without a cigarette but tonight I decided to have one as I'm messing around in the kitchen after the lights have gone out. I'm making hot cross buns...

BBC 'direct' schedule today with lots of maundering and lots of trouble putting tapes over to the BBC. I had been told that there was a message for me but didn't get it till the conditions were nearly too bad to hear. I said, 'Hello,' to Eleanor who asked who I would like to hear next to her. 'Enid, of course,' I cried. 'Well here I am darling, I've been listening to this all the time,' said Enid. I'm afraid I was too taken aback to make much use of the next few minutes – especially with conditions so bad. I had to strain to hear that Enid wanted to know how I was and not where I was. After asking what I was going to do for Easter, I told her 'fishing,' which she could hardly believe...

I mentioned that I'd said to Taffy at lunch that I'd like to hear Enid on the schedule and that it was a double shock for me. With quickly failing conditions I could only guess that Enid said something about 'this wonderful opportunity' and that 'it won't be long now.' But, if only I had been given a clue! That sort of surprise is fine for the perpetrators in the planning phase, but a disappointment to all afterwards. I could have so looked forward to speaking to Enid if I'd been told at the start of the schedule and I could have said things I wanted to say. Also, I could have been on the spot when conditions were good. And earlier, they were very good! That's only a thought though. I thoroughly enjoyed those few minutes and I'm thoroughly enjoying the lively impression she has left on me...

Friday 19 April, 1957

... In the morning I dug out my Sno-Cat which had got iced in and had drifts covering the tracks and one drift extended as high as the bonnet and had spread solidly over the engine...

Milo growled at Bunny today who was pretty put out about it. Milo will get a beating, I fear, if he does it again – especially on the trail...

Saturday 20 and Sunday 21 April, 1957

Gash hand Saturday and included big job of digging through four feet of snow on the roof of the porch in order to remove the 3ft square cover over the lavatory. The 44 gallon drum then had to be hoisted up about 8ft and for this we used the Fergy Hi-lift loader in two moves...

Friday, I removed the faulty starter motor from my Sno-Cat and found, on stripping it, that it had a U/S solenoid assembly so today removed one from a spare starter motor. Although slightly different I managed to fix it on my starter... I have sealed everything on it to make it quite drift and anti-freeze proof.

Nothing much happened today... Taffy says South Pole have had -68°C.

We hear Rhino has become engaged to [his girlfriend] Sally (who is still using his bedroom). Our telegram congratulates him and says we are glad he is half-way to getting his bedroom back again!

Tuesday 23 April, 1957

... I took the long seats out of the body of the Sno-Cat and brought them into the living room where they make the wooden wall bench-seat very comfortable...

Wednesday 24 April, 1957

Northerly with fair amount of drift today...

I've started making a fish trap that David Pratt and I have been planning to make. I'm using two spare sets of stay rods for the Aga, some welding rod and 1" wire netting...

Thursday 25 April, 1957

Strong northerly bringing plenty of drift...

I spent most of today in my little workshop welding together the frame for the fish trap and covering it with wire netting...

Friday 26 April, 1957

Gash-hand with George today and a very fine day outside... I finished off the fish traps in between times today. Now have only to fix the hoisting ropes...

Tonight made rum, honey and orange cold punch, but it tasted dreadful. The bitter taste, I figured, came from storing thick orange juice in a lime bottle which had contained washing detergent...

6

WORK AND PLAY

On the other side of Antarctica, Sir Edmund Hillary had been busy with his team. While he and the Ross Sea Committee were subordinate to the London Committee and of course to Fuchs, Hillary's approach seems to have had an air of independence from the start, despite his lack of polar experience. Hitherto, his independence had manifested itself to a fairly limited degree, in occasionally questioning Fuchs's decisions on board the *Theron* – much to Fuchs's irritation – and in adopting what was arguably a more professional approach to training his men prior to their departure from New Zealand. Once in the Antarctic, however, he would reveal an ever-increasing willingness to make his own decisions without reference to Fuchs, or to either of the committees.

The Ross Sea Party had arrived in Antarctica in early January and with American help had identified Pram Point on Ross Island as a suitable site for a base. Once established, they went on to lay two depots and to undertake surveys by land and air to find a route onto the Polar Plateau. By the time the Ross Sea Party hunkered down for the winter, Hillary had fulfilled his responsibilities up to that point both efficiently and properly.

Saturday 27 April, 1957
Hut cleaning this morning. Clear day outside with light southerly. Part shape of mirage sun to north-east this morning, but only small amount of glow.

Fixed hauling lines to fish trap and loaded it on [a] Canadian sledge then camouflaged it with [a] load of wood wool…

After David Pratt had cleared and washed up the lunch things we took the lot down on a Weasel. I had two 6' crowbars and we pretty soon had a hole about 2ft 6ins x 4ft in the new ice near the hill just off the old ice where the break-away occurred. The ice was a soft sort and about a foot thick. We baited the wires down there and fixed four of them in the trap then lowered it down through the hole, trying to keep it level. It's down about 50ft and the two wires are joined and hung over a length of timber...

When we got back Bunny asked if we'd been down to feed the horses. David played mystified and explained we took a load of rubbish down to burn. Suspicion has been aroused so we hope more than ever that we get some fish.

Sunday, 28 April, 1957
Sadly disappointed today. It's easy to guess why...

David Pratt and I left early from lunch to visit the trap. We were quite excited with expectation when we hauled it up but there was nothing in it...

We have more hope of getting some fish if we get down to about 100 feet or lower. We hope to keep trying, possibly to 300 feet...

Monday, 29 April, 1957
Very good day for outside work... David wanted to know when we were going down to the fish-trap. So I got the thin steel rope down and reeled off about 360 feet which I wound onto an old cable drum. After a false start when Bunny wanted David, we left at about 4.45 p.m....

When the trap came out it was thickly matted with ice flakes but inside we found a catch this time – shrimps! Not normal shrimps, but very similar – Euphausiacea – (krill)... and we collected 380 of them. The inside of the trap had a huge load of ice flakes as well, so, after cleaning it all up and attaching the extra steel rope we let it down to its full length of about 230 feet...

On the way back the tin of krill fell over and they were in a scattered heap on the floor, a few having gone down into the hull, but I collected nearly all of them up together with a lot of dirt and powdered Onozote.[58] When the Weasel was parked I picked up the tin but it slipped out of my leather mitt so once again they had to be collected up. We're keeping them in their frozen state till we get more, but we think we'd better do it with a hand net...

Cook tomorrow for four days.

---

[58] Onozote: a form of expanded rubber often used for making buoyancy aids.

Tuesday 30 April, 1957
First day of cooking done…

Tonight at about 2030 hours David and I went down in the Weasel to look at the trap. We hauled the lines up with the Weasel till the join at the bottom 50 feet where there now was a colossal tangle of wire loops. We don't know how they occurred unless a seal had been having a game. Inside the net, alas, was nothing (except our bait)…

We still keep the project secret, ever hoping to give everyone a surprise, so it was an intriguing conversation at lunch when Bunny suggested a trap should be made to try to catch some fish…

On the wall when I got up this morning was a poem called 'A Grace' – about Homard stews – and fish and chips!

A GRACE

We thank thee, Lord, for vulgar food,
For trotters and pig's cheek
For steak and onions, with their crude
But appetising reek!

Potatoes in their jackets make
Us plain folk honour Thee;
And thou art with us when we bake
Fresh cakes for Sunday tea.

Thy people's praise is overdue,
But see, dear Lord, we try
To offer thanks for Homard stew
And tasty, sausage fry.

Now wait a minute, Lord! Don't miss
The last word on our lips:
We'd thank Thee most of all for this -
A gift of fish-and-chips!

Anon.

No one admits to writing this but I think it was Bunny…

Wednesday 1 May, 1957

Second day of cook done, including ten loaves, two cakes and two puddings and puff pastry sweet and savouries and marshmallows. Unfortunately the marshmallows went sticky, even with icing sugar on them. I guess the sugar wasn't boiled quite long enough...

Weather mild with northerly wind and snow, continuing snow from east, then south, then east again – not suitable to go down to inspect the trap.

There's a little check going on over the tilt of the hut. Since the end of last year we've noticed that the met room has tipped down (north-east corner) and it's now quite apparent that the whole hut is tipped to the north. A level placed on the living room floor reads about ¾° tip down to north, although the hut is level in length (east to west). It seems that the main drift weight on the north side is compressing down that side, but Bunny puts a tentative theory that we are descending on a wave movement as the ice progresses north. It seems doubtful that a chasm is causing it...

Thursday 2 May, 1957

... I told Bunny about our fishing and he was very interested, so tonight he, David Pratt, George and I went down in the Weasel...

Eventually we were able to pull up the trap while George took several flash photographs of operations. We weren't very lucky having only about six krill in the trap this time. Probably the ice shale had kept them in the trap the time before last at 25ft. We had a job keeping the ice clear of the surface and soon we were able to see all the krill swimming around at various depths in the beam of our torches. David caught some with a hand net hastily made from his net scarf, but Bunny's net was of cloth and didn't let the water through, so he wasn't very successful. We had about 20 though and brought them back in a can of water...

I collected the 380 krill in the tin from my workshop and tomorrow will prepare some for specimens and the rest for David Stratton's tea as it's his birthday...

Friday 3 May, 1957

Last day of cooking done and bouquets from all quarters. Large ones too, but it wouldn't have been so if it hadn't been David Stratton's birthday. I had two chickens for that, but I had also planned for the meal, so we had a six-course one, apart from coffee and tea. My poor old feet complained and I didn't even find time to take a cup of tea at tea time.

To start with were five different pastry savouries, then soup, fish (salmon), chicken with spinach, Brussels, baked beans, spaghetti, butter-creamed potatoes, stuffing and chicken sauce with peas, then peaches, pineapple and cherries and Genoese (I think) sponges decorated with cream and chocolate inscribed 'A APPY BERFDY' on one and the other 'AND MENNY OF EM' on the other.

David started the morning with a miniature cherry brandy and got people to drink a bottle of gin and lime by lunch while still routine work continued.

With dinner tonight were three bottles of Kopke port and a bottle of sherry and afterwards a bottle of whisky and a bottle of gin. There was also rum, but no-one got around to that. A party ensued and we practised various acrobatics and John Lewis and David Stratton played 'Moriarty'.[59]

I forgot to mention that I boiled, after washing out the rubbish, the 360... krill, but found that they were empty except for oil, a very tiny amount of flesh and the small tubular assembly of intestines. I only opened five and two had about a dozen round eggs inside them. The whole basinful I put before David Stratton just for fun...

Tonight we've got our first real wind this year, around 50-60 knots from the north...

Tuesday 7 May, 1957
... Meeting tonight – mainly to go over to a 7-day cook period, scrub out on a Sunday and have the afternoon to relax, if not busy.

Wednesday 8 May, 1957
Temperature rather low today... John Lewis bet Ralph we won't get -46°C in May. I wouldn't be surprised if we get it tonight and I'm sure we'll get it this month. They have only a bar of chocolate on it (the usual currency)...

Bunny, John Lewis and Peter have started on the tunnel for a new entrance to join the existing one. Bunny started it some weeks ago. Geoff with the Muskeg and me with the Weasel both took loads of sawn snow blocks away...

---

[59] 'Are you there Moriarty?' is a parlour game in which two blindfolded opponents try to hit each other on the head with a rolled-up newspaper or similar.

The recent 60 knot wind has extended the whale-back from the west end of the hut to well past our Sno-Cat crate store about 200 yards away. A huge wind-scoop right round the hut now leaves a bank about five feet high on its east side and about three feet high on the other...

I found out the other day that my telegram bill is about £56/16s/6d.

Friday 10 May, 1957
Quite a notable day for temperature. Started around -40°C and has tonight gone just below -51°C.

I worked outside all day as the cold wasn't bad with only a few knots of wind from the south. Started my Weasel on choke at only second attempt and told the engine what a beautiful thing it was. Towed the Muskeg to start it and commenced making safety ropes to go round Weasels...

Roy's next diary entry refers to an 'IMP' – an Integrating Motor Pneumotachograph – designed by Allan Rogers in order to study the energy expenditure of men at work and at rest.

The device was by no means pleasant to wear, consisting of a rubber mask that covered the nose and mouth and a back-pack. In the interests of science Geoff Pratt later volunteered to wear it every day and night for a week, save for meal-times. Not surprisingly most expedition members proved less co-operative.

Saturday 11 May, 1957
... I helped David Pratt rig up a sledge for a strain gauge test on another sledge which Taffy was to pull while wearing an 'IMP'. At -47°C and about 12 knots southerly it wasn't too pleasant. Taffy towed his sledge loaded with a full jerry can and four piles of Weasel bogie wheels. The strain gauge was attached in his pulling rope and wires from it led to two 6v accumulators and the test equipment on my sledge. So I had to haul this sledge and keep it level with the strain gauge to keep the wires from becoming taut. At that temperature (and above) the insulation easily snaps. This meant hauling backwards and it's no wonder that I fell over backwards twice. The circuit took 8 mins.

George took several flash photos of all this...

Tuesday 14 May, 1957
Gash hand today...
... Bunny went down on skis this morning to dump half a dozen bottles in the sea – Hannes had prepared messages inside the bottles giving date, position and asking finder to notify [the] Scott Polar Research Institute...

Wednesday 15 May, 1957
Not very nice this morning with southerly wind so was glad No. 1 generator was due for 250hr overhaul...

Yesterday Ralph and Gordon did the finishing of the new main workshop roof and covered in the east wall so it shouldn't be long now, but the little lathe room still has to be built as an attachment...

Tuesday 21 May, 1957
... A darts ladder tournament has started and everyone is keen. In the draw George was at the top and I second. Taffy crept up one, challenged me and beat me, so I'm now third.

George won't play Taffy till tomorrow because he wants to be champion for a whole day!

Thursday 23 May, 1957
... Having been challenged by David Pratt (No. 4 on the list) we played off our darts match and I won the first two legs and, next, hope to tackle George with the possibility of removing him from second place where Taffy put him last night...

As it's John Lewis's birthday, Taffy made a sandwich cake, which Ralph iced, for tea. Tonight we had port (Kopke) after dinner and now have whisky or rum (with gin before dinner).

Ralph, just playing darts, has had difficulty in getting double one, so George said he'd do better with the lights out – so he put them out. Just after, Ralph said, 'Right, it's there. Put the lights on.' George put the lights on. His first dart was in double one! ...

Saturday 25 May, 1957
Northerly continued today at over 40 knots and temperature remained high, averaging -10°C, though the drift had virtually disappeared.

I didn't do so much today, but gave Gordon a hand in the [new] workshop cutting and putting up sheets of soft board to line the roof... David Pratt has been continuing with fixing up light and power fuse boxes in the workshop.

I visited the dogs this morning. All well and happy but Milo has a nasty streak and always has [had]. Snapping and snarling at old Joe in the next alcove calls for reprimand, but he refuses to accept it. It appears to be positively dangerous to hit him as he dodges quickly and shows much vicious challenge...

Yesterday Ralph took the wind speed of the up-draught from the bath drain hole. Using a hand anemometer he found it to be momentarily nearly 8 knots, having been forced by the wind strength through the snow beneath us. This was with 50 knots in the open...

Sunday 26 May, 1957 (written Monday)
Northerly continued but I was gash [hand] so it didn't matter...

About an hour before dinner I started printing [photographs] in the darkroom for the first time... I did seven by dinner, an hour later. From 9.15 p.m. to 11 p.m. I did another 22.

All are full plate from 35mm, so the grain shows a bit (not having a top-line camera). They are mostly iceberg scenes from Theron, *South Ice with wind generator and mast and the Southern mountain group which I did a series of photographs of, from the Otter...*

Monday 27 May, 1957
... Have started making skittles for midwinter indoor sports...

Wednesday 29 May, 1957
... South Ice have had bad winds which blew down Hal's 25ft instrument mast. Too windy to use the wind generator for charging and the pop-pop too fumy while they work in the tunnels.

Sunday 2 June, 1957
Lazy day due to 9 a.m. lie-in and then hut cleaning. I cleaned up engine room and hut workshop.

Cleaned up a new heavy-duty Weasel gearbox and found it far more robust than the old sort...

Made two more skittles this afternoon, making 10 including one spare. Also made a ball for the game, but it is a bit too small. Made a larger one from a piece of pickaxe handle which was fine and a good weight, but it split part-way through. I glued it, clamped it and put a ¼" wooden peg through, also glued. Haven't cleaned it up yet...

Monday 3 June, 1957

... Today, brought over No. 2 Weasel to investigate fitting of new heavy duty gearbox. I had to work out modifications which meant drilling and filing two holes in the gearbox rear mounting cross-member of the Weasel...

The propeller shaft had to have its internal spline-shaft reduced in length by an inch although I just managed with only ¾" (not quite enough). After filling with oil and re-adjusting the gear selection rods, the whole thing worked perfectly and synchronised gears were splendid...

Caught Taffy smoking this afternoon. I went through the radio room to get to the loft and Taffy, standing by the radio, self-consciously looked at his right forefinger and rubbed it in his left hand. This was a spontaneous act revealing guilt, for often I point out that the nicotine on his, a 'non-smoker's' fingers, is more heavily stained than mine and I still smoke (though only between 2 and 5 per day). As soon as I saw this act my suspicion was aroused and looked in vain for a cigarette. Then a tiny whisp of blue smoke curled up from under his desk. There was no fuss. I walked round him, reached under the desk and fished out a cigarette tray with a lighted, half-smoked cigarette on it. 'This is a sad day for you Tam,' I said. 'Indeed it is,' he agreed. Twenty-four bars of chocolate!

Tuesday 4 June, 1957

This morning I went in there and he was just drawing on a cigarette. He owes about 120 bars of chocolate now. Hannes lost 12 bars to him for the first week of the month, so Hannes challenged him again, this time 50 bars for a week. This bet Taffy lost in two days, so paid up 10 bars of the 50. These 10 were from 12 that Peter gave Taffy out of compassion for his being completely chocolate-less.

So he owes 72 bars to three of us and another 40 to Hannes – making 112 bars... Allan has bet him another amount for 48 hours and Hannes double-or-quits on the 50 bars for 48 hours. High finance! ...

Wednesday 5 June, 1957

Quiet day as Allan decided to spend his first day after a week's cooking doing some dentistry on me. While he prepared all his tools and instruments I finished off the period inspection of No. 2 generator.

From about 11.30 a.m. to 1 p.m. he took out the old filling in No. 2 top right. From 3.15 p.m. 'til 5.45 p.m. I had two injections, part of the pulp drilled out and a filling of penicillin powder and gutta-percha... A proper filling will be put in later...[60]

Thursday 6 June 1957

Cold day with -43°C this morning...

Decided to get kerosene in today and had to start No. 2 Weasel with heater. Temperature (coolant) gauge read about -43°C or lower and the engine practically didn't turn at all [but] after... heating... the engine started quite easily...

This afternoon, I decided to do something about the delay in progress of the skittle set. I got a length of... wood and shaped up a nice post for the ball to swing from. Finished off the pin block tonight...

David Pratt beat me at darts tonight and I came down to place No. 6 as we can now challenge to two places above. I had a return match and lost. Tomorrow David Stratton plays me from place No. 8. (Soon be at the bottom!)

I opened the dog tunnel first thing this morning. The smell was so overpowering that I was nearly sick but the dogs were so cheerful in their welcome that the smell was soon forgotten.

Taffy paid me the equivalent of 12 bars tonight, including rolls of fruit sweets, 'Rolo', 'Toff-O-Luxe', etc. He has won his two bets against 48 hours no smoking, so he's due for many bars now from Hannes and Allan. When I get my other twelve I'll find some way of letting him have it back.

Ralph expects to have the workshop finished tomorrow...

Friday 7 June, 1957

... I noticed a very odd thing today when George and I emptied the gash water butt in the pit in the tunnel. I always listen to the water when it tumbles 20ft to the bottom of the pit as it sounds just like

---

[60] Gutta-percha: a tough latex resembling rubber produced by certain Malaysian trees.

The Motor Vessel *Theron* trapped in ice in the Weddell Sea, January 1956. Vivian Fuchs's ill-judged attempt to cut the time taken to reach the expedition's planned base site resulted in a delay that threatened the success of the whole enterprise.

Photograph ©Antarctica New Zealand Pictorial Collection.

The members of the Trans-Antarctic Expedition Advance Party, left to right: 'Taff' Williams (partly obscured), Hannes Le Grange, Tony Stewart (standing), Ken Blaiklock, Rainer Goldsmith, Roy Homard, Peter Jeffries. Not photographed: Ralph Lenton. These men would become the first ever to over-winter in Antarctica under canvas.

Photograph ©RGS (with IBG).

Roy Homard with one of the expedition's four US-made Tucker Sno-Cats. Maintenance of the expedition's vehicles would be Roy's primary responsibility; however, he showed a vital willingness to turn his hand to any mechanical challenge. Photograph ©RGS (with IBG).

One of the Sno-Cats after a blizzard – a photograph that gives some idea of the kind of challenge that Roy faced throughout the expedition. Wind-blown snow routinely found its way through even the tiniest of apertures and could fill a vehicle completely.

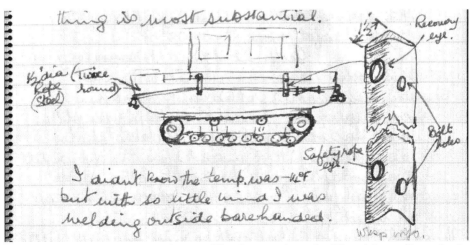

Roy's sketch of some of the safety modifications made to the Weasel in readiness for its journey through the crevasse fields on the approach to South Ice.

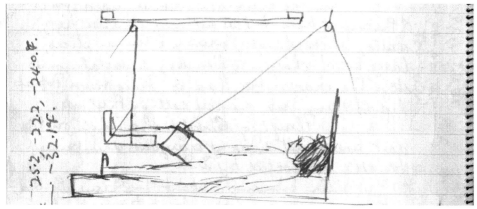

Another sketch from Roy's diary, this one from 25 June 1957, showing Roy in bed with his injured leg suspended by a system of ropes and pulleys.   ©REME Museum.

Crevasse trouble: the first 275 miles of the crossing journey, en route to the expedition's forward base, would be the most dangerous, with the unexplored ice sheet riddled with crevasses that could easily swallow whole a huge Sno-Cat and its trailer.

Photograph ©RGS (with IBG).

Another extraordinarily difficult vehicle recovery. Many members of the expedition thought the continued success of these operations little short of miraculous.

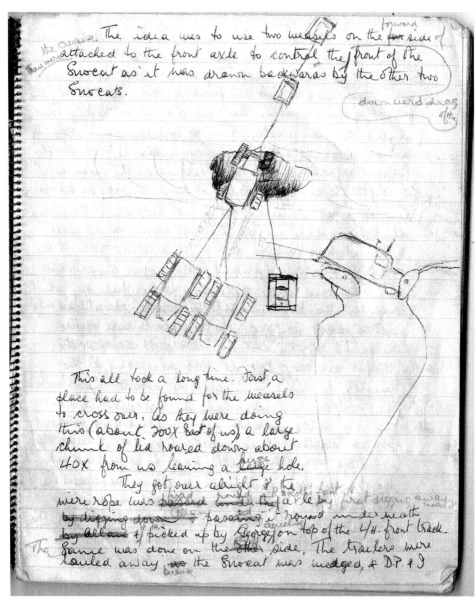

The idea was to use two weasels on the forward side of attached to the front axle to control the front of the Snocat as it was drawn backwards by the other two Snocats.

downward drag of the

This all took a long time. First, a place had to be found for the weasels to cross over. As they were doing this (about 300x East of us) a large chunk of lid roared down about 40x from us leaving a huge hole.

They got over alright & the wire rope was ~~passed~~ ~~under the~~ axle by ~~first digging away~~ ~~by digging down~~ & passing it round underneath ~~by Allan~~ & picked up by George, on top of the L.H. front track. The ~~same~~ was done on the ~~other~~ side. The trailers were hauled away, ~~as~~ the Snocat was wedged, & D.P. & J

Above and opposite: pages from Roy's diary entry for 25 November 1957, showing his sketches of the vehicle recovery process.
©REME Museum.

so we had to pull it far enough to get at it. The ~~careful~~ ~~pontoon~~ came back a bit too far so that its 4H. front pontoon dug into the wall of the crevasse ~~before the~~ ~~thingly~~. This meant a little digging out of the lip in order to free the rear end of the pontoon.

SNOCATS

MUSKEG

Whenever a bit of easing was done with the shovel by D.S. the Snocat sank a bit lower & jammed so we had to allow just an inch, & then the muskeg was able

Both the track & the shovel, the ~~pontoon~~ to slip back it was much easier, then to pull the pontoon up. of the front control rope pulled the ~~pontoon~~ out on to the top, much to the relief of all of us. Looking at the hole afterwards I was more surprised than anything else that we had got the poor thing out. The hole was 15ft. wide. Unfortunately, I don't think D.S. measured the depth, but he had intended to do so.

The measels were free now & our two Snocats

All the gear had been off-loaded from the Snocat & put on the muskeg, so now it was all loaded back in & one by one we made our way round to the probed route ~~out~~ the crevasse & camped.

The crevasse was more like a chasm with here & there these peculiar drifts along ~~its~~ hundreds of yards of length ~~(at least)~~. We sat to us.

Ralph Lenton (left) and Roy Homard (right) under canvas during the crossing. Both men had been awarded the prestigious Polar Medal prior to their recruitment for the Trans-Antarctic Expedition, Lenton for his earlier work in the Antarctic, and Roy for his service with the British North Greenland Expedition.

Photograph ©RGS (with IBG).

The Trans-Antarctic Expedition en route to the South Pole. The Sno-Cats would be the expedition's mainstay, with the other less powerful and less robust vehicles gradually abandoned as a result of mechanical failure and in order to conserve fuel.

Photograph ©Antarctica New Zealand Pictorial Collection.

Arrival at the South Pole, 19/20 January 1958. From this point onwards, in theory at least, the Crossing Party could rely upon the route survey completed by Edmund Hillary during his unauthorised 'dash to the Pole'. ©Antarctica New Zealand Pictorial Collection.

Hillary and Fuchs at the South Pole. Fuchs was dismayed at what he perceived as Hillary's disloyalty in making a journey to the Pole in advance of his own. However, he put on a brave face, telling the assembled journalists that Hillary's attempt had been a 'jolly good show'. ©Antarctica New Zealand Pictorial Collection.

Two of the Sno-Cats parked either side of the Ross Sea Party's de Havilland Beaver at Hillary's Depot 700. The expedition's aircraft had fulfilled the vital roles of aerial reconnaissance and depot-laying. ©Antarctica New Zealand Pictorial Collection.

The approach towards Scott Base, March 1958. Fuchs had estimated that the crossing would take 100 days; in spite of the lateness of the Crossing Party's departure from Shackleton Base and of the myriad delays and hitches en route, it was completed in just ninety-nine.

Photograph ©Antarctica New Zealand Pictorial Collection.

Roy with his pride and joy, Sno-Cat 'County of Kent'. After the completion of the Trans-Antarctic Expedition, Roy would never return to the Antarctic; however, the expedition remained the lynchpin of his career, and he would devote countless hours to the preparation of his meticulously-kept expedition diary for publication.   ©Antarctica New Zealand Pictorial Collection.

the roar of heavy breakers on a seashore. A few seconds later (as we were dallying) a far distant rumble echoed up from the depths.

There was a second lot to empty tonight so we got Bunny and David Pratt to come along. After the roar of the cascade of water had died away we waited. I thought nothing was going to happen. It was a failure. Then, from deep down, started the rumble like distant thunder which died away after about 4 seconds. The time it took to arrive after the water had gone down the pit was about 8 seconds or possibly more. What are we to make of it? Perhaps we are over a chasm that reaches 190ft down to the sea...

Saturday 8 June, 1957
... I spent this morning and half of this afternoon finishing off the skittle game and thank goodness it's done...

Tonight, it has acquired immediate popularity but discussion continues about the post being on the left or right. Allan dropped a surprise bomb-shell by asserting, at the precise moment of the completion of the job, that the post should definitely be on the left and was prepared to bet high on it. If he is right, then I can only say some boards have it on the right. This one for instance...

The [new] workshop looks wonderful now that the old stuff is being removed. The machine bay at the east end is very neat and good being nicely lined with soft board and all seams beaded. The little stove sits in one corner and the lathe, looking very new with preservative (red) still covering all steel parts, against the inner wall, looks very efficient and fine.

We still get dull glows to north around local midday. It is a dying red along the horizon and it is just bright enough on very clear days to faintly show misty silhouettes of distant large icebergs. This glow fades into orange, blue and then night, with stars only a little above the horizon. With the nearly full moon in daytime now it is possible to wander about outside and find places, knowing first the approximate direction.

In the first year Roy had managed without a proper workshop. The makeshift construction that he erected himself was too small to accommodate vehicles so he had laboured in the open, undertaking intricate work upon engines in freezing conditions, with no proper shelter from the wind, and with drifting snow everywhere.

When David Pratt came south, he brought with him an inflatable workshop that could be put into immediate use, but its usefulness was limited by its tendency to deflate when not sustained by the heat of the sun. The impact of this failure would have been lessened if the prefabricated workshop that he also brought could have been erected quickly, but other jobs took priority and construction didn't commence until 30 March. It then took two months to complete, with Fuchs himself admitting that its erection constituted a 'major task' in the prevailing conditions.

Despite the delays, and the resulting need to work in conditions that remained very far from ideal, Roy complained little and described the finished building as a 'fine, large, warm new garage'. In fact, this solid wooden building would be used for little more than five months – after which it would be abandoned forever.

Tuesday 11 June, 1957
Cold day with not too much wind, temperature... dropping to -46°C this afternoon...

I contented myself with opening up the dog tunnel this morning and saying 'Hello' to all the dogs. Some of them are very dirty livers, their alcoves completely iced with urine. They stand outside in the tunnel at the full extent of the chains looking quite forlorn. Others deliberately take care that their alcoves are not soiled. The stench down there is mighty powerful (and more).

Not feeling very bright again this morning – as so often happens here, although last night I didn't sleep too badly. Night before I lay awake from 12.30 a.m. to 2 a.m., then woke up for a couple of ½ hr periods before time to get up. Peter's 'hoot' of a cough helps ruin my 'dropping off' period and then it takes an hour or so to struggle back to that same state. The kitchen doors are noisy too and some-times people come and go as in a transit camp.

Sleeping quarters should be removed from kitchens (where people like to have a last minute beverage and goodnight chatter after lights are out) and from frequently used thoroughfares – especially where doors have to be used by the night weather man, and to use the latrine. Doors should be of a silent hinge type and with noiseless locks or catches. Sleep, being well guarded in a normal home is, in a place like this, least available though needed most...

Wednesday 12 June, 1957
We had a pretty good day today, though it got colder, with southerly dropping. Temperatures -28°C down to -41°C tonight and

wind 6 knots to 15 knots to 5 knots. Pretty clear sky with only a little cloud quietly hanging high up, lit by such a bright full moon that our shadows on the snow were black and clear.

I worked most of the day on the garage pit walls and uprights...

Ralph is painting out the living room with white fire-resisting paint – to have, I hope, a more homely and warm colour later. With Midwinter's Day only nine days off there is only just time to get this done and the mahogany bar set up. This latter was to have been a workbench at South Ice but couldn't be included for time and weight...

David Stratton dug up supplies of cigarettes, tobacco, bottles and chocolate and today issued [the] next six months' chocolate ration which normally would be due 1st July. Taffy paid all his losses on his non-smoking bets... I got rid of 12 bars of plain for 9 bars Caramello from Bunny. Taffy eats only Caramello for preference and with so little left of any sort, I'm hoping to get a little stock of Caramello to give him at midwinter.

Tonight David Stratton put out two bottles of Malmsey but I didn't feel like imbibing and had a little lie down to relieve a sore eye... Allan had a look and found something stuck to the left eye on the edge of the iris. It took some moving but at last it came.

I was relieved enough to have a drink and start a sing-song with Gordon, from our song sheets. On the strength of this racket Ralph got another bottle of Malmsey...

Thursday 13 June, 1957
After tea Allan removed the gutta-percha from my front tooth, refilled it with penicillin powder and put in a base filling before capping it. It still needs a top trim-up and another layer due to a last-second hitch in its shaping as it was setting...

David Stratton and Ralph [are] painting white undercoat along south wall and part of roof of living room and have started a coat of cream...

Sunday 16 June, 1957
... Good weather, but it didn't matter much, for I was in the garage and had a red letter day.

Due to the upheaval in the living room because [of] the painters, there was no scrubbing out today so everyone rather had a day off. I was anxious to make a start on the Weasel so went across in a fresh northerly with drift and snow... In the garage I went ahead with the Weasel, clearing out everything and undoing all the cab holding-down attachments. I also ran the heater for an hour as the Weasel was cold and full of snow while its roof and walls inside had layers of ice as well as drift. A tropical downpour ensued.

The temperature in the garage had been -13°C when I went in, but, with the fire and heater going, it rose to 1°C in an hour. After break I had several helpers to move the cab off the Weasel and it fitted very nicely on its side along the wall next to the coal bunker.

During the rest of the day I've removed the floor, propeller shaft, gearbox, battery box, windscreen heater, petrol tank, engine side cover and instruments, etc., VCR (voltage control regulator), oil filter, fan and engine. I am glad I got the engine out but I had to work on till 10.30 p.m. to do it. I had the pleasant assistance of David Stratton some time before dinner and also after dinner till 10.30...

The mahogany bench/bar tonight looks very fine against the west wall of the living room. The wall is a nice cream with the Queen's portrait in the middle. On the polished surface of the bench is a blue mug containing Ralph's large bunch of imitation flowers (via Magga Dan). It looks a real homely touch.

Monday 17 June, 1957

... Good weather continues with light northerly and mild temperatures.

I worked in [the] garage to 10.15 tonight. I started the morning by collecting likely spares from the old Sno-Cat crate. All the gaskets will be replaced on the Weasel even if no other replacements are required...

I've stripped the engine of everything except the sump and clutch plate. Celeron timing gear is not in any way damaged so I had only to replace the cover gasket. I noticed that the crankshaft pulley had a crack by the keyway – I seem to remember this in BNGE. Cylinder block cleaned of carbon and I have ground-in two valves – but I think I might as well use new ones as they will only be wasted – there being no chance of using them otherwise. There is always the spare engine too in emergency...

My knee has been slightly swollen... This evening it is bigger than ever and a bit painful. Although I've done some kneeling this worst bit occurred after bending over the engine for a while with my knees tensed backwards. Allan says that only rest can do anything – so I guess I shall have to put up with it...

Tuesday 18 June, 1957

... Good weather continues, though light southerly...

Through the day I've been working on the Weasel engine and made good progress... I've ground in all the valves... I've replaced the sump gaskets and the clutch plate...

George is willing to do a gash day tomorrow so that I can get on with the engine... Worked till 10.15 p.m. and wish I could sleep and eat there with nothing to interfere with this work...

David Stratton came in, de-coked the cylinder head for me using a screw driver and a Wolf wire brush... He reckoned it was good sport.

Wednesday 19 June, 1957

... Good day again though a little cooler with a light southerly and clear sky.

Work [has] gone well today with no major snag... tomorrow I hope to get everything else assembled and the vehicle running.

We've got two cooks this week. John Lewis doing normal cooking while Ralph is preparing everything for Midwinter. We have a beautiful 15lb turkey (ready packed in polythene and frozen) and it's the finest looking thing I've seen. We also have a huge piece of pork and some kidneys and a couple of fine Xmas puddings. One is Ralph's, home made by his mother and the other from Harrod's. We also have 5 bottles of 1878 wine from a wine grower in Jamaica, as well as some bottles of champagne.

For the last 3 days a series of very loud, single, double and multiple explosions has been going off in the dark as Gordon continues his research into a suitable pyrotechnic display for 21st June...

Thursday 20 June, 1957

... Thank heavens the Weasel engine plan worked. I just got it all finished in time. Everything back in place, everything works, and the engine came to life at the first press of the starter – and it sounded beautiful... The vehicle is ready to run out of the garage apart from the cab – so I can enjoy midwinter with a clear mind. It's meant four late nights and no lunch today but it has been worth it and anyway a compassionate cook (John Lewis) sent ham sandwiches and pickled onions across by Gordon who was going out past the workshop anyway to wire up his firework display. He's done over a 100 connections for his set pieces, etc.

David Pratt and I managed to tidy up pretty well in the workshop and will finish off tomorrow ready for a two hour champagne cocktail house-warming party from about 1 p.m. to 3 p.m. This keeps everyone out of the way while Midwinter table is being arranged...

During today somebody's put up all the decorations and the living room is very attractively hung with numerous criss-crossed cut concertina chains, double coloured twisted crêpe paper, bunches of balloons and strings of coloured fairy lights all round the walls.

Shackleton has received about twenty Midwinter cables (which I haven't read yet) and a long play (through courtesy of GPO – gratis) from 64 Victoria St... I haven't read this either. I have received three Midwinter greetings telegrams – one each from the two families and a nice one from Enid.

Friday 21 June, 1957
... Writing this on Saturday – and don't feel a bit like it. As yesterday and this morning were such a success I hate to think of no record at all in my diary.

A 9.30 breakfast of bacon, tomato, beans, and fried bread started the day, but before this I went to the workshop and lit the fire.

After breakfast David Pratt and I had a hectic time preparing the workshop for the cocktail party. I had all the prints pinned up upon the soft board panelling showing last year's Midwinter party in the Sno-Cat crate and also some portraits of the other blokes. These were very suitable in expression to mix in [with] a large pin-up of an 'Esquire' girl entitled 'Bewitching'. On another wall were the pictures I took in Halley Bay...

David Pratt had pinned up some large, beautifully coloured prints of various world-wide views that he got as a bound set in Madeira. These were in the machine bay. On the bench in here were the eats – salted nuts, pâté de foie gras puffs (Ralph made), cheese straws (also Ralph's) etc.

On the bench in the workshop were gin, lime, vermouth, Bristol Milk, and our champagne-brandy cocktail. We also had the HMV record player here. Scottish country dancing and [a] Charlie Kunz medley were the favourites and some even danced reels etc. George and Hannes took many flash photos and the whole thing was very happy and successful...

I blew up a fairly large meteorological balloon on the Weasel exhaust and this was an exciting diversion to see how big it would get (2 metre diameter). What a thick, filthy, pall of fumes suddenly enveloped the rear of the Weasel when the balloon burst! Opening the roof-vent soon cleared the air.

Guests arrived from 1.05 p.m. onwards, guided through the darkness by our flare-path of a dozen tins of burning oil. Bunny showed how to bend a bar by striking it hard over his forearm then partially bent it straight by striking it across his thigh. To finish off, he used Ralph's thigh, but the first strike sprang poor old Ralph into startled life and sent him hobbling away nursing one leg with both hands and wearing a look of extreme anguish on his face.

Gordon put on his fireworks at about 2.20 p.m. It consisted mainly of an opening explosion, several Very lights and some ground-flares, some of which changed colour and one which spurted a cascade of silver sparks for half the display in company with a large red flare – which went on forever I think.

Back for Midwinter dinner which started about 3.30 p.m. Everyone was feeling in fine style. George took a couple of photographs of us all in our places and then the turkey was brought in for Bunny to carve...

Miniature liqueurs – from crackers and separately wrapped – added to the wine, champagne and brandy poured in our glasses, but the miniatures were not called upon. Crackers, containing lots of noisy instruments added to larger musical instruments of last year and those used on Magga Dan, *so there was no shortage of noise once toasts had been drunk, led by Bunny's toast to the Queen. The HMV did almost continuous service...*

My knee was worse and Allan said he might have to put it in plaster (and today I think I might need it!), but he said he would give me the freedom of the day. In spite of this rather painful knee handicap, I was able to make full party business once a couple [of] hours of rest on my bed after dinner had restored vitality.

Noise, music, records, games, etc. kept going with various characters re-appearing from darkened bunk rooms after short recuperation periods. Great volumes of nuts seemed to be descending over someone's head for most of the time, while torpedo battles raged with noises so very realistically produced by Ralph using the amplified loud-hailer... Sadly, the thing got rather lost after our submarine became airborne...

It was a mighty fine party and it wasn't till 4 a.m. that the last of us, Ralph, Allan, Gordon and I, went to bed.

Tuesday 25 June, 1957
... Have got a lot to catch up with.

Saturday evening turned into rather a party again. People were gradually beginning to feel better and when I distributed my box of Xmas crackers... people all got together in the living room again.

In the afternoon I had used part of the buffet table to lay out my Chinese figs, dates, sticks of rock, orange and lemon slices, large box of chocolate liqueurs, sugared almonds etc. The cracker box had a Pixie House pop-up lid so I amused myself setting that up.

Playing 'cricket' and 'Shanghai' on the dartboard got nearly everyone drinking forfeits concocted by David Pratt.

On Sunday I spent the day in bed – not only to get over the last two days, but because it was more than time that I gave priority to my bad right knee. It came up last Monday and got gradually more painful. On Friday morning it swelled up again and was very painful, with slight bruising on the inside of the knee and oedema down the shin.[61] On Saturday conditions were the same with the bruise having spread on the inside of the knee. On Sunday bruising discolouration reached down to the ankle but not round the back of the calf. On Monday two pulleys were rigged up over my bed to support my leg in its most restful position and to allow fluid to run back down. Pain, though bearable, was continuous and is only relieved with the leg up...

Saturday 29 June, 1957
... Seven days in bed on my back and my leg slung up for six of them was no hardship I must say. I had to unhitch my leg for sleeping and it gradually got more comfortable – till today when I've been allowed to get up for the evening after Allan had wrapped nearly the whole leg in three inch wide Elastoplast...

A day or two ago temperatures went down to -40°C but it has been pretty good on the whole...

---

[61] Oedema, or dropsy, is the medical term for fluid retention in the body. Fluid build-up causes affected tissue to swell. It can be localised – for example, as the result of an injury – or more generalised.

Sunday 30 June, 1957

... First full day up and no trouble – knee quite comfortable in its bindings. I worked on No. 1 generator all day with David Pratt doing its de-coke and valve grinding...

I had a wander outside and to the workshop tonight. Quite mild and only very light wind from the South. I saw some fine aurora about 10 p.m. (corona) with shafts and curtains forming a huge shining stockade reaching upwards in a circle just to north overhead of us. The form was changing all the time and soon it had faded very much. A little later it came back fairly strongly but then I came in...

International Geophysical Year commenced today.[62]

Wednesday 3 July, 1957

... Have finished No. 2 generator's 1000hr overhaul except for welding the broken fuel tank mounting. Glad to have finished the silencer and exhaust pipe cleaning – a job I didn't look forward to. Got more out than I expected. It shouldn't be necessary to do another 1000hr overhaul on the Enfields after this – I hope.

Got myself thoroughly filthy and had to change all of my underclothes tonight. As the engine room was up to 30°C even underclothes were too warm...

George has pinned up the 'after-Midwinter' prints and made them appear as ghastly as possible. These show me in bed next morning refusing a drink while wearing a paper hat.

Bunny had me playing shove ha'penny tonight and proved himself to be a very skilled player. As a novice I wandered off for a wash when Allan took over and then listened to records of 'Mikado' with Peter in the kitchen.

Allan re-wound only one bandage around the knee this morning. The ankle was still swollen, and is still tonight.

This afternoon he did some dentistry on myself and Taffy. He put in a full filling in place of half of one which came out from No.1 upper left (or 'Right' as the dentist looks at it).

Friday 5 and Saturday 6 July, 1957

... Oedema persists down the shin bone on the inner side and pain at the bottom few inches... This morning Allan put only a cotton bandage on, but is thinking of putting my leg in plaster.

---

[62] In fact, the IGY ran from 1 July 1957 to 31 December 1958.

Tuesday 9 July, 1957

... Minimum -40°C.

Southerly all day today still with a beautiful red glow over the silhouetted ice bergs to north and a long low arc of dark cloud framing it all...

David Pratt and I worked on suspension [of Weasel No. 1] today. He replaced all 8 rear bogies while I fitted up a larger 13 leaf spring with heavy U-bolts. I had to cut slots in the hull to allow the U bolts to come up. Also had to remove the top leaf.

'Calling the Antarctic' tonight had bad conditions and David and I didn't stay for it but went back to work. We finished early enough for me to get my bath at 10 p.m. I just managed to get all my washing done by 11.10 p.m.

My knee has a slight pain to the right of the kneecap, the knee being generally swollen and a large oedema at the top part of the right side of the calf...

Thursday 11 July, 1957

... Today David and I got on with the Weasel, but mostly he was Weaselling to take away 15 boxes dug up by Bunny and John Lewis. George filmed the second sprocket assembly and of course Enid will certainly remark on the hands full of grease... I used the oxy-acetylene 'Sapphire' to heat the axle and of course there was plenty of smoke. The flint gun wouldn't work and David lit the acetylene with his lighter and his hand seemed to be enveloped in flame. George thought this was good stuff...

Southerly came up again today with drift and temperatures dropped to -43°C.

Friday 12 and Saturday 13 July, 1957

... Both Weasel repair days with southerly wind and low temperatures...

It was a party night, Saturday, as it was Ralph's birthday and it wasn't very long before we were well away. With dinner we had Sherry, Madeira (1878) and Kopke port. Afterwards we had two bottles of whisky and one gin. Everyone joined in a game of cricket on the dartboard and I had produced three paper hats which were being worn by Ralph, Geoff and me. Taffy sat in a canvas chair reading a very large book.

Pretty soon John Lewis had quietly lit Ralph's paper hat from behind and the flames were large and long before Ralph felt the heat and tore off the hat.

A little later, Taffy leapt off his chair and his book crashed to the floor. A novelty candle had been placed on some books under his seat and it took a long time for the heat to penetrate.

In the same darts game, while my attention was distracted by much barracking, I felt a scorching heat at the back of my head and quickly snatched off my own burning hat. I think the third hat went the same way on another head.

John Lewis did an impressive trick by holding a lighted match in the dark and blowing neat Appleton's rum at it. This produced an immense bomb of near-white flame edged all over with little flicking tongues of fire. It lasted only a split second and made quite a roar. He did this three times, each time making a larger flame. I noticed a little later that his eye-lashes were singed.

During the latter couple of hours of the evening we developed our own jazz band to help out the record player. Toy saxophone, clarinet, etc., tin trays and saucepans, tins of dried peas, and a tea chest fitted up with a length of string and a broom stick. A triangle was really a steel marlin-spike hit with a knife-sharpening steel. David Pratt had a saucepan-lid tied to his right foot and played on an inverted meat-roasting tin with two sticks [while] using a saucepan... as a side drum. Allan alternated with Ralph playing the 'big-base' and using drum sticks on it.

George took a lot of flash photos including one of me using Allan's hypodermic needle behind him as he crouched over his drum playing his concentrated best for the camera. Allan let a whole tape run on the recorder after announcing into the microphone that this was the scene on Ralph's birthday, Saturday 13th July, 1957. It was a little upsetting to find this morning that the tape is quite silent.

The party broke up just after 1 a.m. when the lights went out and George dispensed bacon on fried bread...

Sunday 14 July, 1957
... Minimum -39°C.

Woke up about 9 a.m. when the generators came on and soon dozed off again. Taffy brought me a cup of tea, so I had that and the port. Later David Stratton brought me another cup, then Peter told me that breakfast was being cleared away, so I got up, but only had tea and coffee. Time was 11 a.m....

Monday 15 July, 1957
... David Pratt and I have finished the [Weasel] track today but it has been far tougher than we could manage on the trail. Getting the track tension spring down was a most difficult job...

Northerly blizzard all day with speed up to 35 knots and gusts to 40 this morning. Tonight it has eased off considerably...

Tuesday 16 July, 1957
... With cooking coming up tomorrow I spent most of the day making a bracket to use with a special jack to adjust the track tensioning spring...

In the evening I tried it out on the track spring already tensioned and it worked fine.

Wednesday 17 July. 1957
... Minimum -39°C.

First day of 7 days cooking and it went very well. I made some 'imiak'[63] but it's hardly got time to be ready for Saturday evening.

Southerly blizzard today with temperatures in the minus thirties centigrade and wind around 40 knots and more...

Thursday 18 July, 1957
... Second day's cooking a success and my little jam cakes were so popular that the complaint was that there were not enough.

Imiak coming along fine, but I think it needs more yeast as it seems to have almost stopped working, while the liquid remains sweet.

Temperature down to -43°C today but southerly only around 12 knots...

South Ice on this morning had a double trouble and I was handy in the kitchen to speak to Hal and Ken. Hal explained that the pop-pop was partly in pieces and Hal had dropped a valve cotter in the sump and was talking about removing the generator but hadn't the right tools. Also, the wind generator was producing only 4 Amps...

---

[63] Immiaq: a beer brewed in Greenland. Presumably, Roy had become familiar with it during his year with the BNGE.

I was able to talk about these things for a minute or two and conditions faded. Another schedule was hastily arranged and we started again but in a matter of seconds conditions faded right out. Twice since, no contact has been made but Taffy read out my list of instructions...

Friday 19 July, 1957

... On Thursday night David Pratt had his bath and Ralph doctored a bath cube... with Aqua Flavine[64] which turned his bath bright yellow. David had his own back by dipping Ralph's pyjamas in it. Next day most of the bath room was stained yellow and the bath has an interesting two-tone effect.

Saturday 20 July, 1957

... Fourth day of cooking done and used Enid's mother's Xmas pudding, Bunny having two helpings, but it just went round nicely.

Tonight bottled my imiak in six bottles and have about two gallons left to drink tonight.

South Ice have [their] wind generator working alright, trouble was worn propeller bush which I had asked them to look at...

Temperatures today -44 °C, with southerly wind...

Sunday 21 July, 1957

... Wonderful night last night and imiak pronounced a success, people generally started to go to bed at about 2 a.m. and I a little after 3 a.m.

Ralph and Peter were ribbing each other and when Ralph grabbed Peter's legs and pulled him out of his chair he had to run like mad to the kitchen and barricade himself in together with John Lewis and another, who were already in there. Peter heaved his shoulder to the door and then we got the wonderful notion of having David Pratt push the door to allow Peter to go through the loft down into the radio room and into the kitchen via the little passage. This he accomplished pretty quickly and quietly crept up behind Ralph who was straining to keep the door shut. John and the other chap moved aside and Peter stepped in to help Ralph hold the door. Then the fun started with Ralph receiving the shock of his life. A quick rough and tumble and the action was brought to a satisfactory conclusion and the duellists entered the living room for

---

[64] Acriflavine: a form of antiseptic.

further refreshment to the most joyous roars of laughter from the accessories to the action...

Outside a strong northerly worked up into the 40 knots... with a maximum of 64 during the night but the temperature had gone right up to just below -18°C...

Monday 22 July, 1957
... Strong northerly continues... No. 1 Weasel is finished but can't be got out due to the strong wind which makes opening the large workshop doors impossible.

I forgot that after the Saturday night party Ralph, who was night meteorological man, took a Tilley lamp at 2 a.m., went to the workshop armed with brush and red drab fire-proof paint pot and painted nearly all of the orange Weasel red. David Pratt arriving in the morning (after a party night) couldn't believe his eyes...

Tonight, while washing up, Geoff, who only sings pom-pom-pom-pom whenever he sings at all, got going, and John Lewis (also washing up) and I joined in. Unknown to us, Allan had the tape recorder running by the kitchen living-room door and made quite a long recording...

Tuesday 23 July, 1957
... Last day of cooking finished and I feel reasonably happy...

Temperature remained good until tonight and wind dropped a lot. I had a look outside this morning to see very definite signs of returning daylight. All objects around the camp were visible – though without detail – in the quarter light...

Peter taking over cooking from me – about as happy as I was.

The Weasel is now out of the workshop and preparations are being made to bring in the Muskeg.

I heard the washing-up recording tonight. It's a shocking noise.

Wednesday 24 July, 1957
... Scott Base on tonight and coming through very clearly... Ed might be pushing on about 800 miles it seems, using the Fergies. Wouldn't be surprised to find Ed and Fergy at the Pole...

Thursday 25 July, 1957
... Minimum -29°C.

Gash hand with George today. In between I was at the workshop making and welding a new battery carrier frame for the Muskeg.

This I finished tonight and David Pratt and I packed up at 11.15 p.m. ...

I had to trim Ralph's beard tonight, separating his beard to form a top chin beard and huge mutton chop whiskers so that the flying oxygen mask used with the IMP will fit him.

South Ice came through well this morning after an impromptu party the previous night. Ken said they had a check on the liquor stock and found they have to drink an awful lot to get rid of it all before the soaks arrive...

Friday 26 July, 1957
... Minimum -45°C.

Poor night's sleep and felt droopy all day. I spent most of the day making nuts from bolt heads and threading 'U' clips for Nansen dog sledges...

Yesterday I stopped in the middle of drying up the lunch dishes and went straight to the radio room where I sat down and wrote a telegram to Enid: 'Always thinking of your patient waiting makes me want to tell you I love you very much.'

Sunday 28 July, 1957
... Telegram from Enid yesterday saying, 'Message was much needed tonic deepest love.' So everything feels much better...

With -51°C today and 20 knots southerly, it's making things a bit uncomfortable... Temperature going down again tonight so we may get a new record.

Monday 29 July, 1957
... We did get a record low temperature last night of -53°C...

Wednesday 31 July, 1957
... Gash hand with George today... I did a little pottering in the kitchen to help and also got 2 gallons of imiak started...

This morning we had a good deal of early morning light for a short time and to north the orange glow was very light and promising...

This afternoon and this evening I did a bit more drift-proofing on the Muskeg with David Pratt and Ralph...

Friday 2 August, 1957
... Yesterday was quite nice with light southerly and fairly low temperatures. Today much the same...

First thing I did was dig up seven bags of coal and warm up the Muskeg to bring them to the workshop. Remainder of the day had been spent on the engine cover modifications [for Weasel A], adjusting the clutch and steering bands and checking over things generally. It has only been run about 14 miles here since its overhaul in UK...

Gordon threw an orange smoke bomb in the workshop today making us furious. George had gloves on and threw it out again. In retaliation David Pratt and I took a large can of water to the RAF place while they were helping on digging out sacks of coal. We used the water to turn the Dexion bundles that they are using to make a shelter, into solid blocks of ice. They won't have got those apart in a hurry. Also, a tin of Dexion nuts and bolts we iced-up solid, ready for Gordon to collect. He looked in the tin but noticed nothing and took them away. We haven't heard anything about it.

Very fine to see light increasing. Everything visible and even details of distant objects...

Saturday 3 August, 1957
... Very nasty day outside with strong southerly and low temperatures. Wind at 50 knots with -43°C was not pleasant to be out in, especially with thick drift.

This morning I overhauled No. 1 generator so didn't have to venture out till after lunch. Just before lunch I siphoned the two gallons of imiak from the large aluminium pan into a two gallon polythene bottle and it filled it right to the top. Allan fitted an IMP mask to my face for future imping and intended to do one for an hour today while I worked in the workshop but it didn't get done. He wanted to do two more to complete a century.

This afternoon things went pretty well in the workshop. We got a Weasel track off and an idler and axle assembly complete...

Tuesday 6 August, 1957
... Gash hand again so didn't get very much else done...

David Stratton had 7 or 8 dogs out today for a run, but each time had to let Squibbs out with one as it was the only way he could catch them. Squibbs would always come when called, bringing the other one with her. Young Marø had a fight with four others but, though a bit bloody, was quite happy. Squibbs, having galloped madly for two hours... found it all a bit too much and was sick twice.

Wednesday 7 August, 1957

... Weather has been good with very light northerly wind, then almost calm from the south and tonight a light wind freshening from the north bringing some light snow with it. Too cloudy this morning to see any glow to the north but there was plenty of diffused daylight about, which made everything quite clear...

I got on with fitting the new Atkitrak [to Weasel A]. Ralph was away on the Fergy. George had been [on] night met duty and David Pratt was with 'Wrack-and-Ruin'[65] towing the Auster to a new park place. So I had to shift the removed Balata Goodrich track on my own and manoeuvre the new Atkitrak into position on my own. By the time I had lifted and pulled the track over the rear sprocket and brought the end up to the front I was sweating.

Since then David Pratt and I had a devil of a job trying to get the four connecting straps bolted together, but we managed. I don't know how it would be at -40°C or -60°C, but certainly the rubber would be very stiff...

Saturday 10 August, 1957

... Outside a strong southerly brought heavy drift and low temperatures...

Learned that Ed had an accident on Friday and broke his leg but don't know how. I guess he's furious and George[66] says he's the worst patient he's ever seen.

I've had nine [air] letters so far and five of them from Enid including four of nearly 200 words each. What a wonderful girl to have. She makes me the envy of all here who care about receiving letters.

---

[65] During the second winter most of the vehicles that would take part in the crossing had been named. The four Sno-Cats would now be known as 'Rock 'n Roll', 'Able', 'Haywire' and 'County of Kent'; the Weasels as 'Wrack-and-Ruin' and 'Rumble', and the Muskeg as 'Hopalong'. Only weasels 'A' and 'B' remained unnamed. Roy chose 'County of Kent' in honour of the county of his birth.

[66] George Marsh, British medical officer to the Ross Sea Party.

Sunday 11 August, 1957
... -52°C tonight, so David Pratt and George have won a dinner each from Hannes who bet it wouldn't reach -51°C again this year. Southerly still bringing drift though wind dropping steadily tonight after being 40 knots.

I spent morning de-icing lavatory and porch and part of afternoon making outer door fit...

I took on Hannes's bet that temperature wouldn't go to -54°C...

Monday 12 August, 1957
... I won the bet with Hannes who now owes me a dinner, for we had a new low record of -55°C last night... South Ice had -43°C and South Pole -21°C...

Scott Base schedule tonight revealed that Ed had not broken his leg and knew nothing about it... The rumour started when a message of condolence was received from the Australian Base... David Stratton reckons they overheard Ed last week talking about the American base where several had [suffered] broken legs...

Being gash hand today has held up work quite a bit, but in between I've been working on the radio frame in Weasel A...

Tuesday 13 August, 1957
... -51°C today and wind strong with drift, but suddenly this evening the southerly dropped to very light. This was just what we wanted, for Weasel A was finished tonight and we were able to take it out and bring in Weasel B. I feel rather proud of the radio surround which now sports a table on top and is all very firm. Safety belt fitted, heater tank repaired with fibre washer and such other little finishing jobs have been swiftly done but I think the vehicle clutch plate is either not new, or else the clutch toggle levers need adjusting...

Wednesday 14 August, 1957
... Still -46°C and southerly but plenty of daylight till evening. Most people think they saw the sun refracted above the cloud bank at the north horizon around local midday. A bright short streak, waving with haze, appeared just over the cloud bank two or three times...

Official date for reappearance of the sun is 21st August...

Friday 16 August, 1957

... Made some rubber bushes for No. 1 generator today... and fitted both idler axle assemblies [on Weasel B]. Also reversed right-hand track and finished fitting it...

Bouncer is allowed loose in the tunnel due to his sore neck from mange. He daren't go past Mutt and Jeff on one side and Ivik on the other. He did once try a hypnotising act on Ivik, David Stratton tells us. He put his face up to Ivik and growled and wagged his tail and Ivik growled back then suddenly gave up and looked away while Bouncer relieved himself in Ivik's cave and came out again.

Next day he tried it and Ivik latched on to Bouncer's snout causing him to howl in pain. David Stratton separated them and Bouncer hasn't tried that one again. He did however, get into Tio's cave and grabbed her seal meat but she grabbed him by the throat and he was glad to escape. So now he stalks up and down his couple of feet of tunnel as though he's the King Dog, and is content with that.

Saturday 17 and Sunday 18 August, 1957

Saturday... minimum -42°C, Sunday... minimum -20°C.

Yesterday was a big party night and also my bath night so diary didn't get done. Weasel B's tracks and suspension were finished off yesterday so I felt free in mind for a party. David Pratt isn't sure, apparently, if his birthday is 17 or 18 August but it was clearly best to have it Saturday night. The party was also by way of celebrating our change-over from winter routine to daylight working life...

There was plenty to drink last night and for dinner, I put out six bottles of imiak (4 August vintage). We had three chickens for dinner and an ice cream and loganberry sweet etc. David Pratt had put out a couple of his cheeses (Danish Blue and Cheshire) and a huge pot of Hong Kong ginger.

He had saved a large (one gallon) wicker-work jug of Madeira wine which, unfortunately, had frozen and cracked. However, Ralph thawed it and collected it in a large saucepan. David Stratton, on gash, thought the pot contained water with the lid on, so put it on the Aga to boil before washing. Ralph found it gushing steam from under the lid and took it off. Poor David Pratt looked mortified when he heard. Cooled off it didn't taste too bad...

Fooling around, darts, cowboy dancing, record playing etc., kept getting [an] extension, first from 12 midnight to 1 a.m.... we packed up at around 3.15 a.m....

It wasn't until 10.55 that I got up... I was on gash with George... Bunny started to scrub the floor on his own and was later joined by Allan while a couple of bodies were unable to appear until lunchtime.

This morning David Stratton went on skis to the hill edge and showed Taffy the way to ski-walk. Whenever I looked out north I could see a figure spread out on the snow, but he kept to his skis all the way there and back...

Tuesday 20 August, 1957
... Geoff has worked out that the sun should have been a little visible on Sunday, partly more yesterday and wholly today. If the atmosphere had been clear today the sun would quite certainly have been well above the horizon. (This would have included all the refraction, mirage and anything else you like, of course)...

Tonight, conference with Bunny, David Pratt, David Stratton and myself, on vehicle procedures in the 'field'. Very good but we require another session still. I enjoyed this and only hope all vehicles are ready in time. Biggest problem I think of is how to attach safety rope to Sno-Cats...

This conference was in anticipation of various journeys to be undertaken by vehicle and dogsled in September. These were of a scientific and exploratory nature:

(1) On 1 September four vehicles would leave to investigate a chasm south of Shackleton as well as taking the opportunity to add fuel supplies to the 50-mile depot established the previous November.
(2) Two weeks later, a dog team would be flown to the Theron Mountains to carry out survey and geological work.
(3) Near the month's end two dog teams would be flown out to the Shackleton Mountains to try to find a vehicular ascent of a formidable feature known as the 'Ice Wall' that could be used in the crossing. This would be followed by a survey of the mountains themselves.
(4) At the very end of the month, the vehicle team, comprising four vehicles, would attempt to reach South Ice, using information supplied by the dog teams.

Inevitably, things did not go to plan.

7

ALARUMS AND EXCURSIONS

Thursday 22 August, 1957
... Conference tonight on vehicles, driving procedure, radio, etc.

I don't like the idea of not flagging the route all the way to South Ice at all... any deviation (old track marks obliterated) of any sort could find new concealed crevasses.

This is my only concern after tonight's discussions in which Bunny and David Stratton did not agree with me. Bunny was unable to understand why a vehicle would not be on the same route over any distance from here to South Ice (except in known, flagged crevassed areas, which David Stratton says is all that's necessary) when it has a compass and tracks to follow. My examples of BNGE experience didn't carry any determining weight. Track marks readily drift over.

I started to write today's diary before the conference and Bunny said at the time, 'Tell Enid, "thanks for lending you to us."' I thought that very nice and said you would like to read that, Enid.

Monday 26 August, 1957
... I worked on Weasel B all day which now nears completion... David Pratt got Sno-Cat C going tonight after Bunny, Allan and Geoff had dug it out. Otter also being dug out...

Tuesday 27 August, 1957
... Dreadful day in -40s °C with -52 °C tonight and a wind over 30 knots southerly, all day bringing thick drift. This has done the Otter digging a lot of no good. The huge piles of snow dug out yesterday have now collected drifts of their own as well as drift filling up where all that had been dug out. I haven't been to look but I'm sure it isn't almost ready to tow out, as it was last night.

In the workshop we can't take out Weasel B, which is about finished, until the weather changes. Then the Fergy comes in...

Delighted to read Enid's letter for this month. Very amused and very heart-warmed.

Wednesday 28 August, 1957

... Minimum -52°C...

The Sno-Cat had warming-up troubles... Eventually it was running ready to pull the Otter...

A rope spreader of a baulk of timber with angle iron brackets and shackles was attached by ropes to the suspension and the fuel drum chain hauling gear attached to the shackles. Onto the lifting ring of the chains was attached a 70ft Terylene 3-inch circumference rope (ready made up for vehicle safety rope). This was hooked onto the Sno-Cat. Going ahead, after repeated attempts, did not move the Otter skis and all that happened was that the Terylene rope stretched like a piece of elastic and pulled the Sno-Cat back again.

Dinner was delayed till about 2030 and hot rum grog was ready. This, altogether, made everyone very sleepy but they went out again and fixed up a wire rope, cutting with a saw under the skis again and putting timber under them to stop them sinking back down. At last it was dragged free into the clear.

I'd had another dose of fumes and my eyes were sore as well as feeling very tired, so I went to bed immediately after dinner. The boys came in about 11 p.m. so lights were out at about midnight and we had a late breakfast and I had some rest and sleep for a change.

Thursday 29 August, 1957

... Outside we've had around -46°C and average 30 knots southerly so it's been rather nasty. Thank goodness the Otter was moved last night. Its old hole is filled in.

Geoff has finished his 7 days 'Imping' and it looked as though it had worn him out. Allan is like a dead duck with [so] little sleep. Geoff had to wear the IMP for 7 days, taking it off only for food. Even when sleeping he wore it and Allan had to sleep near him to make sure the mask stayed on. Geoff turns in his sleep with a huge lurch and doesn't notice the mask being dislodged. The exhaust valve makes a rattling burp and when it stops, Allan wakes up, pushes the mask back in place and lies down again...[67]

Lots of auroral activity today due to biggest sun spot disturbances ever recorded, a couple of days ago. 'Worldwide alert' now on...

Friday 30 August, 1957

... Change during the night brought strong northerly and drift with snow. Temperature rose of course so the very thick drift didn't really matter. So far we've had gusts of up to 46 knots, but mainly it keeps to around 35 knots.

Being gash hand today curtailed my Fergy repair work but I still got some done...

Bunny informed us tonight that our new departure date will be 7th September. I hear that this was alluded to tonight, on BBC news.

I cut hair for John Lewis and Allan tonight and did Gordon a few nights ago, also George.

Saturday 7 and Sunday 8 September, 1957

... Ellsworth on today – expect to arrive in about a week to discuss plans. They hope to use our route if they can't find a way around the chasm.[68] *They say one of their Otter's tail has been crushed with the weight of snow – the elevators I believe. (They have three – one in a crate). Possibly damaged digging it out by tractors? Two Dakotas are visiting early in November and we have been asked if there's anything we want flown in. We shall be giving Ellsworth a Sno-Cat clutch plate.*

Monday 9 September, 1957

... Minimum -23°C. Sno-Cat repairs continue...

---

[67] Unfortunately, on his return to the UK Rogers discovered that the breath samples collected during his laborious work with the IMP had been contaminated and rendered useless as a result of defective ampoules.

[68] The US IGY party under Finn Ronne planned to make their own inland traverse. Given the relative proximity of the British and American bases on the Filchner Ice Shelf it made sense for them to share survey data.

Meeting tonight to clarify the situation that has arisen due to the weather and vehicle repairs. The chasm run is now cancelled but plans for the present vehicle programme are unaltered...

Wednesday, Thursday, Friday 11, 12, 13 September, 1957

... I've been busy on making a very sturdy front safety rope assembly of three inch angle iron [for the Sno-Cat] and David Pratt has... been welding up the angle iron bracket. George has been filming these operations and taking flash pictures...

Tomorrow would have been the day for the Theron mountains trip, but that will have to come later.

Bunny spoke to Ellsworth the other day and learned that Finn Ronne will try to come through on our reconnoitred route round their chasm 17 miles inland and then on to here. When Bunny asked what he's doing about safety ropes he clearly hadn't thought about them... He said he'd reconnoitre by helicopter to direct the vehicles.

I spoke to Bunny this morning when he visited the workshop about flagging the route so that three Sno-Cats following the route on the second journey could be sure of being on safe ground without rope attachments, but he feels only known crevassed areas need be flagged.

Sunday 15 September, 1957

... Quite nice this morning with little wind, so Bunny and David Stratton were able to take two lots of dogs on a little training. As they had some last year it wasn't completely hopeless and there were only a couple of fights...

Sno-Cat repairs continue as before...

Ellsworth have agreed to allow the two DC-3s[69] to get 3 new fans of five blades for our Sno-Cats. Ellsworth hope to fly their 2nd Otter in here next Wednesday...

Monday 16 September, 1957

Quite nice day with only light southerly...

I have nearly finished safety belts on Sno-Cat C. All fittings are now made and attached and parts of full length seat cut away. Now engaged on repairing seat with canvas and Bostik.

---

[69] The Douglas DC-3. In the UK, the military version, the C-47 Skytrain, is commonly known as the Dakota.

174

David Pratt [is] still re-enforcing safety rope attachment with electric welding but having tough time getting suitable welds.

Taffy called in to do some aerial re-arrangement of Sno-Cat C and Geoff has been doing some more seismic gear fitting...

Scott Base on tonight. Ed's party have made the depot at the foot of Ferrar Glacier for a geologist run and another party have discovered some of Captain Scott's rations...

Tuesday 17 September, 1957

Cold with strong southerly and lots of drift, so our aircraft work is held up some more. There is still a lot to be done to get snow out of the aircraft and they need warm weather to get results from their heater. All mechanical work has to be done on the planes outside so weather is vital...

Rather a crisis has been discovered at Halley Bay. For about a month Robin Smart has been ill. He fell over on skis, and a camera hanging round his neck rammed into the bottom of his ribs on the right side. Since then he hasn't been well and yesterday he nearly lost consciousness. He is pretty poorly and in bed and Joe McDowall is running the Base. He and Allan had a long talk this lunch time and it has caused a great deal of worry. Robin thinks his liver has been torn and fluid collecting round it has broken out, going to the bottom of his intestines. The scare is that peritonitis may set in and an operation is likely. As he is their doctor as well as Base leader difficulties arise and it seems that an aircraft will have to be flown there. Our Otter isn't ready if Allan has to bring him out. The Auster isn't ready either but it couldn't carry a sick man. We don't know what facilities the Americans have, but no doubt we shall talk about it on the next schedule...

Thursday 19 September, 1957

... Frantic work commenced to get something airborne. David Pratt removed the Fergy tracks but it was no good in the soft snow, so he had to get out Weasel A to tow the Herman Nelson heater about for the RAF – and also the Auster. It was this evening that we suddenly realised that the Auster was in the air when Ralph called into the workshop (He was working on Weasel D just outside the door). Gordon had a bit of a fly around and then John went up. Tomorrow, after an hour or so local flying Gordon will take Allan up to Halley Bay.

Sno-Cat repairs still going on...

Robin still holding his own and hopes are running that his system will do the healing without an operation...

Friday 20 September, 1957

Sad day here, but not to last long, we hope...

Gordon took off with Allan at eight minutes to twelve and, at his estimated time of being in the vicinity of Halley Bay, they hadn't seen it. Gordon flew on for one and a half hours and no sign, so flew south for an hour, then had to land with dusk setting in and only one and a half hours fuel left. This was about 5 p.m. They have no tent, but have warm clothing and sleeping bags. Luckily, with an easterly wind here of 10 knots and temperature -27°C, they should not be too badly off, but if the weather got bad they'd have to dig into the snow – without a shovel.

Gordon thinks he flew around Halley Bay promontory, but we think he mistook it for one further north... Advice to them will be to fly south and all agree.

It had been quite a laugh to everyone when Allan, wearing all the clothes he could get on struggled into the plane. Good thing now, of course. But, having to sit next to the pilot in an Auster is a very cramped business and most uncomfortable. Also, it's chilly.

Tonight, Bunny had a talk with John, David Stratton and Peter and later we were all called in. I was in the workshop and got four 'cuts' on the lights, so came straight up. The whole position was explained and now two shifts are working to get the Otter flying, which may take 3 days.

Tonight, John, George and Geoff are working on de-drifting all internal parts and in the morning Bunny, David Stratton and Peter will be on. Tonight, therefore, David Pratt and I got our heater out and two lead lamps with 12 Volt bulbs and two batteries. These are operating in the Otter while, outside, Tilley lamps supply light...

In the meantime Taffy had been trying to get Ellsworth to give them the alert. For two hours he was unsuccessful in getting any US station but then got the South Pole Station. Then luckily Ellsworth broke in, so Bunny was able to tell them the position here. They are eager to do all they can of course and hope to have an Otter on test flight tomorrow and will afterwards be ready to come to our aid. Finn Ronne was very good in suggesting that if their assistance was used, no publicity would be made of it...

Halley Bay have a beacon for homing on of course, but, unfortunately they had a London schedule today, while the *seriousness of the position was not foreseen, so the beacon was not always on while the Auster was going north to them. They at times received the beacon signal but were unable to get a setting...*

Saturday 21 September, 1957

Nothing heard from Gordon today except an early message around 8 a.m. which was not clear enough to understand... We learned this afternoon (lunch time) that the American No. 2 Otter is not ready to fly.

Weather report from Halley Bay suggested no flying is possible due to much cloud, so it is hopeless for Gordon who probably also had cloud. No doubt in that case he was wise enough not to go near the radio but stayed in his sleeping bag. Hope he kept the battery warm beside him...

Night-shift worked on the Otter with the two heaters and the job was carried on by the day-shift. This continues with tonight's shift. At least the heat in the aircraft doesn't get lost overnight. All frost throughout the hull, under the hull insulating lining, has been dispelled and also under the instrument panel. The tail and tail planes have been melted out and mopped up and next comes the big job of getting the snow out of the wings. Possibly in a couple of days' time it will be near to flying.

We don't know what trouble the Americans have got, or how long it will take them to be flying...

In the workshop David Pratt and I have finished Sno-Cat C... Last night we finished at quarter to twelve and tonight at twelve...[70]

With the shift work everyone does a bit of everything. This morning I cut snow for the kitchen, all sorts of people have collected plates and washed up and Taffy and I tonight, on finding pies and vegetables etc. in dishes and pots, put them in the oven and on the stove, hoping we were doing the right thing...

Wrote out telegram to Honeybunch,[71] *'Transpolar' London for sending 7th anniversary flowers to Enid and large box of*

---

[70] There was no expectation that vehicles would play a part in the recovery of Haslop and Rogers – or in the provision of medical assistance to Robin Smart. Fuchs believed that he had sufficient labour available to ready the TAE's aircraft without interfering with Roy and Pratt's essential work on preparing the vehicles for the journey to South Ice.
[71] Eleanor Honnywill.

chocolates for her, but due to crisis and therefore radio obligations saturated, [it is] not yet sent...

Sunday 22 September, 1957
Today David Pratt and I repaired the last of the A-frames for the Maudheims... Have also made sets of aluminium threaded holding studs for the E2 compasses complete with 2 dozen copper nuts. I am now working on holding attachments for the other Sno-Cats' safety belts...

Halley Bay were having high drift and 30 knots some hours before we got it, so no doubt Gordon and Allan got it first (assuming them to be north of Halley Bay). Hope they are comfortably dug in. They have one small Primus and some paraffin, but the stove will use either kerosene or petrol. They have food to last up to 28 days at a pinch and for normal requirements, up to about 25 days.

Nothing heard yet of Ellsworth's trouble, so Bunny sent a signal... to say we don't expect to be able to fly before Tuesday at earliest (not including weather) and how is their Otter progressing, etc.

Apart from the concern over Allan and Gordon's comfort, the new worry is for the Auster in 30 knots winds and not able to be lashed down or turned into wind. It could be easily blown away...

Taffy got Bunny's message out today concerning the Auster and also my message to Honeybunch for 7th anniversary flowers.

This morning Bunny saw our first bird visitor. He said it's got a good memory as it landed on the seal meat dump. It was a bit too far away to identify but thinks it was possibly skua...

Monday 23 September, 1957
... Outside our weather has been very bad with strong northerly, lots of snow and plenty of drift...

Tuesday 24 and Wednesday 25 September, 1957
... Very nasty northerly yesterday with lots of snow and very thick drift which held up Otter work.

Asked Americans if they have any Hepadine drug. They have, but their doctor was immediately worried about its use. However, it has been prescribed for Robin's new trouble, thrombosis, by professor of London University College Hospital.

Americans were flying yesterday and were on their way, unknown to us, when they asked for weather report here. They had just met whiteout conditions half-way here. We had the same, so they turned back... Luckily, today we had decreasing northerly and better visibility later in the day so we hope for good flying conditions tomorrow... If they are able to be flying tomorrow they'll come here and take Bunny up with them to try to find Gordon and Allan...

Our own Otter is coming on well with today's weather...

Thursday 26 September, 1957
Fine day for outside work – but useless for flying... Halley Bay's weather is very poor and so's Ellsworth's. We must have a break soon...

Friday 27 September, 1957
Horrible weather with bad visibility all day and low cloud... It seems unlikely that the weather will be good enough for flying tomorrow.

Today the [Otter's] engine was ground-tested satisfactorily and rudder assembled. Now, controls are to be tested and ailerons checked...

Saturday 28 September, 1957
Pretty awful day again with northerly, snow and poor visibility, although the sun brought silvery brightness through low scudding cloud showing high cloud well above during part of this morning.

Hannes said yesterday that there would be a chance of flying weather tomorrow and this is our greatest hope yet, for tonight the Otter is ready for flying...

Bunny had a message from Sir John Slessor today saying that the Committee of Management did not wish Bunny to fly in the relief plane. Tonight Bunny is composing a message explaining why he feels he must go.

David Pratt and I have been getting out more Weasel spares from the old Sno-Cat crate and new Sno-Cat crate and sorting them in the workshop...

Sunday 29 September, 1957
Weather quiet with very little wind, and overcast. Fortunately visibility was just about good enough for John to do a test flight

this afternoon in the Otter for about half an hour. It was very good to see it flying and everyone is very happy about it.

Better still was the welcome surprise this morning when Gordon came up on the Auster's radio... Conditions soon got too bad for much information, but we learned that they are 'OK', as Gordon puts it. He also said about rations, 'OK'. He still thinks they are about 35 miles South of Halley Bay, but as we think he's North of there, he agreed to stay put. He had his Auster engine running and had apparently run it at times to keep his battery up, but it has meant using fuel, so he has about one to one and a half hours flying left. Better he stays put and uses the fuel for battery charging and for cooker. He knows that our Otter was then nearly ready to fly...

Ellsworth on the air at lunch-time. Said they were willing to do the trip to save our Otter for its other journeys, but quoted regulations concerning conditions under which they could and could not fly and today's weather was not suitable...

Bunny's message to Sir John Slessor says he's categorically stated to the Americans that if their plane is used he will go with it. If our plane is used, he will, in deference to the wish of the Committee, send David Stratton with John. He states clearly that the Committee will know that in future, where an element of risk may be expected, he will not withdraw from such situations.

John's aircraft is loaded with 1900lbs odd, including three drums of fuel, rations, oil, etc. and two bottles of imiak for Halley Bay. Ron, their operator, had heard of it and Ralph had promised them a bottle.

Monday 30 September, 1957
Big promise that today would see everything ended well, but, at the last, we had failure.

Early we had a thin streak of light on the horizon to the north, over towards the base of Graham Land, this very slowly grew and suddenly we had the American Otter arrive at about 11.25 a.m.... They brought the Hepadine and also their Herman Nelson heater... We used it to warm our Otter before it took off with John and David Stratton for Halley Bay...

At 4 p.m. John took off, although Con Jaburg[72] reckoned that, with his heavy load, little wind and soft snow, he'd have a job

---

[72] Conrad 'Con' Jaburg (1931-2015), US Navy pilot serving with Operation Deepfreeze at Ellsworth Station.

getting off. However, John was cunning and took off 'across' the line of sastrugi in order to go into what wind there was and so was airborne in a normal length run. He flew overhead and rocked his wings while we waved, then headed off to the north-east into the blackest sky imaginable. Although we had bright sunshine and blue sky, over there, where all the cloud was getting pushed to, it looked like a huge thunderstorm brewing up. Vahsel Hills were not visible by about 20 miles I should think. Anyway, by 5 p.m. John had said he really was in 'clag' and would have to turn back if it continued for a further half hour.

He was forced to turn back. His visibility was down to about 2000yds flying at 200ft, and could only just make out the edge of the ice-shelf, while he got forced further and further west by poor visibility and cloud. He flew over many icebergs which loomed up and eventually he was in such bad weather and so far out over the sea-ice that he had to turn back. Icing of the wings, tail, rudder, skis, etc. and frequent snow flurries made things very risky, and when the 'stall' warning light started to come on, he got slight relief from that worry by switching it off...

Tuesday 1 October, 1957
Thank heaven for good news at last. The generator was run last night from 3 a.m. onwards to keep in touch with Halley Bay for weather.

In between times Ralph broke in on Scott Base and learned from them, after giving our news, that one of Ed's parties had discovered a depot box remaining on the Ferrar Glacier from Amundsen in 1910.

By 6 a.m. Halley Bay had reported clear weather so Bunny came round and woke up John, David Stratton, Peter and George who all went off to prepare the Otter. They were still removing ice at 10 a.m. and possibly longer. At about 11.30 a.m. John and David took off from here... They went through rather thick stuff for about 1½ hrs, icing up again, 'but not as bad as yesterday, thank God!' as John said. At about ten to two they were at Halley Bay...

After re-fuelling, they came south to zigzag in a search to Dawson Lambton Glacier without seeing the Auster. They turned north and searched again seeing groups of a few hundred seals – and at last they found Allan and Gordon...

Gordon, true to his doctrines, fired a green Very light into the air – 'okay to land'. I believe he would have done so if it took away his last heartbeat.

We heard from John that they were both well, fighting fit, though a bit thin and still had saved seven days survival rations and a quart of paraffin.

This morning when Gordon came on the air he was told that the Otter was getting ready to fly. He asked for confirmation that the Otter would fly, because if it didn't, he would.

The Otter and the Auster (after re-fuelling presumably) flew into Halley Bay 'in formation', where undoubtedly they were all made very welcome. The two doctors, Robin and Allan, are having a good pow-wow and both of the survivors are in a change of clothing. Apparently Robin is a bit better, for he was talking on the radio today...[73]

Lately David Pratt and I have been packing up at 10 p.m. or so instead of 11 p.m. We are both always tired and could do with a good long sleep. Today we've been still working on Weasel spares and I've been still repairing and testing radiators...

Wednesday 2 October, 1957

... Flying conditions rather too poor for the aircraft to take off at Halley Bay, so they are staying on... Both Allan and Gordon are quite well today after a good meal last night and a party. Allan drank can after can of beer. They have both lost their pot bellies...

There was talk tonight about getting on the trail to South Ice. Geoff has still three days at any rate on his gravimetric photographs and seismic shoot before he's ready to go and we still have about three days on Sno-Cat spares, tools etc. In the meantime we hope to get the sledges loaded in order to be ready to go off as soon as possible...

Bunny wants to do 36-48 hours in the Theron Range for geological specimens and also, later, up to two weeks of survey in the Onaways group...

---

[73] Dr Robert 'Robin' Smart (1914-1986) made a full recovery, eventually retiring from the Army Medical Services with the rank of Major General.

Thursday 3 October, 1957
... At Halley Bay the weather was bad this morning and later they decided to fly, then the Auster wouldn't start. When it was got going it was too late.

Bunny's a bit on edge about both aircraft and four people all away at this time when we are trying to push the first journey into the 'field'...

Friday 4 October, 1957
Big day with return of Allan and Gordon. Heard over the radio from John that they were over Vahsel Bay and would be in soon. At 1325 local time the Otter came in with John, Allan and David Stratton and about 25 minutes later Gordon arrived in the Auster. I didn't meet either plane, but of course met the two very fit survivors when I came up to the hut from the workshop.

David Stratton tells me that they (Gordon and Allan) were about to set up, if necessary, for the summer, having a route down from the shelf to the sea-ice by way of a snow ramp about a mile away, where they hoped to get a seal and possibly a penguin.

They had started the first day by digging a shallow pit about 5ft by 4ft and using their sleeping bags in there with a cover over the top. To dig, they used a sheath knife and a flat piece of metal. Later they deepened the hole, widening it as they went down, making a sleeping berth each side and alcoves in the snow walls. They would have used seal blubber, for lighting, with a wick. They used only survival rations and Gordon had two bars of chocolate and Allan one. They didn't feel hungry, so much as empty, as Gordon said. They continuously looked after the aircraft, always turning it into the wind...

It got very cold in the sleeping bags which became stiff from frozen vaporisation from the body and the cold came from below as the sleeping bags were straight onto the snow. Gordon reckons that, apart from a couple of fairly decent night's sleep, he spent most of each night kicking his feet and turning over in an effort to get warm, feeling the sleeping bag sticking to the snow...

For me it was a big day because Enid and I spoke by radio telephone... It was really quite wonderful to talk to Enid and all day I've been hearing in my memory, over and over again, her voice and the things we spoke about. Surprised to hear that she was leaving on 17th January, arriving 18th February, giving two months in NZ before we expect to get there. Lucky girl! ...

Saturday 5 October, 1957

... This morning we got the news from Halley Bay that Robin had got permission from IGY in London to send two of his chaps along here to help in all our work. So John took off with Ralph as companion, picked up Fred Morris and Ivor Beney and came straight back after re-fuelling.

Before our Otter left here the American Otter arrived with Finn Ronne, Thiel (seismologist), Walter Davis (vehicle mechanic), Walter May (met man), and Sumral (met and seismology). We all got together and we had a talk with Davis about vehicles and how to temper his clutch springs... Before they left, David Stratton spoke to Chuck about a couple of flying crash helmets he's promised us for vehicle driving. David ended up by having the four helmets on the plane. They include cloth insert with built-in ear phones. They have also brought a crate of canned beer each time and also a lot of packets of frying chickens and steaks...

I have been completing Sno-Cat spares and fitting spare radiators to Weasel roofs and now making canvas satchels to carry spare gaskets in the Weasels...

Over the next few days preparations continued. Soon the first vehicles would set out for South Ice – but how would they cope on a 270-mile journey over treacherous, crevasse-strewn terrain? With constant faults and total breakdowns, they had proved a nightmare to Roy in the first year – though matters had improved in the second. Bearing in mind their critical role in the expedition a brief review seems appropriate.

The Weasels that had arrived in January were named simply 'A' and 'B'. A problem with Weasel B was soon found as its steel tracks had been fitted the wrong way round and needed turning to bring less worn surfaces into use. The two engineers broke or bent no less than five wrenches undertaking this difficult job. Weasel B's brand new radiator, handmade in Sweden, also proved a disappointment when it manifested leaks in its honeycomb and needed replacement. Roy then spent days testing and repairing radiators more generally, for these were a known weakness in the Weasels' design.

In addition to replacing No. 1 Weasel's differential, Weasels 1 and 2 had heavy-duty gearboxes fitted and routine maintenance work undertaken. Their engines' side covers were also adapted to make access much easier – 'a long modification but a thousand times worth it'. Finally, safety work was undertaken, including the installation of safety harnesses similar to those used in aircraft and safety brackets and ropes that allowed the vehicles to be roped together like climbers: a vital modification when travelling through areas riddled with crevasses.

Overall, and despite the fact that Roy would later describe Weasel B as 'a huge waste of expedition money on a junk box', there had been no really serious breakdowns among the Weasels during the second year and they had proved to be useful workhorses about the base.

As expected, the four state-of-the-art Sno-Cats had proved far superior, with none having given serious trouble so far that year. Again, routine maintenance was undertaken and safety modifications made.

The Muskeg tractor was a rather basic vehicle with no headlights and terrible insulation but it proved reliable, and was much the fastest vehicle when not hauling a load. Occasional engine problems were mainly due to ice and, 'as it was never intended to be used in drift', there was constant snow penetration. Nonetheless, Fuchs said of the Muskeg: 'As a base vehicle, it was excellent...'

However, up to this point, the vehicles had not completed any serious mileage, with their movements limited to hauling equipment and supplies around the base and occasional seal hunts. The imminent journey to South Ice would be the real test of their capability and reliability. If they failed, the crossing of Antarctica would fall at the very first hurdle. With this thought ever-present, at 5.45 p.m. on Tuesday 8 October, Fuchs, Roy, Geoff Pratt and David Pratt swung themselves into their cabs, started the engines and set a course for the Shackleton Mountains, 200 miles away across the Filchner Ice Shelf.

Tuesday 8 October, 1957
Nothing much yesterday, but mainly continued preparations for the journey.

Today, however, we've moved, somewhere between 6 and 7 miles south to recce the route to South Ice: the main journey to come later...

During six miles we went down and up five depressions running east-west and these were about 500 yards wide in undulation form.

Bunny overheated all the time in leading Weasel A and both he and David Pratt got stuck in soft snow through poor track grip.

Bunny's has the light-weight Atkitrak and David's steel tracks. Mine had no bother at all with Goodrich Weasel tracks.

Eventually we were more or less forced to stop to attend to Bunny's overheating engine. Geoff and I had a large meal of Pemmican first, then I went to David Pratt on Weasel A and carried on the repair. The two fan belts are Colink and were very slack. I took two links out of the main belt and David had removed one from the dynamo belt. After re-adjustment they seem fine. To do the job meant removing the engine side cover of course, which in itself is quite a job, but was made easier and quicker by my earlier modification.

I finished at a quarter to twelve…

When we left base George was filming and nearly everyone was out to take photographs and wave 'Cheerio'.

Now to sleep – feels a bit chilly beneath me. We've got our tent against the Sno-Cat and have a 6W lamp plugged in.

Fuchs, Roy and David Pratt were all driving Weasels, while the fourth man, Geoff Pratt, took the wheel of a Sno-Cat.

On their way to the Shackleton Range they must skirt the Slessor Glacier before reaching the Ice Wall, a 1500-foot-high near-vertical barrier created by the movement of the Recovery Glacier. A potential ascent had been observed from the air and between 11 and 13 October Stratton and Blaiklock would be flown out with a dog team to survey and flag a route for the vehicles. If a route was located and negotiated successfully, the vehicle team would still need to cross the Recovery Glacier and manoeuvre through rocky peaks known as the Whichaway Nunataks – the location of Blaiklock and Stephenson's near-catastrophic geological expedition in the previous March – before finally reaching South Ice.

Fuchs was anxious to get this exploratory job done quickly and then return to Shackleton by air with the engineers, leaving the first vehicles at South Ice. He then planned to begin the full crossing on 14 November, confident that this schedule would give his party a decent chance of reaching Scott Base on the far side of Antarctica before the Ross Sea froze over. As he knew from painful personal experience, a frozen sea could well render relief impossible and result in he and his team being trapped for another winter.[74]

Unfortunately, the stranding of Haslop and Rogers on their mercy mission to Halley Bay had caused much delay and a great deal remained to be done at Shackleton before the final push could begin. All of this meant that Fuchs could allocate only fourteen days to complete the journey to South Ice – a journey of 270 miles over largely unknown terrain. He would later describe this section as 'the worst part of our entire journey across the continent'.

It is noteworthy that the day of the vehicle party's departure, 8 October, was also the day that flights to South Ice resumed, and it was now possible to effect some changes in personnel.

Wednesday 9 October, 1957
We had hoped for a good day today, but it wasn't to be. Weather was fine but a misfortune befell my Weasel...

After a couple of miles when we'd got going well at about 7 or 8 m.p.h. I was jerked to a stop and the Weasel was spun half left. I couldn't understand it till I saw a guide roller broken off and jammed between the track and the back axle. This was about 1335 hours and Bunny was well on ahead. David Pratt noticed and turned back, while Geoff pulled me straight. Since then, till 10.15 p.m., David and I have been trying to get the track off and the roller removed. We succeeded and tomorrow will get the track back on...

On closer examination it became apparent that, caught in the moving track, the upper-track bearing roller had fouled the drive sprocket, bending the axle in the process. Less than 8 miles from Shackleton and one of only four vehicles had already been disabled. The engineers agreed that such a major repair was impossible in the field, meaning that Roy must limp his Weasel back to the workshop at Shackleton. 'It is a great disappointment to Roy', Fuchs wrote with masterly understatement.[75] Nonetheless, Roy remained undaunted, believing that he might be able to

---

[74] In the austral summer of 1948-9, the ice in Marguerite Bay failed to break up, trapping Fuchs and his team of ten men for an unplanned year at Stonington Island. They were not relieved until February 1950.
[75] Fuchs, diary, 10 October 1957. Quoted in Haddelsey, *Shackleton's Dream*, p. 154.

complete the repair and then race back to catch up with the rest of the vehicle party.

Thursday 10 October, 1957
Back at Shackleton...

It was decided to let me come back alone and I left about 1345hrs. After 2.7 miles I arrived at our previous night's camp. I could see black dots far in the distance and thought it was a party with a dog team, when suddenly I was right on it and found that it was some small empty food tins. Poor light makes everything white and dull and distance is impossible to judge without previous knowledge of what an object really is.

Here I lost our track and kept on going on my compass (E2). After 6.3 miles from my breakdown I came across one of Ken's flags, a wood slat with a red and black flag on it. At 6.7 miles from my start I sighted most of Shackleton but it disappeared as I went down an undulation, although in the blended grey-white light without shadows it was not possible to see any rise in the surface. I sighted Shackleton and lost it through four undulations, but saw only the masts at these intermediate times. After doing 8.4 miles I found another flag and arrived at Shackleton after 8.8 miles.

Gordon put on a meal of beans, toast, bacon and bubble and squeak and then I got down to the workshop, where I had Ivor to help me.

Ralph and Fred brought along angle irons to bend the axle straight and we got ahead with the job but had to pack up at midnight when I decided the other axle would have to be bent too. The first track only needs re-tensioning. If the other hadn't needed attention I would have gone back tonight.

At 8 p.m. we heard that the team had done 19 miles from base and were still going. Only if they have bad weather tomorrow can I catch them up. Otherwise I can't go on alone hoping to catch them as it will mean being in bad territory.

Friday 11 October, 1957
Wearying day. Finished off left-hand track and got on with right-hand track and straightened the support tube. Nearly got the track back on...

[Vehicles] are about 40 miles on now. Wish I was with them...

The Vehicle Party had now travelled too far for Roy to reach them overland, but his disappointment didn't last long. On Saturday 12 October Fuchs instructed him to fly out and re-join them the next day, saying later that he needed Roy 'to strengthen our party'.

Sunday 13 October, 1957
Have arrived by Auster...

The whole area, for miles in all directions, is closely patterned with short wide crevasses... It's certainly no good going on where it gets thicker and to the east. It is also worse as it gets nearer the ice stream this side of the ice-covered hills. It means going back to 50 mile depot and turning off west for a couple of miles or so before going south to get around the stuff we're in...

Since my arrival here, continuous, bangs, cracks, rumbles, booms, explosions and roars have been going off incessantly and some of the big roars make the whole place shake. A bit awesome when a big one goes off just below. It seems to have quietened now. Time about 2.30 p.m. I arrived here at about 11 a.m. Possibly the landings of the Auster started off all the disturbances...

With all three vehicles hitched together, we made plans about signalling and I elected to sit on Bunny's roof with a flag to signal 'STOP' if a vehicle should get caught in a rope... Silliest thing I ever did was to sit on the roof of the leading vehicle in a crevassed area while vehicles were roped together and safety belts worn, but it got the party moving...

We did the 4.7 miles to 50 mile depot in 1hr 17mins... I got very chilled...

Monday 14 October, 1957
... No move today for visibility is too bad...

On the far side of the continent, Ed Hillary and three companions set out from Scott Base on 14 October driving three tractors and a Weasel. Their purpose to establish a vehicle route onto the Polar Plateau and lay more depots in support of the Crossing Party. This work progressed well.

Tuesday 15 October, 1957
With no move yesterday we got in more sleeping than we ever would normally...

We got away at 2 p.m. on a compass course of 300° for about four and a half miles... After 4.2 miles David Pratt had to stop for a broken oil pipe to his filter (Weasel B). An hour later we are off again, but just had to tighten a bogie support arm bolt on Bunny's left-hand rear assembly...

We had a good run but in very poor visibility. Bunny is most anxious to get on, though worried about not being able to see the surface.

We've done about 25 miles today... It snowed for most of the run and with little wind it has settled softly and we've camped in very soft stuff, up to 8 inches deep...

Wednesday 16 October, 1957
... At last we're moving – at 11.55 a.m. Hanging about from 9 a.m. rather annoys me.

Unfortunately, after going along well for 10 miles, Bunny stopped to report noise coming from his Weasel engine, thought to be noisy winch drive. My first listen compelled me to diagnose 'big-end'. We decided to go on, lightening Bunny's load...

We heard news this morning on 9 a.m. schedule that five Argentineans had arrived at Shackleton base with a Weasel and a dog team. They had called in for an overnight stop on the way to Vahsel Bay area and left a hunk of Argentine beef with the boys at base...

In spite of the big-end we made good progress over 40 miles today, putting in a 100 mile flag on the way...

These last 10 miles have been rougher going than before so perhaps we are soon to see a change of scenery. I expect tomorrow, if we get going, to see something of the Slessor Glacier rising up before coming to the Onaways.

I find our rations inadequate and am hungry for most of the day, therefore, quite bad tempered at night before being able to eat...

Thursday 17 October, 1957
Another slow start, leaving at midday...

This morning we were able to see good miraged images of the Theron and Shackleton Mountains. The Therons are a long way off to our left (east) and Shackleton Range (probably Corner Mountain of the Onaway Group) about 25° east of our course ahead. Deep soft snow all the way for days covering all sastrugi and anything more unpleasant... We stopped at 9 p.m. after doing 36.4 miles...

Gordon flew out to us… He landed very well, but very close to the Sno-Cat as he set down. Bunny wanted to take a photo of it landing with the Sno-Cat and two Weasels which were giving line of direction for landing. So we got our two drums of 10W oil and also [my] diary, tooth brushes and paste. We also got some air letters. I had one from Enid and one from Dad.

I drove Bunny's Weasel about the last 9 miles and all the time Shackleton Range unfolded… a huge chain of mountains complete with upward mirage extensions, looking extraordinarily attractive and impressive in the faintest glow from the sun which we cannot see for cloud. This Range must be about 60 miles from us…

I've just realised that the mist-diffused sun to the south that looks rather like a huge poached egg, hasn't set tonight… It may have been up on 24 hour rounds for two or three days…

Geoff and I have been having [a] big scoff all day as we learned this morning that we start a new ration box tonight and we thought we had two or three days to go. Chocolate, biscuits, butter, dates, sugar etc. went fast while driving and tonight we've had one and a half rations each of Pemmican butter, milk and sugar.

On 18 October Stratton and Blaiklock, who had been flown out with their dogs on 11 October, reported that they had completed a reconnaissance of the Ice Wall and were able to provide route guidance. In his diary, Roy merely observed, 'Hope they know the difference between dog teams and vehicles with sledges!'

Saturday 19 October, 1957
Late start this morning was expected, though not as late as it turned out to be… Geoff started having trouble with the Sno-Cat due to low batteries. Subsequent, borrowed batteries were wasted – and all because he had forgotten to switch on the electric fuel pump… Afterwards he got on all fours in the snow to be kicked by each of us in turn.

Got moving about 2 p.m. with Bunny and I alternating over 10 miles each in the leading Weasel. 'Twas in my second turn, after about 34 miles today, that we ran into crevasse country as we approached to about 20 or 30 miles from the Onaways. There was a notable change of surface shade which I thought to be cloud shadow, but I sat up to take notice, although the crevasses gave no surface indication of their presence.

I noticed that David Pratt's Weasel (following 200 yards behind to the right of my track) had stopped and then the Sno-Cat stopped and all three bodies peered down behind the Weasel. I guessed the trouble and started to walk back when I noticed I'd broken through a narrow one about a foot wide so I went back to Weasel A for a crevasse prodder. Walking back to Weasel B again I found another that I'd broken open about 3-4 feet wide.

Bunny decided to camp, so I brought Weasel A and sledge back and here we all are, on the edge of Heaven knows what and at least 20 miles from the slope up around the Onaways.

David's crevasse is about 4-5 feet wide and very deep. Only his Weasel broke through and he stopped with his sledge on the other side...

Sunday 20 October, 1957

Camped last night on hard snow – much better than the messy, soft stuff we've had for so long. We had a crack about two inches wide running under the Sno-Cat beside our tent and considered that that meant we were clear of anything bigger for a bit each side of it. Bunny and David Pratt moved to what they felt was a safe spot and this morning David put his foot down one which ran in a line with their tent.

Bunny had a go on the radio at 9 a.m. and Shackleton reported cloud and snow, while South Ice had cloud and one mile visibility. This arrived at us blotting out the mountains. However, it was decided to go back five miles and then go west. First, there was the business of turning round again. After plenty of pulling back and forward, a bit this way, a bit that and then pulling from a different angle and so on, all vehicles and sledges were facing in the right direction to retrace our tracks...

We retraced our trail for five miles then did five miles west and are now preparing a new course parallel to the one we've just abandoned...

After about two miles we started breaking open crevasses again, but only narrow ones. Since then we have had to stop to get over a wide one which Bunny broke open (4-5ft). David Pratt took his Weasel over a clean part and then hauled his sledge over on a long steel rope (as per BNGE practice). The Sno-Cat came over alright where the crevasse narrowed, which could be seen by looking along under its lid. Then we all roped up while Bunny skied and probed half a mile ahead. I led in Bunny's Weasel and felt it falter on one bridge so was able to warn David Pratt by hand signal. Bunny took over and we are going along roped up without probing. We passed one large open hole on our right (about 5ft x 8ft) but we didn't break through any extension that it may have had.

Well, the day ended with a little excitement anyway. We had gone on, roped up, for 6.1 miles breaking open several very narrow cracks and a couple about 18ins to 2ft wide and were beginning to think we had a chance of getting into clear ground again, when I noticed Bunny's vehicle, (through David Pratt's windows) to be down a crevasse. We all stopped to investigate. Only his front idler wheels and front pairs of bogies held him up at the front and at the rear only the buoyancy tank and the trailer 'A' towing frame held him up, so he was well and truly suspended.

I took some Kodachromes at 1/25th at f4 before we started recovery work. Old BNGE method proved to be wholly successful. The first thing was to do a sound basic probing for the other vehicles to cross. Luckily a spot was quickly found only twenty feet from the crevasse. Geoff's Sno-Cat crossed with trailers and then he unhitched. A steel rope was connected from his rear tow hook to the front eye of the Weasel. The Weasel had been left in gear (forward), so when the strain came on the steel rope the vehicle was put in neutral. The Weasel was hauled forward and up the lip of the crevasse quite smoothly and easily and the sledge was then a foot or so overhanging the lip. The vehicle was held here while Bunny lay on the rear buoyancy tank and undid a safety rope shackle and the tow eye, while I, on the crevasse lip, undid the other shackle on the right-hand side of the Weasel. The trailer was still connected to David Pratt's Weasel by a three inch Terylene rope and the Weasel in gear. Detached from its trailer the Weasel was hauled quite clear.

In the meantime, David Pratt's Weasel was still roped up, so now he was able to unhitch and bring his sledge across the safe bridge. Bunny then took his Weasel back over and towed his trailer back away from the crevasse on a steel rope. Being now well clear, he was unhitched, turned round and the sledge towing frame hooked on the Weasel in the direction we were going before breakthrough. It came safely over the good part by the crevasse and all vehicles were once more together.

So now, with the great gaping hole just a few yards away, we are camped... I don't know if we will stop here till we can get an air recce, but I think even that might tell us very little as the crevasses aren't at all apparent on the ground – except a few. Looks as though there are about 30 miles of it to get through before we arrive at the known and obviously bad part!

The operation to recover the vehicle had been time-consuming, difficult and dangerous and conditions were such that Fuchs decided to set up an air-depot nearby rather than have aircraft fly what was now 200 miles from Shackleton, so that air support could be readily available. This camp was established by Haslop, with Lowe as ground crew, on the evening of 23 October and the Auster began its reconnaissance work the next day.

Thursday 24 October, 1957

... The Auster took up Bunny and David Pratt in turn for good long runs and it has certainly given a very much clearer idea of what we have to try to get through. Ahead of us, going a little south of east towards the Shackleton Mountains we now have about 8-10 miles of crevasses. After that we seem pretty clear again. These 8-10 miles might take anything from a day to a week – can't say, but no doubt we'll have some bother here and there.

They also looked at the route up the 1000' Ice Wall which had been marked by David Stratton and Ken. It looked pretty disheartening to Bunny, till he saw the alternative routes and realised they had chosen the best...

After 1.9 uneventful miles of no crevasses we struck one. Bunny broke through and David Pratt couldn't pull round far enough to get over to the left of the hole, so we had to unhitch him and shackle a wire rope to the other end of his sledge so that he could pull it back far enough to turn left and straighten on the firm part of the crevasse. Geoff was able to follow alright.

A little later David Pratt broke through and got across, then stopped with his sledge just managing to span the gap (which had almost filled in with broken snow-bridge and squashed down lips). He was able to pull his sledge over alright. But Geoff's steering valve gear had frozen so he couldn't steer left to get round the hole. We rigged up a wind shield of canvas and applied a blowlamp to the valve compartment of the steering cylinder. As soon as it was warm Geoff was able to steer left and quickly straightened up to go over a firm bridge.

After 3.7 miles we camped... We decided that we should probe right across this crevasse area and I shall take it in turns with Bunny to probe and drive...

On 25 October they probed nearly all day, with the team taking turns to prod and poke each yard of snow with 6-foot aluminium poles before allowing the vehicles to move slowly forward. Once a crevasse had been identified, they attempted to break a hole in the centre of the lid and, if they succeeded, they marked the area as being impassable and went on to test an alternative route to either side. 'Just what that means in terms of monotonous labour is hard to describe,' Roy wrote shortly after the expedition, 'quite apart from the never-ending risk of disaster'.[76] On the 25th they covered just 1.7 miles, with a meagre 1.5 on the 26th and the same on the 27th. This was slow progress indeed.

Despite the crevasses' impact on the expedition's timetable – to say nothing of the danger they presented to life and limb – Roy found the gaping chasms fascinating and, having taken suitable safety precautions, he decided to take a closer look.

Monday 28 October, 1957
... It is very beautiful inside these things, and yet, I've never had my camera with me at the right time. I could see about forty feet in one direction along the crevasse to where it split itself up into three smaller ones going in different directions, so this seemed a good place to cross, while at the other end the crevasse curved inwards, i.e. wider under the main lid, so I didn't bother to look far along there! ...

On 29 October they at last reached the far side of the crevasse field and could surge forward to meet their next obstacle: the formidable Ice Wall.

Tuesday 29 October, 1957
Bit late this morning... Didn't matter as we three just had to wait till Bunny had skied a good way out and then we were to drive the vehicles out to his marker sticks. In the meantime we had a brew-up...

---

[76] D.E.L. Homard, 'The REME Contribution to Polar Exploration', *Journal of the Royal Electrical & Mechanical Engineers*, 5, No.1 (1959), p. 3.

Bunny and Ralph had a long natter about operations here and at Base. Ralph's sent off a 2000 word thing to the office via the telephone circuit so the news up to date is now all at home. I learned that I might soon be flown back to Shackleton – Bunny was telling Ralph, but I haven't been told yet...

After un-roping we went along very happily for another 6.8 miles before stopping at a flag on David Stratton's bottom traverse before the hill climb. A few miles earlier we had seen the cairn and were headed for it, but abandoned that one when we saw a couple of flags to our right. Having reached it, we turned right again. At 0.1 mile further west there was the bottom corner flag where we had to turn uphill to the left.

For 1.4 miles it was pretty smooth going and a quite gentle uphill slope, then we came to rougher surface over a steeper climb. We wasted a lot of time and energy looking for crevasses which I was sure weren't there from what I'd seen from the air and from the fact that David Stratton and Ken had already flagged the route and probed it. We found nothing but I got my clothes very damp from sweating. I suppose we went up for about three quarters [of a] mile. By the time we got back down again the vehicles were getting cold and Geoff's steering had frozen up again.

Over the first part we had two soft patches where old crevasses had filled in and Bunny got stuck, sunken right down on the right-hand side. The Sno-Cat unhitched and towed him out as well as David Pratt and his sledge roped up behind him. Later we came to another large soft area whose surface gave way and Bunny's big end was now making a loud clatter. I guess the white metal bearing had beaten away and now it's steel to steel. He dropped his sledge and we roped it to Geoff's Sno-Cat trailers. For the first time the Sno-Cat failed, spinning its tracks on the snow, starting to bury the right-hand front one. So he unhitched and towed David Pratt's Weasel and sledges clear first, then cleared his own two trailers and then took out Bunny's trailer...

Earlier, we had seen a little black dot moving ever so slowly along the flat below the ice hill, behind him was a little string of black dots and leaving a tiny bright white trail behind them which faded into nothing towards [the] Onaways. Before we could see them over the curve of the hill we could hear the dog drivers urging the dogs to do the right things. Then the dogs appeared under control of David Stratton and Ken. We exchanged sincere pleasantries and decided to get on up the hill. David Stratton missing no opportunity to take every little advantage of modern travel, hitched up his dogs and sledge to our third loose sledge ready for a tow up the hill. He took the precaution of making a quick release hitch that would release his sledge and team the moment he pulled out a piece of wood. (Just in case!)

We trundled on up to the large filled-in crevasse which was re-prodded earlier and here we caught up with Bunny and David Stratton. Everything passed over this huge sagging filling alright and the Sno-Cat and dogs joined Bunny a bit further up at the 'corner flag' which marks the trail to go east along the hillside. The Sno-Cat had to go back to recover David Pratt and his sledge who were stuck again in soft snow.

And here we camp…

Although it came as a considerable relief to ascend the Ice Wall with so little difficulty, the party's slow progress to date was causing Fuchs a great deal of anxiety. He had predicted that the run to South Ice would take just fourteen days, with the vehicles achieving a daily average of 20 miles. Instead, they had been driving for three weeks, and had still not so much as sighted the chimneys of the forward base.

There was much work still to do at the main base and the date for starting the full crossing was barely more than two weeks away. Ideally, Fuchs wanted Roy in two places at once but decided that his number two engineer would best be used preparing the vehicles at Shackleton ready for the main event.

He therefore instructed Roy to go with Ken and his dog team to the air-depot so that he could fly to base from there. This overland journey on 30 October was demanding but it did provide Roy with an opportunity to try driving a dog team. He and Ken stopped briefly, and when Ken skied ahead searching for old tracks, Roy tried to get the dogs to go after him. He quickly discovered that dog-driving is not as easy as an expert like Ken made it look:

Wednesday 30 October, 1957
… They took not the slightest bit of notice, but just sat and lay around eyeing me with mild curiosity. I tried coaxing, pulling them, brandishing a rope, shouting. No good. I had to call Ken back and soon they reluctantly got up and moved. Ken kindly explained that they have to get used to a new voice…

197

Roy had to wait many hours at the air-depot before leaving, because the two dog teams had first to be flown to South Ice, so that they were in position to survey ahead of the Crossing Party later on. He got back to Shackleton at 8.55 a.m. the following day and after some much-needed sleep he started work. The focus would now be mainly upon vehicle modifications and, fortunately, Ivor Beney and Fred Morris were still on hand to assist. First in line for attention was David Pratt's Sno-Cat.

Meanwhile, news came through that Fuchs had been forced to abandon his Weasel, leaving the Vehicle Party with just one Weasel and the Sno-Cat. This was worrying. If the heavy Sno-Cat should get stuck in a crevasse, it was unlikely that it could be recovered using a single Weasel and the expedition would be thrown into jeopardy.

Friday 1 November, 1957
... Ivor's working on the heat shield modification for the fuel pipes and Fred's finished the windscreen modification to let the heated air out of the top of the windscreens and make them more easily removable. We are now trying to find a way of fitting the batteries and battery box inside the vehicle... In the meantime, I'm halfway through with a modification to the heater housing...

I believe the vehicle team did twenty-three miles yesterday and have been over very rough sastrugi... I understand they have about seventy miles still to go to South Ice and are due to start on crevassed areas of glacier.

Sunday 3, Monday 4 and Tuesday 5 November, 1957
Can't bother thinking of what the last couple of days have been about except that we three worked on the Sno-Cat 'A'...

We finished Sno-Cat 'A' today, while Ken, Gordon, George and Allan dug out my Sno-Cat... One extra modification that we did to David Pratt's Sno-Cat was paint it white inside and put a Perspex window in the roof. It makes it very bright inside now, as before it had only a rear-door window.

The Otter, with Gordon and Ralph, left this afternoon taking fuel to South Ice and dropping three ration boxes and steaks to the vehicle team. The Weasel had been stuck in crevasses a couple of times and when the aircraft arrived, it was down again, having gone down back-end, though some of it is still above the snow surface. David Pratt, I'm told, expects to have it out at 3 a.m.

We hear Ed is doing well, being ahead of schedule.

Wednesday 6 November, 1957
De-snowing of my Sno-Cat with Peter's RAF heater continues while we get on with other work...

Gordon came in for a short while to do some stitching to safety belts. George changed the plugs and leads... and did some stitching. Fred's modified the front seat to fit over the safety belt attachments and blanked-in an open patch under the seat. Ivor's made safety belt parts and fitted it up as far as possible and is now fitting instruments to the dash. I've fitted dynamo and drive belt and made a Dexion frame with shelf for the radio. So things are coming on, but I have forty items on the list and some of them are rather lengthy...

We hear that the vehicles are still in the clag, having moved only two miles in three days. Probing continues...

Thursday 7 and Friday 8 November, 1957
... My Sno-Cat work still goes on with we three and Gordon quietly doing jobs... Ivor, Fred and I don't do gash or cooking, due to work on the vehicles since I returned, but we work till 10.30 p.m. each night. They are a magnificent pair to have working with me and their being both completely insane only lends a cheeriness to the continual work...

I had a bath at last yesterday and did four lots of washing; so much in fact that I had to do the rinsing today...

Saturday 9 and Sunday 10 November, 1957
Two more days on this Sno-Cat of mine and out of the list of forty-four jobs about six are still being done, or still to be done...

Tonight is Jon's birthday celebration and also a special dinner for our last Sunday here, of chicken, 'fresh' potatoes and tinned Brussels sprouts, with Madeira wine. After, we had 21-year-old whisky, brandy, gin, ginger wine and sherry, with a bottle of wine that Jon produced. There have been water pistol fights and talcum powder fights, the powder being packed in polythene plastic bottles which are squeezed for use.

The vehicle party were a mile past Whichaway at the 1.30 schedule today and had encountered more crevasses and heavy sastrugi...

Monday 11 and Tuesday 12 November, 1957
*Getting more and more chaotic with the rush on vehicle repairs –
and diary suffering too...*

*Our strong northerly blew itself out last night... Great new drifts
have been formed that could be serious if more comes before we
leave.*

*Certainly 14th November as our departure date is nothing like
possible and although Ken tried repeatedly to get Bunny today, it
wasn't till 11 p.m. that Bunny came on to speak about the situation.
He said we could not leave later than ten days' time. I reckoned on
more like twelve days or more. My Sno-Cat is ready to go out – that
is without doing a lot of desirable things to it which aren't quite
essential.*

*So tonight Sno-Cat 'B' could have been in, as Ken and his gang
had dug it out, but the blow was struck when I found that the starter
motor was burned out... Now, I'm having to make up a starter from
spare bits...*

*Captain Finn Ronne has sent a message that we can have the
Weasel parts required if we can collect them. Now we want to ask
for a Sno-Cat starter motor.*

*The Vehicle Party have now got through the very 'Ugh' area and
are going past the last of the Whichaways so could be at South Ice
tomorrow tonight. Preparations are ready for the Otter to go and
collect them...*

*It was very disappointing today that the GPO telephone circuit
was unsatisfactory... It was so difficult to understand what poor
Enid was saying and it was made worse with work worry and lack
of good long sleeps. Hope on Friday it will be better...*

Wednesday 13 November, 1957
*Got my Sno-Cat out at last in another northerly bringing more
snow. It seemed to achieve something just to get it out even though
Sno-Cat 'B' wasn't ready to bring in.*

*Fred and I fitted the starter back on to 'B' after I'd made one up
from three different starters including a 12-volt one. It was most
unpleasant lying under the Sno-Cat working bare-handed with a
spanner on a fixing nut in a small space up between the clutch
housing and the starter body with the wind blowing snow and drift
through. It worked though...*

*While we were working on the Sno-Cat outside I was called to
the radio room, to find it full of people talking or listening to the*

BBC who were doing recordings. Allan said I was to talk on vehicles in the field and crevasse work, recovery, technical stuff and so on, but George was already doing this so after waiting a while I felt it was quite unnecessary for me to have left my work. George was thoroughly enjoying talking so I said, 'Goodbye' and left, to get on with something slightly more important.

I believe Allan was a bit upset, but so was I...

Roy was so busy and exhausted that he failed to mention in his diary that the vehicle party finally reached South Ice on 13 November. This was an achievement of great significance but it had taken far longer than had been hoped. Now, Fuchs wanted to fly back to Shackleton right away, but the weather closed in and instead he spent 14 November – the day originally scheduled for the beginning of the trans-continental journey – kicking his heels at the forward base.

Thursday 14 November, 1957
Strong northerly wind today around 35 knots with snow and drift...

Telegram from Enid today sending best wishes for the journey and thoughts of our meeting. Bit previous, but no doubt due to irresponsible information sent out from here.

If conditions are suitable the Otter will fly to South Ice tomorrow with fuel, etc. and pick up the vehicle team...

Friday 15 November, 1957
Just starting this at 11 p.m. as the Vehicle Party arrive by Otter...

We heard the plane arrive at about 10.15 p.m. It had taken off at 10 a.m. this morning with Jon and Ken with a load for South Ice and called at Ellsworth on the way back. I hope they've brought my Weasel spares (and possibly a Sno-Cat starter motor) and some beer. Probably Bunny has spoken about arrangements for the future of our base and gear left here.

I had a long-shot hope this morning that Sno-Cat 'B' would be out tonight and Weasel Wrack-and-Ruin in. It was a hard target to meet and I'm afraid I drove my two lads just a bit, but they understand alright and we made it. We've been at top pressure for a long time and today we mustered a last spurt. The Sno-Cat is out and the Weasel is in...

Telephone calls today were fairly good and Enid and I were able to carry on a conversation for six minutes and I know I thoroughly enjoyed it and would have liked more. If Enid had been on the phone at home I would have had another call put through from here. I loved every minute of hearing her voice and seeing her in my mind. I'm glad she could hear me clearly...

Saturday 16 and Sunday 17 November, 1957
I didn't get to bed till 4 a.m. this morning due to David Pratt and me settling down to departmental conversation. I enjoyed talking about it all, but trouble was thinking about getting up in the morning at 8 a.m.

Yesterday we three worked on Wrack-and-Ruin though I hadn't much zest. Fred got on with changing the battered windscreen while Ivor and I removed the rear spring to fit two new U-bolts.

In the afternoon Bunny had us all in for a conference. First he outlined the journey to South Ice and next explained the necessity of stating a departure date and keeping to it as long as possible instead of revising it several times. We discussed our departmental positions and I gave my estimate of six days plus packing personal gear. We are allowed to send 30lbs via the Americans and Halley Bay. I don't think I shall do much letter writing, but Enid will have all these books to read sometime in the future.

David Pratt has been working out fuel consumption and require-ments and finds it a bit of a problem as we can't carry all the fuel we need and all the equipment other departments hope to take...

Bunny has put up a notice – 'Departure date 24th November. Vehicle work will cease on 21st November. Best of Luck!!'...

Monday 18 and Tuesday 19 November, 1957
... Tonight the Weasel, Wrack & Ruin, is finished except for tidying up. It's had a lot of good work and new parts put in on it and should prove a good goer...

The tenting and driving lists have been posted up today. I am driving and tenting with Ralph, so first I shall have to put him through some driving instruction on the Sno-Cat...

Rotten northerly all day with snow and drift, getting worse tonight with 40 knots...

Wednesday 20 and Thursday 21 November, 1957
Two days of good weather...

Yesterday we finished off George's Weasel and sent it out and David Pratt brought in his Sno-Cat...

George is taking pride in his Weasel, fitting canvas bags to the roof for photographic equipment etc. On the front, in large blue letters he's painted 'WRACK & RUIN' and on the rear 'ERMINTRUDE'. I believe this is one of The Times' code names for George...

Friday 22 and Saturday 23 November, 1957

This rush goes on, but to make matters worse we had a 'Farewell Party' last night. On top of that there's the headache of packing kit for the trail and kit for home. Weight allowances make the whole thing overwhelming. Our test runs of the Sno-Cats today brought a new crop of work.

Thursday I made attaching bars to connect the sledges together and also one to connect a sledge to a Weasel, so Bunny and Co. fitted them and had slight modifications done to them. Started loading Sno-Cat spares into my bus and a 24v MacFarlane charger and then sorted out my tool kits and special vehicle tools.

Our Farewell Party was quite a fine meal of roast beef, fresh potatoes, asparagus etc. with plums and custard after. Port and Old Malmsey were in full supply and Bunny gave a toast to the Queen, then to 'absent friends' including families and business contacts, schools and donors, etc. He later gave a short talk about the Expedition, its aims, his wish to do this since 1948, our having been chosen and so on.

Not much partying went on after dinner, but I had a little too much brandy and felt pretty bad all morning...

Today I started sorting out my kit! By mid-afternoon I still hadn't finished, but had arrived at the desperation stage. Too much I wanted to keep, but also too much weight...

We heard the news on BBC overseas tonight, which mentioned the TAE leaving tomorrow.

8

SOUTH TO THE POLE

Sunday 24 November, 1957
Big Day at last! We've moved, and this time on a date previously specified.

After years of planning and preparation, the Commonwealth Trans-Antarctic Expedition had at last begun its epic journey. In reality, though, the event was probably something of an anti-climax, with the whole team dog-tired after the frantic race to get away.

The Crossing Party set off hauling 20 tons of food, fuel and equipment. By following the tracks and marker stakes along his proven route, Fuchs hoped to increase his speed and to shave 70 miles off the distance to South Ice. He would not have the assistance of the dog teams as they were now at South Ice in readiness for the journey to the Pole, during which they would serve as an advance survey party; however, air support would be available if required. The second journey to South Ice was still going to be hazardous, but with the party's departure delayed by ten days, the greatest challenge would be completion of the traverse before the end of the austral summer. A premature onset of poor weather could still force him to abort his journey part way through.

We didn't get off till late, but it could have been later and we worked right up to the last. We, or some of us, didn't get to bed till 5 a.m., being up to finish packing, etc. I didn't get to sleep till about a quarter to six, so felt dead tired all day.

Vehicle packing, last minute repairs, additional building in the vehicles, making wire safety ropes etc., all went on till we left at about 6.43 p.m. (local). Just as Bunny was about to make his pre-starting instructions the Argentineans turned up! That fairly hustled things along, but, while Bunny was talking, the Argentineans had walked to us and started shaking hands all round.

*I had given Allan a quick run through on Weasel C, 'Rumble',
this morning and he was alright on that. George has the other
Weasel D, Wrack-and-Ruin, and Steve the Muskeg. Bunny and
David Stratton were leading in Sno-Cat B, 'Rock 'n Roll', David
Pratt and Ken next in 'Able', then me with Ralph in 'County of
Kent'. After us came the two Weasels and Muskeg. When we had
all said goodbye we moved off to where George stood on his
Weasel roof Wrack-and-Ruin with a tripod and cine camera about
a quarter mile south of us. He filmed us as we passed one by one.
Fred and Ivor said goodbye and I was sorry they weren't coming
with us. Bunny had given them each a Smith's travelling alarm
clock. Geoff Pratt and seismic Sno-Cat 'Haywire' were left at
South Ice after the recce journey, 13th November, 1957.*

*David Pratt's Sno-Cat has had a last minute bench and vice
fitted into it but I hope we don't often have to use it. His vehicle is
towing two Maudheims with eighteen drums and other gear, and
behind a Nansen with two drums on it. Ken rode on this to try to
keep it upright, but in the first couple of miles it had tipped over
three times. During our sixteen odd miles it turned over all too
often, but we shall use these drums first...*

*We camped at about 10.30 p.m. I think and I got on with repairs
to my ignition as soon as I could. This finished around 12.15 a.m.
and then supper. It was nearly 2 a.m. when I settled down to sleep.
Boy, were we tired.*

Monday 25 November, 1957
*What a day, so nearly fraught with tragedy or disaster. It started so
well too, with everyone preparing to be ready for moving around 9
a.m. By 9.30 I thought we were about to move -- a record! Then
Allan said he'd got no oil in his sump. This was disquieting as I had
thoughts of leaking sump gaskets. David Pratt shouted something
about Jon having time to do a Rammsonde,[77] but the oil job was
quicker, as I found it was only a loose union for oil return from
filter to the sump.*

*When we did get away, at 10.30 (local) we made good progress
for about seven miles, passing, on the way, a flag and then turning
off to a flag and then left to another flag and a beacon of two wood
struts. This marked a 20-30ft filled crevasse with open sides. This*

---

[77] A Rammsonde is an instrument that measures resistance to
penetration in order to determine snow density.

205

was alright and Bunny and David Stratton probed a bit. We were clear after half a mile. About one and a half miles further on was another small belt of crevasses. We stopped for probing and lunch before going on...

In poor light we went on, not being able to see any surface irregularities and suddenly Rock 'n Roll started climbing uphill, up what I thought was the horizon. It was a huge snow drift which David Stratton hadn't seen and belonged to a very large crevasse. When, later, the light improved we could see lots of these things around, like wide extinct volcanoes. The one we were going up made us think, so Rock 'n Roll came down again by turning round in a circle on the side of the drift! We all swung off to the right for 150 yards and crossed there.

One and a half miles further on I, in the last vehicle (so that I can pick up strays), noticed Rock 'n Roll, in the lead, to be at a nasty angle and not changing its position. The other vehicles were between me and it, but I could see well enough to be sure that Rock 'n roll was down. And down it most certainly was! I hope never to see the likes of it again. When I looked at it I thought maybe we can never get that out. The right-hand front pontoon was right down inside and all the other three partly in.

As a preliminary, photographs were taken and discussions took place on deciding a recovery method. First, everything was removed from inside the Sno-Cat and eventually a plan was made which, most fortunately, was successful.

The idea was to use two Weasels on the forward side of the crevasse. These Weasels were attached to the front axle to control the downward drag of the front of the Sno-Cat as it was drawn backwards by the other two Sno-Cats.

This all took a long time. First, a place had to be found for the Weasels to cross over about 200 yards east of us. As they were doing this, a large chunk of [crevasse] lid roared down about 40 yards from us leaving a huge hole. They found a crossing place alright and the wire rope was fixed round Rock 'n Roll's front axle by first digging away under it. Allan passed it round underneath and it was picked up by George crouching on top of the left-hand front track. The same was done on the right-hand side. The trailers were hauled away because the Sno-Cat was wedged, then David Pratt and I hooked up to Rock 'n Roll's rear. The Weasels, to start with, were left in gear with no drivers. Their resistance was to stop the Sno-Cat dropping hard onto its vulnerable underneath parts when the front pontoons came off the far lip of the crevasse.

We pulled under heavy load until the under-structures of transfer case, steering rods, steering hydraulic cylinder and propeller shafts to front and rear axles were resting on the near lip and by then the rear pontoons were mostly on top again, while Rock 'n Roll hung nose-down in the crevasse.

The drivers got in and released their Weasel clutches while we, in the towing Sno-Cats, pulled. It came fairly well and then it was time to stop and fix a strong rope to the track of the right-hand front pontoon hanging loosely over the crevasse. The other end was attached to the Muskeg, which hauled the rope until the pontoon was tipped up at the back in order to be able to ride up the near lip. As the tracks revolved it was necessary for the Muskeg to move in slowly, but retaining sufficient rope tension to keep the pontoon end up while the Sno-Cats pulled.

The operation went well and the right-hand front pontoon started to ride up the lip. Now it was the left-hand front pontoon which had to be pulled up by the Muskeg, this time pulling in between the two Sno-Cats. This pontoon was still over the crevasse so we had to pull it far enough to get at it. The casualty came back a bit too far so that its left-hand front pontoon dug into the wall of the crevasse. This meant a little digging-out of the lip in order to free the rear end of the pontoon.

Whenever a bit of easing was done with the shovel by David Stratton the Sno-Cat sank a bit lower and jammed both the track and the shovel, so we had to allow the casualty to slip back just an inch and then it was much easier. Then the Muskeg was able to pull the pontoon up. The Weasels were free of the front control rope now and our two Sno-Cats pulled the casualty out on to the top – much to the relief of all of us.

Looking at the hole afterwards I was more surprised than anything else that we had got the poor thing out. The hole was 15ft wide. Unfortunately, I don't think David Stratton measured the depth, but he had intended to do so. The crevasse was more like a chasm with here and there these peculiar drifts along the hundreds of yards of length visible to us.

All the gear had been off-loaded from the Sno-Cat and put on the Muskeg, so now it was all loaded back in and one by one we made our way round to the probed route over the crevasse and camped.

The whole recovery operation, from the time of stopping to camping took about six and three quarters of an hour...

Tuesday 26 November, 1957

Only about 13 miles yesterday and not doing too well today, having been held up by crevasses unexpectedly. So far we've done nearly six miles, from about 10 a.m. to 1430 and no sign of moving from our present spot...

We are not on the original vehicle route, quite stupidly, which was to have proved a way for the main party. Roughly we are following Ken's dog run, instead of a bit further west. Although the last few days of warm weather have softened the crevasse bridges, it cannot be solely blamed for unexpected crevasse difficulties.

Rock 'n Roll was [the] cause of a hold-up till 5 p.m. Over a bumpy crevasse lip the jolt was apparently too much for its right-hand battery pad and it split around its side seam, losing 23 pints of coolant. David Pratt fitted a new pad...

When we got going eventually, at 1720, I came along at the end. We were passing over several filled crevasses which sagged with the compression of the snow bridges by the weight of the vehicles. Hal, in Weasel C had just passed over such a one and I was about to roll onto it. In fact the bonnet obscured the concealed crevasse from my view when a movement out of the right-hand passenger's windscreen snatched my attention and I realised that the lid of the crevasse had fallen in, in front of me.

My first thought was that if the Weasel had gone over it then it wasn't too big for me to do so, but instinctively I pressed down the clutch and knocked the gear lever out, but the Sno-Cat still rolled under its own weight, as the previous vehicles had sloped the lid downwards, so I grabbed around under the instrument panel for the transmission hand brake. When I'd got that on, I didn't know if I was on the edge, or hanging over it, or still rolling. When I looked up I was very relieved to find that I had stopped 3-4 feet short of the edge. Sno-Cats ought to have a footbrake – even if only to transmission.

Ralph was asleep in the back, so I called, 'Ralph, the bloody bridge dropped through in front of us. I only just stopped in time.' He roused himself immediately with a grunt, took one look outside and said with much emotion, 'Hoo! Bloody good show, Roy!'

The rest of the vehicles were 300 or 400 yards ahead and mistook our arm waving signals, so went on. I expected to need a

Sno-Cat to tow my sledges back far enough for me to get my Sno-Cat out, but as they were all so far away I tried backing them and luckily, when they jammed in a zig-zag, they had gone just far enough to allow me room to go forward to near the edge again and then back round in a part circle. Then I was able to drive forward and round my sledges and fix my winch rope to them to tow them well clear. Then I hooked them to the back of the Sno-Cat again. David Pratt came up in the Muskeg to see what was wrong but that became quite clear when he saw the 12ft-wide gap going down into the depths. From his side it looked as though it tapered off to my left, but that was only a small branch crevasse. From my side, when I lay down on the edge, I could see a main cavern affair joining up at an angle. The whole thing was pretty grim, so Ralph prodded a good way to my right and I got over safely about thirty yards from the hole.

When I caught up with the others we went on a bit through pretty uggish country and then camped for the night in the thick of it... This was about 8 p.m. – earliest yet...

Wednesday 27 November, 1957
Another uggish day in crevasse country, though not as thick as the eleven mile stretch below the Ice Wall, but containing some old un-filled caverns which could spell disaster. So it's been a day of probing and moving, roped up... making three miles today...

Light to fairly strong southerly these last two or three days, bringing temperatures down from -4°C to -14°C. Should help make bridges safer (we hope!).

Thursday 28 November, 1957
Another dreadful day. Clouded over all day with strong northerly and snow. Light was so bad that no surface shapes could be seen, so there was no indication of crevasses. Sun did try to break through for about half an hour this morning but it was vanquished and from then on snow fell. Yesterday, while we had our light southerly, base were having 40 knots of it!

Still in the 'ugh', so it meant continuing the probing. We probed from 10 a.m. to 1 p.m. then walked back for lunch. We were then able to drive our marked obstacle course for 1.6 miles, ending at 1710 hours. Seven hours work to travel 1.6 miles! Then of course, more probing, this time to get the vehicles 0.7 of a mile in three hours. In wind and snow and poor visibility it's not much fun, because it is wearying work pounding a rod through iron-hard layers of snow and ice all day long. We are still finding a few small crevasses, with the odd large and dangerous one here and there – and not always with a visual surface indication – so it means probing if we wish to get the vehicles through...

We hear... that Ed has reached his 480 mile depot. Very good going.

Friday 29 November, 1957
Another probing day, with little progress in poor weather. Very bad visibility, continually clouded over, and snow with a light northerly. Tonight it is almost calm, tending to turn southerly, with light snow still falling.

Radio good tonight, with base coming through well on voice... The Otter is standing by to fly to Halley Bay and will afterwards bring mail and other things we have asked for.

We have reached Depot 50...

Bunny's Sno-Cat is showing trouble on the left-hand front pontoon. The lips of some of the rollers are nearly worn away and the rollers are wearing the side of the pontoon and the outer edge of the bearing rail.

At Depot 50 four and a half boxes of man rations and five boxes of dog Pemmican were dug up from around the beacon while George filmed this 'historic' occasion. Light was very poor though.

Saturday 30 November, 1957
... We've done 26.7 miles by my vehicle clock which is pretty good considering that we didn't start till after 5 p.m. (and ended at 2335!). After camping and eating, time is now nearly 1.30 a.m. and we will be up at usual time in morning.

We were roped over our probed route for about [the] first one and a half miles, then roped over un-probed route for a further 2½ miles. There, at the second flag, we altered course to (I think) 175° where, some of the time, we saw faint traces of the earlier vehicle route. No crevasse trouble at all on the proper route and progress good except for Weasel C overheating and boiling off some anti-freeze...

Sunday 1 December, 1957
Quite a good day, that could have been even better, but for a slightly depressing ending.

With last night's late ending, I got to sleep at about 0215 and awoke to the call of the alarm clock at 10 to 8 and made breakfast. We made a pretty good start at 0945 and went on, with several halts till 1945 tonight, having done 41 miles. Our main halt was at the petrol that we had dumped off Bunny's sledge on the last trip when his 'big-ends went'... The fuel depot was nearly ten miles away from last night's camp, making up to 84.4 miles since base. It should only have been about eight miles to the fuel, but we had to alter course to 217°M for 1.8 miles when the drums were spotted way over to our right. Bunny's classic remark while the re-fuelling was going on was, 'The depot is off course.'

100 miles mark today...

Having arrived here, after 41 miles, at 1945 hours, Bunny wanted to complete 50 miles. This was scotched because someone announced that Bunny's left-hand front pontoon was breaking up. Not true, of course, just a cover plate over the sprocket drum wearing through... The worse trouble is the rollers wearing against the guide rails on the inside of the pontoon. Anyway, tonight, David Pratt has started to take it to pieces to see how much damage there is and what's causing it. At base we have a new pontoon which can be flown out...

Monday 2 December, 1957
Big maintenance day due to repairs to Bunny's pontoon and track...

Tuesday 3 December, 1957
... Big day and no serious faults. 65 miles today. I woke up at 6 a.m. to make breakfast for Ralph and myself and we were all away at 0750. We stopped tonight at 9 p.m. My speedo reads 67.1 miles today, so probably it is around 66 miles, excluding local work.

We had deep soft snow all the way which hid large hard sastrugi underneath, so we had to go rather carefully over some stretches. After 10 miles we stopped at the second flag of the day and a solitary snowy petrel flew over us, going north of course. We stopped for lunch from 1245 to 1335 and had a few minutes at each five mile flag. We have been able to follow readable remains of our old tracks so it made things easier and faster...

Uneventful journey apart from Bunny's Sno-Cat starter relay sticking on a couple of times. We started off in plenty of sunshine, but cloud stayed over to south-east and by tonight we have full cover. They've lifted enough to be able to see the Onaways clearly, though still wreathed in clear shaped cloud and mist, making it all quite arresting to the eye. The Ice Wall is obscured by cloud and ahead of us, slightly more on a southerly route than our day's south-east, is the 11 mile 'ugh' stretch, all ready for tomorrow…

Wednesday 4 December, 1957

Near disaster again today. We all moved off towards the 11 mile 'ugh' stretch except George who filmed our leaving camp this morning from a tripod on his Weasel roof.

Allan was in front of me and I was last. He was making slow progress due to fuel trouble, so, after about 5 miles, after the others were seen not to be waiting for us at the 7 mile flag (from camp) I checked over his fuel system and found the carburettor filter choked with sludge. We went on and broke over or through bridges of four crevasses up to four feet wide and caught up with all the others who were stopped.

Here, after only 7.3 miles we found Rock 'n Roll (Sno-Cat B) with its rear pontoons and back, down a crevasse about eight feet wide. It was serious because we could see its left-hand front spring attaching arm was snapped on the rear steering platform. Also in the drop, the first sledge 'A' frame had been pulled right down into the crevasse and the strain was too much. Bunny and David Stratton felt the lurch as the tow hook bolts snapped. David Pratt tried pulling her out, but his tracks failed to grip. But first, everyone was probing for a spot to cross the crevasse and, in time, both David Pratt and I crossed comfortably with our sledges.

Our next attempt at recovery, after Allan had dug the lip away from the transfer case, was successful. David Pratt remained attached by a double wire rope to the spring attachments on the front axle and I had a single rope going under his Sno-Cat to his tow hook. We were able to pull out the casualty quite easily…

We have removed the broken steering platform and are… making sure that our spare new one fits alright – Tucker doesn't exactly make standard interchangeable parts…

Thursday 5 December, 1957
... At 1 a.m. last night Admiral Dufek[78] spoke to Bunny from South Pole Station, having flown there yesterday. I didn't hear it but Ralph put it on tape. I understand Dufek said something about the eyes of the world being on us and that, 'I know you can make it.' South Pole Station are greatly looking forward to receiving us and will 'roll out the red carpet and champagne'.

Friday 6 December, 1957
Slow day with everyone prodding except David Pratt and me. We got away to a slow start to cover the route as far as yesterday's prodding got to. This was 1.8 miles without any incident worth recording. Progress was made unnecessarily slow by David Stratton walking ahead on skis, over the route probed yesterday. I lagged back so as to do about a comfortable 5 m.p.h. and stopped again when I caught up with the others. Like this I did it in four hops.

The order of procession was altered to save further Sno-Cat casualties. Bunny went first in Allan's Weasel, then George, then Steve in the Muskeg. These three were all roped together. Allan came next, driving Bunny's Sno-Cat Rock 'n Roll, as named by David Stratton, then me and last David Pratt who was still cleaning out pontoons when we left. Besides Ralph, I had Hal in the back as refugee passenger from Allan's Weasel...

Saturday 7 December, 1957
Big probing [day], with progress as good as could be hoped for. We first covered the route probed yesterday, doing 1.7 miles, then probed till 1330. Driving over this section gave us 1.2 miles and the next lot of probing this afternoon and evening added a run of 0.9 miles, making our journey today 3.8 miles, but really only 2.1 miles belong to today.

It's tough going probing every two or three feet and much more often in suspicious or bad bits. Any crevasse more than about 2ft 6ins gets a detour and so does any narrow crevasse which har-bours a cavern running off underneath from its almost closed bottom lips. Our course winds snake-fashion the whole way, for

---

[78] Admiral George J. Dufek (1903-1977), commander of the US Navy's Task Force 43, responsible for the logistics of the USA's contribution to the IGY, codenamed 'Operation Deep Freeze'.

there are perils to be avoided every few yards. Sometimes we divert round one side of a bad spot for about 30 yards. This means, at any diversion, that the section probed immediately up to this spot is, wasted, and a new route must be probed to get over to the safe spot. This is the loss of much time and labour, but the loss of time is our greatest concern. However, for the safety of vehicles even time doesn't count.

Some of the things we've had to divert the route round have been monstrous caverns which could greedily accept a Sno-Cat and for a long way down. The depths of these are not to be estimated for they deepen from inky blue to a blackness where no light penetrates from the holes we make for inspection in the surface. We have come across several of those terrible-looking three-cornered things, ugly and huge and always more terrible to see than a straight deep crevasse. Luckily there is usually a way around these without going too far off the route. The smaller ones which happen to be on the route, or which we accept on a diversion round a wide part, collapse and sink down as the two Weasels, Muskeg and Sno-Cat Rock 'n Roll go over. When I get on, with the weight of my load in the back, my rear pontoons go deep and push the bridge right down, making my two heavily laden sledges snow-plough their way up and out. This always leaves a nasty mess for David Pratt's Sno-Cat (so far unnamed) to get through. Sometimes, where the bridge has broken through or has squashed down too steeply he has had to go over to one side, after Ken has probed to see that it is safe. It's quite exciting to feel the back of the Sno-Cat lurch down, generally to one side or the other and step on the accelerator and feel the engine pull the lot up and out...

It's time I changed my socks – they're beginning to smell like stale mice-nests again...

Sunday 8 December, 1957
Sno-Cats in crevasses is becoming so commonplace! Today David Pratt's went in and did a first class job of it.

We probed, as usual, this morning and ended our first stretches at about 1230 hours so there was no point in doing a second leg before lunch, because it would take us up to about 3.30 p.m. Our progress this morning was much slower as we were going through worse stuff and hours have had to be spent in probing for safe diversionary routes round shockers. I had one area riddled with caverns and one I opened up was the triangular sort, but I'd *opened it right over its centre... It was about 12 feet by 30 feet and went down into blackness. This was not one of the larger ones, but merely one whose walls I could clearly see and down whose centre I could peer. The others had been so big, and with such thick lids, that I had seen only a portion of the insides of them...*

We had our 'lunch' and moved off, this time in beautiful sunshine with blue skies. We got over the two worst patches alright, but leaving many badly squashed-in bridges and also some broken ones, then suddenly I saw a figure waving its arms reflected in my mirror about 500 yards back and also noticed David Pratt's Sno-Cat looking squat and still. It was pretty plain that I was wanted so I unhitched and Hal, who'd come up from the trouble, and I, probed a route for me to turn on. Sno-Cat B, Rock 'n Roll, had also turned and the two Weasels were being got ready to come down too.

We had a casualty alright, for the Sno-Cat was all four paws inside, with the front ones partly up on the forward lip of the crevasse. The rear was held up by the back of the vehicle which was jammed about four feet down inside against the crevasse wall.

After much discussion a plan was agreed upon. Strangely enough we were to use snow to fill the crevasse under the Sno-Cat, then use crevasse bridges for the rear pontoons to come down onto and ride out on. Unfortunately, we weren't able to fill all the space under the Sno-Cat, for a deep black hole fell sheer away down to one side, so the mass of snow that we shovelled in was only under the front of the vehicle and the right-hand rear side.

The right-hand crevasse bridge was lowered down... (weight 1cwt, 24lbs; 14ft long and to take 2 tons) with its front end propped against the forward crevasse wall under the right-hand front pontoon and the rear end supported by snow blocks and a steel wire rope up over the top to a 'deadman'. Steady ropes were fixed from the bridges to anchors sledge-hammered into the crevasse walls. The left-hand bridge needed more arrangement as it had only a sharp slope of snow under it. The forward end was propped up just high enough on a vertical petrol drum with one laid horizontally on top of it and the rear end, sloping downwards, nestled into a step cut into the rear crevasse wall. This end was also supported by a wire rope up to the top and a 'deadman' buried.

It was found that the 'A' tow frame was taking no weight, so the pins were removed each side of the sledge and the two sledges

215

drawn away by a Weasel. (A route had been found round the crevasse for the two Weasels to cross). The safety steel rope from the back of the Sno-Cat was still attached. This runs in loops under the sledges and, at the rear end of the sledges, is attached to a Terylene rope when necessary. So this steel rope was used to attach a Weasel, and from its rear, another steel rope was attached to a second Weasel. This was a check or control on the Sno-Cat to stop it dropping in with a crash. On the front end I (County of Kent) was attached by a steel rope to the front axle of the casualty and from my tow point a steel rope was taken forward under me to Rock 'n Roll. The Weasels had taken in the slack and David Stratton and I pulled. Our tracks only spun. So the Weasels dipped their clutches and the casualty steadily slid up forward but down in at the back. While the rear pontoons were still against the rear wall and the forward ends of them were on the bridges something had to give and it was the bridges. Both moved forward a few inches. When all the weight of the rear pontoons came on the bridges they both sank a little, but the left-hand rear, resting now on only part of its step in the Ice Wall, broke the step and dropped, but luckily the 'deadman' held the weight and kept the bridge from twisting over on the side of the snow pile. The casualty however, making alarming swayings towards that side, gave near heart attacks to the onlookers. If it had swayed off, the Cat would not have been recoverable for it would have been upside down jammed in a very deep dark hole.

However, as it was steadily drawn up the bridges, the discrepancy between the levels of the bridges decreased and with the front pontoons up on top, with a good forward pull, it was clearly a successfully salvaged Sno-Cat. With it up on top, no damage was found...

Monday 9 December, 1957

A day with a difference. Some good cheer, good weather and a little progress without too much trouble.

We started our usual morning prodding session, with Ralph and me on the first stretch from the vehicles. We were unlucky and had a bad area which took several diversions to get through and round.

When we were half way through, the Otter arrived, with John, Fred and a lot of spares we'd asked for, plus two drums of fuel...

A small packet of letters yielded only one each for most of us... Later, David Pratt was opening a parcel of Sno-Cat spares, labelled 'Weasel spares' and found a whole lot more letters.

Everyone cheered up immensely and sat down to a reading session. I was only in a tattered string vest, but George included it in some filming of people reading their mail from home…

[All] vehicles got through safely for today's 1.4 miles…

Tuesday 10 December, 1957

… The day started with the usual probing and driving, but we had such a good session that on the first leg Allan and I did two sections (each about 300 yards) and helped on two other sections. We were able to drive on 1.8 miles.

We had stopped for lunch at 2 p.m. before driving on and once having completed that little drive, we all set to, prodding again. This took us to 8 p.m. when we all went back for some tomato soup laced with Pemmican. We started off again at 9 p.m., this time doing 1.5 miles. Up to this point we had proceeded with David Stratton and Hal guiding on skis and with Weasels and Muskeg roped, and without probing. Now we hauled the skiing guides on board… We passed over only very minor crevasses and no trouble. A little earlier, when Hal thought a broken crevasse bridge might cause me bother, to save time he leaped into the air to test another part and shot straight through up to his armpits.

After the first 3.3 miles we rolled along cheerfully with the two skiers a long way in front and after 11 miles came to a tall flag below the Ice Wall… I can't say [we will] climb up the 'wall' in the <u>morning</u> because today a big time change has come about. We have gone onto GMT and will also work at nights when temperatures are lower and surface a little harder… The amount of UV about is doing great good and a bit of harm. My nose is sorely burnt underneath (from snow reflection) and so are my lips, while my ear lobes are frost bitten…

Tonight, being cook in our tent, I was stabbing the block of Pemmican in order to break it up for quicker solvency, when I missed, and stuck the pointed sheath knife neatly through my left thumb. Fatigued and hungry I suppose. It'll be alright…

Wednesday 11 to Thursday 12 December, 1957

Working at night makes the diary cover two days and if I don't write it down as two, I'm bound to either lose or gain a day sometime.

Our beautiful long sleep was very nice, but everyone was waking up after a few hours…

Ralph got the South Pole Station and learned that Ed had recently done a day of 52 miles and had 63 miles to go to Depot 700. It will be interesting to watch subsequent developments.

My thumb has not been too troublesome but I have to be very careful. The slightest pressure stops me like a hornet sting. It didn't prevent my driving thank goodness, so up we came, up the hill, with Weasels and Muskeg roped in front. We had less trouble than last time, only Bunny getting stuck in soft snow once and he might have got out of that, but he stopped when he felt the back sink.

There was a diversion round to the right of the big crevasse two miles up [the Ice Wall], although I could see no change as we went by. This was as high as I'd been last time. We went on up, over two monstrous crevasses, both filled in solidly and being about 40-50 feet across and probably 80-100 yards long, but the lips grew indistinct and may have extended further. The second one looked worse because to the right of us where it had sagged the most, it was joined by another similar crevasse and a wedge shaped island of snow and ice was left standing up between the two depressions.

After 38 miles from the bottom of the hill camp, we came upon the abandoned Weasel and Maudheim, abandoned on 31 Oct on the recce trip. The Maudheim was half buried, but the Weasel was not and it hasn't a scrap of drift inside. We started to strip off all that we felt would be useful, including both Atkitrak light-weight rubber tracks. In the meantime Bunny had gone off uphill for a recce. I took on a Canadian trailer from Jon's Muskeg and put the two tracks on it while Jon took a load on the Maudheim.

After only 1.4 miles (of uphill traverse!), Allan in leading Weasel Rumble broke through in line with a crevasse about 4 feet wide with his left track, and the Weasel lay over on its side. There was a lot of hoo-ha about what to do and how to do it but of course, it came [out] perfectly simply by the conventional method, although some with no experience insist on doing everything not quite as has been proved best by others long before...

Here then we camped, about 3 hours late, at 11 p.m. Ken took sun shots last night and this morning.

Thursday 12 to Friday 13 December, 1957
If anything terrible were going to happen to us I suppose it should have happened today, but it didn't and things have gone quite well. First of all we've done 21 miles. Secondly, we should be out of

trouble for (I guess) about 20 miles, and, thirdly, we got out of this last lot without a lot of trouble.

We probed a route clear from last night's camp before starting off at midnight (GMT). This took us past the most monstrous hole I've ever seen. It is the one which appeared next to the first vehicle team to go through (on first trip), when the colossal bridge fell in with a roar... There is not the slightest doubt that two London double Decker buses could be put into that hole with room for another two on top. I hadn't my camera with me, so I missed a momentous opportunity.

We still had to cross the chasm, downhill, in order to get round it, but we chose a place half a mile further along. It was safe... We passed over frequent bumps and ruts across our route for another five miles when we came to a chequered flag stuck in what was once a fair-sized cairn, but which the wind had eroded away to make it look like a very old large bleached sponge. Here the Weasels were un-roped.

The sun was being wiped away by quietly sweeping clouds from the north-east... light and shadow were beginning to blend into that depressing state of flat whiteout. However, Bunny, in leading Weasel Rumble saw a depression ahead, so stopped to investigate. It seemed alright so we went on. Half a mile further on the same thing happened... Ahead, and leading uphill to the right where a flag was stuck, was the first of four large depressions. Bunny, David Stratton and one or two others probed along the lip of this one towards the flag and pretty soon we'd all joined in. At some spot below the flag Bunny said the bridge was only a foot or two thick and that the hole underneath could easily take a Sno-Cat.

We probed across all four of these chasms and apart from some very soft snow for twelve feet, more sagging in parts, and some narrow cracks along the lips, they all seemed aright. From the first to the fourth they spread over 0.3 miles. The near lip of the fourth depression was the only sign of the bridge giving way... Bunny and David Stratton skied ahead then till Bunny got aboard Rock 'n Roll after 0.6 miles and David Stratton went on. He went right on to the turning flag under Corner Mountain of the Onaways Group, 1.7 miles from the fourth depression. Here things were safe and the Weasels, having turned right under Corner Mountain, un-roped while Rock 'n Roll went into the lead to follow a compass course. From there to camp is 5.7 miles, all uphill still, and most of it, especially the last half of that distance, very bumpy from hard smooth mounds of sastrugi or pressure,[79] *but cushioned a bit by a fair covering or filling of snow...*

Corner Mountain seemed to take us a long time to pass; it's a massive chunk that I always want to call 'Tre Klover', having three main rock masses, divided by huge ice formations. We make the most of these mountainous features – they're some of the last we shall see for a long time...

Friday 13 to Saturday 14 December, 1957
... We left our camp site under the Onaways at 2145 hours and George filmed our departure. We had good sunlight, but the kata-batic winds from the east were cold as they coursed down the ice slope. We'll have that as part of our normal ice sheet conditions...

Hal has been a welcome passenger in the Sno-Cat today, first in the front while Ralph had a schedule in Bunny's Sno-Cat and later, when Ralph returned, in the back on the two sleeping bags, stretched out in a dream...

Hannes and Geoff are getting short of tinned meat at South Ice and I think Ivik has an infected paw from a dog fight. Allan is anxious that a message be sent instructing the use of a penicillin injection as [the] only cure.

Saturday 14 December to Sunday 15 December, 1957
Splendid day with our biggest hopes having come true. When we camped last night we knew we had 2½ miles of 'ugh' to go through and that on the last run it took four days. They had only four men then and had to try several places for a route through, and also four recovery jobs.

This morning they all had started probing except Ralph who did a couple of radio schedules and Allan and I who did maintenance on our vehicles. I greased all my rollers (296) and tightened the nuts on all of them, when I found one was lost. The greasing alone took three hours and two 7lb tins of grease. The others came back for lunch having probed a mile route through.

We started at 0240 hours... There were stretches of one hundred yards where nothing much to bother about was found, but there were patches which took hours to find a way through or round. Patches which, under a series of faint depressions or very mild

---

[79] Pressure mounds and ridges are distortions caused by the gradual movement of ice sheets from the Polar Plateau towards the coast.

dunes, contained nests of very large deep black interlocking caverns. George and Allan spent all [of] six hours on one such patch, while David Pratt and I spent three hours on one and had prodded about three hundred yards of surface... to gain fifty yards of vehicle route. But at last the end flag was reached and we were joined by those returning from it and they helped us connect up our finished diversion with the completed stretch ahead.

When we got back near the vehicles where Allan was still working on the same patch of ugh, we found a forest of sticks and flags, like two wavy lines of fencing, yet suggesting a children's fairground, which, Allan explained represented, the vehicle route over that patch of ugh, but although completed, he didn't feel satisfied with it. By now we were willing to be satisfied with any-thing, but the thought of a late night recovery, on top of the day's hard work, forced some to go back and have a last reassuring investigation.

At last it was decided the risk was worth it... So at 0925 hours we started up in the same formation [with] Bunny leading in Allan's Rumble...

The whole route was safe. It was six hours hard work well done and we covered one and a half miles with only minor giving of crevasse lips. We passed two old camp sites in this run and also several lids which had fallen in of their own accord over large caverns and at last we were clear of the pressure hummocks, and, the crevasses for that area. We stopped at 1000 hours...

Sunday 15 to Monday 16 December, 1957
Miserable, boring day, but not too bad on final results. While all the others did a morning of maintenance, Hal, Allan and I went to reconnoitre the route ahead till we arrived at the flag where the vehicles un-roped last time, 1.2 miles from our camp site. This took from about 2250 to 0150, or, three hours. It was intended to be only a cursory inspection and probe, not a thorough, 'every two feet' probe. We just investigated suspicious surface signs. We found only one crevasse about seven feet wide...

The journey was uneventful all the way, but quite boring. We had un-roped at the flag, but clouds from the north had quickly covered the whole sky during our probing and by now visibility was beginning to get poor. Snow had started falling fairly thickly and visibility got too bad with 'whiteout' to be able to see any surface conditions. As it happened, we were in for a rough time, for the surface turned from light sastrugi to very hard snow surface with medium sastrugi and whalebacks.

It was a very rough banging ride, made so much worse by not being able to see the obstacles in the whiteout. First indication was always a sharp bang as the front of the vehicle met a rock-hard sastrugi and then the rest of the vehicle would have to rock, sway and bang its way over with the sledges crashing over it afterwards. This continued till we camped, having done 17.2 miles today.

With bad visibility the Whichaways were obscured, so Rock 'n Roll was steered by compass. When we got near to camping, the Whichaways could dimly be seen and with a check on the prismatic compass it was found we were too far east.

We had to camp a little early because a mile or two ahead is a crevassed area which we'll have to probe and it won't be the same spot as they went in last time…

Monday 16 to Tuesday 17 December, 1957
Rotten day. We've moved only 5.1 miles… all because of weather.

Visibility was very poor this morning so we couldn't move. It gave me a couple of hours in which to change my distributor while Hal removed a broken 'hairpin' tow-frame from underneath his sledge. Then we moved because visibility had got slightly better.

Being too far east, our object was to go west before turning south towards the Whichaway Nunataks and in this way, by finding our position to be at a required bearing from Little Whichaway, we would enter the crevasse belt at about the same spot as the first vehicles did on our October trip… After doing three miles… we stopped with very bad visibility and fairly heavy snow and no sign of the Whichaways. This gave me an opportunity to finish greasing my Sno-Cat…

It kept on snowing with very airy flakes in only light northerly wind, so it settled softly, concealing any possible vehicle tracks. We were stuck here for five hours, patiently waiting for a break in the visibility conditions.

At last the Whichaways were sufficiently clear to be able to take a course on them, although no surface conditions could be seen… We then went ahead, with David Stratton walking on skis in front for 2.1 miles… Then we stopped; it would be foolhardy to go on unless pressed to it. Also, it was 7 a.m. Pity, because with good weather we could have camped in the Whichaways and had a walk

*on the rock and moraine, looking for fossils. Some were found here
last time...*

Tuesday 17 to 18 December, 1957
*Dreadful day – no move. Very bad visibility for most of the time
and fairly heavy snow on and off driven by a moderate north-east
wind...*

*There have been one or two messages about Ed lately. Miller
and Marsh with a dog team, reached Depot 700 recently while Ed's
party had had differential trouble with their one Weasel and later
had to abandon it due to mechanical failure. They were also held
up with crevasses, I think about 68 miles from Depot 700, but
reached there yesterday. They'll stay ten days to receive the air
drop.*[80]

Wednesday 18 to Thursday 19 December, 1957
*Some progress, in a round-about sort of way, but weather still not
for us.*

*We didn't move to start with, neither did we prod. Bunny, David
Stratton, Hal and Ken went off on skis to find the route and
disappeared south. I got to work on a modification to my engine,
fixing in a thermometer bulb and gauge for engine coolant
temperature, running off 12 Volts.*

*Two of the recce party appeared coming towards us from the
south-east so we got moving...*

*Having got level with a large ice slope between the western end
nunataks we have altered course towards it and camped for the
night. Pity I couldn't have got this down in detail. Worse though, is
the pity that we haven't had any sunshine, being covered overhead
by cloud, swept continuously by an east-north-east wind and for a
lot of the time by snow as well and always with light too bad to be
able to distinguish surface conditions. We've also missed the thrill
of seeing a great deal of wondrous massive forces of nature causing tremendous ice landscapes of rugged beauty...*

*We were all disappointed in Ed when we heard from Halley Bay
that they listened to the news and learned that Ed is going to make
for the South Pole. Bunny, overall leader, knew nothing of this.*

---

[80] Bob Miller and George Marsh reached the proposed site of Depot 700
on 13 December, Hillary on the 15th.

Premier Nash[81] has publicly supported the idea and so have the Ross Sea Committee. They say it's better for him to wait for us at the Pole instead of Depot 700. I hope he ensures enough fuel for us at 700. He will need a lot to get his three tractors to the Pole. The other thing I don't like is the reference to the New Zealand Antarctic Expedition and the British Antarctic Expedition – if the quote is correct as such. The whole thing is The Commonwealth Trans-Antarctic Expedition 1955-58.

The news that Hillary intended to make a bid to reach the South Pole by motor vehicle did not come as a complete surprise to Roy; privately, he had suspected for some time that the notoriously independent New Zealander might make such a move.[82] Fuchs, however, was taken completely by surprise, noting in his own diary that 'I cannot imagine that Ed would have set this ball rolling without letting me know what he wanted to do'.[83] By any standard, it seemed extraordinary that the expedition's overall leader should learn of such a plan only because the Royal Society team at Halley Bay had tuned into a public broadcast. In some ways, Hillary's decision would become the *cause célèbre* of the Trans-Antarctic Expedition, and a subject that Roy would return to later in his diary.

Thursday 19 to Friday 20 December, 1957
This really has been a flag day for crevasses. I can imagine that when the October vehicle party came this way and saw what there is here to have to get through to the Whichaways, they must have been filled with dismay. It is a veritable graveyard of huge dark deep caverns, some being surmounted by memorial mounds of ice. Great areas, looking quite solid, except for frequent areas of depression and some hummocks, often contain more yawning open spaces underneath than solid ice and snow. Many caverns occur in the same area, all so compactly placed that they honeycomb and join up, so that I feel I could walk great distances underground from one craggy broken cavern to another and another in all directions. As an example, it took Jon and I five hours to find a route through about 250 yards and when it was done it was the

[81] Walter Nash (1882-1968), 27th Prime Minister of New Zealand.
[82] See diary entry, Sunday 9 February 1958.
[83] Vivian Fuchs, diary, 19 December 1957. Quoted in Haddelsey, *Shackleton's Dream: Fuchs, Hillary and the Crossing of Antarctica*, p. 204.

windingest route in the world, doing everything but circle back on itself. But everyone had bad areas and we packed up at 10 p.m. without having finished the three-quarter mile stretch by about a quarter mile...

During the morning's probings, David Stratton and Ken had gone well on ahead to trace out the old route, and Ken, skating around happily on skis, and over-confident, got on top of, and in line with, a crevasse, the lid of which gave way, dropping Ken in to stop with a jerk by his arms, while his skis went on down to be lost for ever in inky depths. David came back about half mile for another pair of skis. (Such stupid bindings – no wonder they fell off!)...

We started prodding again about 5 a.m. and one of the early incidents was when Ken took off his skis, laid them across a bridge over a crevasse to peer at its interior through a hole and Ralph arrived on skis to have a look. As his skis came onto the bridge, the whole section fell in leaving Ken kneeling on his skis, perched up in space over a wide crevasse...

After 4½ hours of it we were pretty weary of the fatiguing work and having to do sections of the route again several times in order to find ways around each newly discovered danger. We were glad to totter back and get tents erected. We don't move over dangerous ground late in the day because fatigued men having to make a vehicle recovery late in the day isn't a very sound proposition.

When we'd got back to the vehicles Jon dropped to his arms and face as a bridge went through under him. He is the luckiest man alive today, for it was a large cavern underneath, with a steep snow slide twenty feet down, sweeping into a jet black hole that ended up goodness knows how far down.

Next was myself, because our vehicle and tent is ringed closely by wide crevasses. The centres of the bridges are very thin and I trod on one and dropped through one arm and one leg. Bit of a wrench. Next, five minutes later was – guess who? Ken again, who went through one next to his tent and jammed his leg in it.

Never mind, South Ice tomorrow!

Friday 20 to Saturday 21 December, 1957
Big day! A happy one at the end of it, but it's been hard slogging and anxious. We've got through the last and the worst part of this run to South Ice and are now camped up the steep long hill between

the Whichaways, being very slightly south of them and having one only about ¾ mile away...

Our probing and the journey through the graveyard of ice upheaval is almost beyond description... We probed all morning and finished off the run we were working on yesterday and started over it at 0355 hours. This was for 1.4 miles, then probing started again and this time over the worst ever. The same inter-joining of several caverns occurred in patches with only yards between them but now we were handicapped by huge ice hummocks much more closely located.

The last probe was only for half a mile but it took us three hours with eight of us on it. Ken and I had a really tough one where the old trail ran off the slope of hummocks before joining the short flat part approaching the ice hill between the nunataks. We found the old trail led over a huge cavern, probably the largest I've seen (and Ken, too, says so) which extended about thirty feet under the slope and as far to the left and right of the trail. Where we broke through probing, the bridge was only about two feet thick, yet the Weasel and Sno-Cat with sledge loads, had passed over it. There had become a difference in the terrain however, for the bridges we were able to probe through had previously been so hard that caverns underneath could not be located...

We all got through the whole lot safely, though we all had mis-givings about several parts of the route which went over thin hard shells of ice supported by indifferent pillars of drifted-in snow and had huge black caverns on either side of the narrow bottleneck route. Indeed, at one such point near the end, just before the detour down the ice slope towards the level, all had crossed safely till I came over last. I felt the rear pontoons jerk the Sno-Cat down rearwards and Ralph riding on a Canadian sledge behind my second Maudheim said the first Maudheim fell down with the bridge as it collapsed. The Sno-Cat was on firm snow and so was able to pull the sledges through and up. It was such a relief to be through it all...

Sunday (midnight) 22 December, 1957
Upheaval of our arrival at South Ice still in progress. Time has been changed for work and sleep so that we work in hours of GMT daytime and sleep at the same times as in England, whereas we have been working through the night hours for lower temperatures in crevassed areas. Now, of course, we want the warmth up here...

We started away... at 2140 hrs in sunshine – first for days! – and gradually climbed between very spaced nunataks over terrain which undulated greatly all the way. Only one thing happened and that was when Bunny had to stop with his Sno-Cat engine boiling due to its radiator doors being closed.

We went on till 0150hrs when we stopped an hour for lunch, having done a series of hill climbs for 10.6 miles, passing five nunataks on the way to the west and one to the east. David Stratton took frequent compass bearings on nunataks to check the course... We had been going across medium sastrugi all the time and it was very hard with not much snow coverage. After doing twenty one miles we started getting soft snow so going became a little easier. We were still ascending [a] series of rises and there was about seven inches of soft snow on the surface. After 28.5 miles (total) we started up a steep hill... and after half mile we were about on top – and could see the southern marker flag of South Ice and then South Ice came into view.

Hannes came out to meet us half [a] mile from South Ice and shook hands and welcomed everyone. We arrived at South Ice parking ground after doing 31.3 miles today and a total journey 348.6 miles (on my clock anyway).

At last they had completed the first stage of the traverse and arrived safely at South Ice, having taken nine days less than the first journey. There was still a very long way to go and time was pressing but a few days were needed to prepare for the trek towards the South Pole – over a route that had been neither surveyed nor trodden by man. Meanwhile, it had been agreed that a US Dakota would fly into South Ice, bringing in some of the expedition's drums of petrol from Shackleton and thereby saving a couple of Otter flights.

When Hannes came out to meet us, Bunny issued parking instructions so that we would all be in line to allow the Americans an opportunity to admire 'British methodical neatness', or something. He didn't want us to loot South Ice as he has arranged to hand it over to the Americans at Ellesworth...[84]

---

[84] Fuchs had agreed to pass ownership of the forward base to the United States, possibly by way of exchange for the fuel brought in by the Dakota. For reasons unknown, the transfer of ownership did not occur. It is

Pretty soon after erecting tents, we were all down inside South Ice which has a double-length ladder down a vertical snow shaft to a tunnel about twenty feet down. Tunnels go everywhere, but... it hadn't altered much inside since I was there early this year.

We drank lots of tea with rum in it and had a good old chinwag and about 10.30 a.m. it was decided to get some sleep and be up again when the American Dakota arrived and finish off a normal working-day. The plane actually landed at 3.30 p.m. and I hadn't got to bed till after midday. We all got up, except Hal who had quickly succumbed to Appleton's Rum...

Finn Ronne... brought ten drums of vehicle fuel from Shackleton by way of exchange for South Ice... They didn't stay but a few hours and then were off again. The day started sometime shortly afterwards when fuel drums were dug up and consumption figures worked out and carrying capacity and requirements calculated. I started sorting out the spares in my Sno-Cat...

Beautiful day here with blue sky and sunshine and only a breeze, but being 3,300 feet up makes quite a temperature change.[85]

Monday 23 to Friday 27 December, 1957
Everything desperate and seems much worse than it is simply because I haven't kept up my diary. Every day points of interest occur as well as our progress and all is being lost to this record. (Probably not of value, but there can't be many of them!).

It all stems from the fact that we have insufficient time in which to encompass all our essential endeavours, let alone personal routines and recreations. In fact we are all very short of sleep.

It will be difficult to recall daily activities so it'll have to be condensed. On Monday and Tuesday I had some good heavy work on Weasel suspension. On 23rd (Monday) also we watched (and assisted) the departure of two dog teams with Ken and Jon.[86] *David*

---

possible, though far from certain, that such a commercial transaction was thought to be at odds with the spirit of cooperation that was meant to underpin the IGY.

[85] In *The Crossing of Antarctica* (p. 238), Fuchs gives South Ice's altitude as 'well over 4000ft'.

[86] The task allocated to Blaiklock and Stephenson was to survey a viable vehicle route to the South Pole – an overland journey that had never previously been undertaken from the Weddell Sea side of the continent,

Pratt worked on figures of fuel and oil consumption and re *ments for the journey. Bunny did writing and calculatio*.. *digging out fuel drums assisted by all the rest except Hannes, who did meteorological work and a stalwart job of catering for us lot with lunch and tea breaks... George did quite a lot of filming in between helping me on the two Weasel suspension jobs...*

Ken and Jon, having prepared their sledges, hitched the dogs, which allowed a fight. George filmed the separating of the combatants but the public might not understand the necessity of the technique required. As they started off Eric (the Red) for no apparent reason, turned on his close chum Nanouk and another fight started. During the first fight I got a bit too closely involved and received a double rope round my skull, cunningly wielded by Ken. This caused no ill-effect but to my glasses, one of the arms being broken off. They had been removed by the ropes together with my hat and I trod on them.

Next day, Tuesday, (Christmas Eve), I worked on Allan's Weasel, Rumble, removing both balata Goodrich tracks and fitted the lightweight Atkitrak which had been taken off the abandoned Weasel A on the Ice Wall... At the end of the day the job was complete, so I washed, put on my fir tree pullover and cravat and got down inside South Ice in time for 'Calling Antarctica' programme at 2115 GMT...

Christmas Eve was a poor affair with no party and everyone dog tired. Shackleton and Halley Bay were on air with us and a general exchange of greetings took place. After which we went to our tents.

Christmas Day was little different to any other day except we had Christmas pudding and listened, as well as conditions would permit, to 'Round the World' broadcast and the Queen's speech, which was much clearer. Loading and packing continued until at last we were able to start for the South Pole at 1935 hours, GMT...

After a spell that was especially busy for Roy and David Pratt, the convoy set out for the South Pole some 550 miles away. The South Ice personnel joined the party, along with two vehicles that had been left in November, bringing the total number to eight: four Sno-Cats, three Weasels, and the Muskeg. Weasel B was now operated by Hal Lister while Geoff Pratt took the wheel of the Sno-Cat

---

the journeys of Scott and Amundsen having both begun on the Ross Sea coast.

Haywire, with Hannes la Grange as passenger. Ralph Lenton, meanwhile, drove the Muskeg, replacing Jon Stephenson, who had left with the dogs. Their total load included one-and-a-half tons of food, half-a-ton of lubricant, half-a-ton of explosive for seismic work and over 5000 gallons of petrol.

In ideal circumstances, the Crossing Party would have reached the South Pole long ago; now, already well behind schedule, its progress would be further delayed by the need to complete the seismic survey, the jewel in the crown of the expedition's much vaunted scientific programme. Roy would find the constant delays exasperating, but he was not a scientist and his frustration was probably exacerbated by the fear that, if the Crossing Party failed to reach the Ross Sea before the departure of the expedition's support vessel, he would be obliged to spend a third winter in the Antarctic, thousands of miles from Enid, who was due to leave for New Zealand shortly in order to meet him.

Sunday 29 December, 1957

We moved from South Ice on Christmas Day at about 1935 GMT. George wanted to film the departure with vehicles moving in line, but after we four Sno-Cats there was trouble. The Weasels lagged and Ralph wrecked the sun recorder with the Muskeg. But we got away.

After five miles on course 190° we came across the first of Ken and Jon's five mile intervalled snow cairns. They've done remarkably good jobs, using a snow-saw to cut out hard snow blocks and building cairns up to about seven feet high.

We had dunes and then hard sastrugi ridges which made progress slow and extremely bumpy, while sledges rode up the ridges only to overbalance and crash down on their front ends. A sledge with twelve x 45 gallon drums of petrol on it is some weight...

Boxing Day was a seismic day, while I and David Pratt rigged up the excellent Terylene neoprene-coated shelter which fits over half a Sno-Cat. Then I was able to work on my engine, not only out of the wind and snow (for it was a clouded day of snow and poor visibility) but also in warmth once the weather broke and the sun came through. I was able to do the left bank of plugs and tappets before we had to move. We set off at 1600 GMT with very rough going...

It's no good; I can't write a diary from my vehicle log information, so I'll leave a few pages to fill in as best I can later. All I can remember is that we have been dreadfully short of sleep.

On 30 December the party stopped for maintenance, which continued partly into the 31st. They had planned to abandon the Muskeg and the Weasels as soon as ongoing fuel consumption had lightened loads to the point that they were no longer needed, and now it was time for the first one to go. They chose to abandon the Muskeg as it was the slowest when hauling heavy loads.

Tuesday 31 December, 1957
... Depressing events occurred this day, but the situation, with one hundred miles of luck, is salvageable...

Sledges were re-lashed and all drums re-filled from the Muskeg's load. Also all petrol tanks were filled and after the rest of the Muskeg's load had been dispersed among the other vehicles' loads, the poor, good, faithful Muskeg was parked behind a wall of nine empty drums and left, we thought, for good.

We didn't move till 1955 hours GMT and after only 2.1 miles George stopped with a tremendous load drag on the left-hand side of his Maudheim sledge. Bunny and Allan had gone on before stopping 0.6 miles ahead. The remainder of us stopped. The runner had broken near the front and the broken end was doing a deep ploughing operation. We turned the sledge round and towed it on a wire rope from its ram's horns, while the broken curved end of the runner was lashed up to the sledge top members. It ran very well like this.

Less than one tenth [of a] mile later I broke a dynamo belt and the spare from David Pratt was too big. Then we had a cairn after doing 5.2 miles. 0.2 miles past that Rumble stopped and when I got up to Allan and David Pratt I found very glum faces. Allan was clearly all finished with his Weasel. The right-hand Atkitrak had broken four transverse drive bars and pulled out a connecting link, where two sections join together. The track [had] already lost two guide lugs on Rumble and one while in use with Weasel A. Just not tough enough for the heavy load. No point in fitting the spare track section as it could only be joined with three bolts instead of four.

The answer is obvious. The Muskeg must make a come-back – or a come-forward!

I went to Bunny and the others to explain the situation while David Pratt and Allan went back in Sno-Cat 'A' to collect the Muskeg. This was now 5.4 miles behind them so this would take a couple of hours to get to it, fuel it, and bring it back. On receipt of the news Bunny decided to camp... only 6.4 miles in the day...

By the time I... was siphoning petrol from my tank to feed to the pop-pop [generator], it was midnight and the New Year was coming in. Bunny came running up from his tent with a bottle of cognac and poured a generous portion out into a Thermos flask cup for Ralph and me. Ralph was still on Bunny's radio. Just after twelve I had the pop-pop stuffing amps, into my batteries... David Pratt and Allan had returned to the abandoned Weasel and didn't get into camp till about 3 a.m. after transferring sledge, etc. and taking off things like grease nipples and top guide roller...

Wednesday 1 January, 1958
Not doing too badly... but still damned hold-ups and slowness.

Yesterday Geoff and Hannes left to get twenty-five miles ahead of last Seismic station and we would catch up with them. That's good – they could get some work done while we are still travelling, but the Muskeg and George's Weasel Wrack-and-Ruin are making only about 4 m.p.h. with their loads, so we all have to wait every cairn or two for them to catch up. My Sno-Cat is doing well and easily and could happily take another ton and speed the journey on...

George's Wrack-and-Ruin is finding it heavy going with his ten drums of fuel on a Maudheim, a Canadian sledge with a load of food and photographic boxes and behind that a Nansen dog sledge with dog Pemmican and other boxes.

Bunny took over the Muskeg from Allan as it gets cold in there. I had noticed it labouring badly and Allan hauling on the right-hand tiller all the time and had three times suggested to Bunny that I take its second Maudheim or some of its load. When he took it over for a spell he found how unsatisfactory it was. I had felt sure the Muskeg was being hauled left by its load or uneven towing rope. David Pratt unhitched it, drove it around the ice cap to left and right, left and right, left and right and pronounced it alright except that a brake band might be binding.

Bunny hadn't gone far when he stopped and I had intentionally stayed back a bit so I stopped near him. Ralph went over and explained how easily County of Kent was going in top gear and

Bunny agreed to let me take the second Maudheim. From there on all has been very much better. His steering has been straight and his speed increased from 3½ to 5 or 5½ m.p.h. It had much grieved me to see so much load behind the Muskeg, the way it was having to be steered continually right and at our slow progress. The object had been to lighten the loads of the crossing vehicles and increase to maximum that of the vehicles to be dropped. It was sadly over-done. My Sno-Cat has taken it very well, coming along at three quarter throttle in third gear and occasionally top. Even up a hill it was happy in third...

We went on over light sastrugi which soon turned to medium stuff and started slowing us down. This turned to medium/heavy sastrugi and we had very rough going. I still managed third gear but the other Sno-Cats didn't.

We camped after doing forty miles and felt we'd done pretty well, although our aim had been fifty miles... We stopped at about 2150 hours and had a long night for a change, having to be outside at 9 a.m.

Thursday 2 January, 1958
A few hold-ups this morning. Allan's Muskeg was short of anti-freeze, so some had to be heated up for him... Just as everyone had got away David Pratt said he had a violent coolant leak in his battery box which would take a couple of hours. Geoff had gone off to do a seismic station.

I started at 1040hrs. After a mile we were going uphill which got fairly steep. This wouldn't have mattered much if it hadn't been thickly surfaced with hard medium sastrugi. We were at the top of the hill in two miles and it levelled off a bit, but the sastrugi remained. After eight miles Geoff did a seismic station and it was here, in the middle of his shoot that we (except David Pratt) caught up with him...

We also had a schedule with Ed and this was the first time Bunny and Ed had spoken on air since Base. First contact with Ed's vehicle party was made about a week ago. Traffic between us was relayed by the Pole Station.

At last we all left and it was my job to escort Geoff who'd been having fuel trouble which he thought might be vapour lock. After three or four miles he stopped with this trouble and I checked through all I could on the spot without finding anything definite, although I suspect a three-way tap of sucking air.

At midnight, about a mile later Geoff stopped for Hannes (his passenger) to do his 'met. ob.' Then he discovered he'd left his gravimeter base about five miles back, so we decided to camp as the rest of the vehicles disappeared in the distance southwards...

Friday 3 January, 1958
... We had agreed to be packing up at 10 a.m. but I couldn't get myself outside till 10.20hrs, while Geoff and Hannes blamed the alarm clock for their not being out till 11 a.m. We got away at 1128hrs and were very surprised, after going only about three miles, to see vehicles appear below as we topped a rise. All the tents were up, we could see, as we got nearer, and when we got close enough to be heard, figures began emerging from tents one by one and hurrying around frantically packing up camp. They needn't have hurried – they hadn't even re-fuelled and we needn't have got up when we did, for we were stuck at this camp for two hours.

The other surprise was to find the two dog teams here. So once more all the land party were together – first time since 30th December, 1957.

Just another long hard laborious grind from 1530 to 0100 GMT. Heavy hard sastrugi in huge whalebacks or sharp ridged, deep, hard, rutted scars crashed and banged the vehicles and sledges as they tossed about on them at very slow speed. Not only punishing to vehicles, sledges, tow-frames, loads and lashing, all of which have heavily suffered, but also on [the] drivers who are keyed up to a state of tension the whole time. So far this stretch of sastrugi has lasted fifty-five miles and looks as though it goes on and on...

The dog teams were losing interest and were flagging due to very difficult going and our altitude of about 7000 feet, so they now run with the vehicles which helps them along much better. They can run in fact so much faster and straighter over this sort of country than can the vehicles...

The Muskeg had to take a little of the load off Wrack-and-Ruin who was finding it very heavy hauling. Also he's using a great deal too much oil and petrol...

At 2130hrs Ralph was talking to Peter [Mulgrew], Ed's radio man and they were about to start the last bit of their trip to the South Pole Station. For them it was morning of Friday, or something. We heard them talking to South Pole Station and Peter reckoned they were due in about one and half hours later as they

SOUTH TO THE POLE

thought they could see some flags, cairns, huts and airstrip. On information from South Pole operator it was apparent that they were further away than they thought, so didn't expect to get in till 2 a.m. However, on the 11 p.m. schedule with Halley Bay, Henry[87] said he'd heard on the ship's news that Ed had arrived there, when in fact he didn't expect to get there till about three or four hours later.[88]

The BBC 2 a.m. news gave a lot of similar nonsense...

Saturday 4 January, 1958

Last night clouds which had started gathering from the north-east, had entirely covered us so that we expected, this morning to be what it was – very cloudy, slight snow, windy (as always – from north-east) and visibility too poor for travel over very rough sastrugi. The day, therefore, became a seismic and maintenance day.

We all got on with our various jobs. I greased the anti-lift devices on the steering platforms, changed my 4000 feet [carburettor] jets... to 6000 feet jets... and then got on, with Hal and David Pratt, on Weasel B's track and rear spring... The steel tracks had become too slack for further adjustment, so we took a plate and connecting link out of each. It was 10.30 p.m. when I finished.

We learned from Ken and Jon, who had left us in the morning, that after two or three miles they had struck good going which continued as far as they could see, so we were all much cheered.

We also learned from the BBC that there had been conflicting reports as to the whereabouts of Dr Fuchs' party. An amateur radio operator was reported to have heard that we were fifty miles from the Pole, a Reuter man said he overheard a radio conversation by Ed that we were 360 miles from the Pole, an official estimate in London said we were 200 miles from the Pole [whereas] we are... about 85° south (5° x 60 miles = 300 miles from the South Pole)...[89]

---

[87] Henry Dyer, radio operator with the Royal Society team at Halley Bay.
[88] Hillary's party reached the Pole during the early afternoon of 4 January, 1958.
[89] 85°S is 300 geographical or nautical miles from the South Pole, equivalent to about 345 statute miles.

A good deal of sledge re-packing and lashing was done and Allan serviced the Muskeg which had been neglected in view of its being abandoned earlier on...

Sunday 5 January, 1958
We're all much happier today. At time of writing we've done 23.4 miles and have stopped at a cairn to refuel Weasel B and Muskeg. Bunny and David Stratton and Wrack-and-Ruin have gone on.

Geoff left at about 9 a.m. to get ahead and catch up with the dogs and start a seismic station. We left at about 1000hrs... After about three miles the sastrugi eased off a good deal and we were travelling over light sastrugi. Rough stuff started again about three miles later and continued for two and half miles. Then it eased again and it was pretty good for eighteen miles.

In the meantime we had come across cairn CCX and marked in the snow 85°S. One cairn was modelled on Stonehenge and marked CCXXV. Here Bunny refuelled and the rest waited while I went up the hill for Ralph to collect Hannes's meteorological observations to send to South Ice. As I went uphill the sastrugi got bigger and rougher and some of it seemed like long walls across the hill. Geoff had made a start setting out his gear after 36.8 miles. The dog teams were there and Ken and Jon were in their tent.

Before starting work I had my Pemmican – the only one who did. Here is where the Muskeg was dropped (for the second time), so its load of fuel drums had to be pumped into empty drums on other sledges. I had a go [at] Bunny's fuel system, then drank some two-day-old tea from a Thermos, before getting on to re-shaping my second sledge load of drums.

I came in to do a little paint work to my vehicle name plate and soon started to feel ill. In a short time I was feeling very ill. From 12.45 a.m. to 0530hrs I was being ill all the time, suffering the most torturous and acute huge pains in my stomach. It was the worst thing that I've ever suffered.

In his next diary entry Roy comments in detail on Hillary's unauthorised, and highly controversial, decision to lead his tractor party to the South Pole, and on the no less controversial communications between Hillary and Fuchs that followed. The significance of these events will be discussed in the subsequent commentary.

Monday 6 January, 1958

I don't know much about this day for I was in my sleeping bag in the back of my Sno-Cat and Allan was driving. His Muskeg had been left at the last camp. We made 30.6 miles (less 0.7 mile when Allan had to drive back to pick up the third sledge which had dropped off when the shackle came undone)...

No radio contact again with South Ice, but late at night we learned that the Otter was at Scott Base, having flown last night. Everyone was happy at this. First single-engined aeroplane to fly non-stop across Antarctica.[90]

I haven't written anything about Ed's activities because it has all seemed so out of order, but the facts are pretty well known. His message to the press [was] that he was 'hell-bent for the Pole', while he hadn't even suggested to Bunny that he would like to do the journey. Nash and New Zealand Committee welcoming the idea [while] Bunny's message to [the] London Committee [was] asking if they knew of these plans, etc. Then, almost as if [the] result of eaves-dropping, Ed's innocent sounding offer to abandon [the] Pole trip to lay more depots if required. Our immediate acceptance through Pole Station of this offer brought Ed's message to say it was too late. He had gone so far that he had to go on, which he did.

Bunny had asked that Ed and mechanic should accompany us from the Pole to Scott Base but Ed declined. Also his two mechanics were reluctant to do the late journey considering the risk as being unjustifiable with winter conditions that start early on that side.

Ed had urged that the crossing plan be dropped while we fly to New Zealand from Pole for [the] winter and return to finish the seismic traverse next season. He offered to join us at Depot 700. Bunny replied that we will go on and that Ed needn't join us at Depot 700 – we would wend our way using Ed's charts left at the Pole. Last night the news broadcast the text of Ed's message and Bunny's answer. I believe they mentioned the committee were considering the situation.

If we split the Expedition at the Pole we could never all be got together again as some have only a limited time away from their

---

[90] John Lewis, Gordon Haslop, Peter Weston and Taffy Williams took off from South Ice at 11.48 p.m. on 6 January and covered the 1430 statute miles to Scott Base on Ross Island in exactly eleven hours. Theirs was the first-ever trans-Antarctic flight completed in a single-engine aircraft.

jobs. In my view we could do a much wider-spaced seismic traverse after the Pole, leaving intervals to be filled in from Scott Base next season as the base is to be kept open.

From the outset, Hillary's agreed contribution to the expedition had been clearly defined: to identify a vehicle route towards the Pole from the Ross Sea coast, and to lay depots of fuel and other essential supplies to be picked up by the Crossing Party led by Fuchs. Initial survey work would be undertaken by dog teams, with his Beaver aircraft bringing in the depot supplies. Hillary had approximately sixty dogs – enough for six teams – meaning that he had sufficient capacity not only to meet the immediate needs of the TAE, but also to explore the Ross Dependency more broadly.

In addition, he had five Ferguson tractors at Scott Base, plus a somewhat dilapidated Weasel. The tractors, all on loan from Massey-Harris-Ferguson Ltd, had been equipped with tracks instead of wheels and they had proved useful for lifting and haulage activities around the base, but only the Weasel – in theory, at least – could be regarded as suitable for long-distance work.

Hillary knew from the start that the tractors' grip in soft snow was poor and although Jim Bates, one of the engineers, spent much of the winter of 1957 successfully improving their snow-worthiness, it was ambitious to consider using them for the depot supply work with their unheated cabs and inadequate traction. It was even more ambitious – or foolhardy, in the opinion of some – to consider pushing them all the way to the Pole, but Hillary hoped to get away with it.

Having promoted the tractors against the wishes of the men running the dog teams, Hillary set off on 14 October 1957 with his Weasel and three tractors towing trailers and a caboose. After 180 miles he reached the existing Skelton Depot from where he could start the ascent of the Skelton Glacier in order to access the Antarctic Plateau. The dog teams assisted in finding a route for him and after a demanding and hazardous journey he arrived at the existing Plateau Depot on 31 October. Utterly elated at having overcome some very difficult terrain, he later wrote 'I don't think that ever before, even on the summit of Everest, had I felt a greater sense of achievement'.[91]

---

[91] Edmund Hillary, *No Latitude for Error* (London: Hodder & Stoughton, 1961), p. 138.

The Plateau Depot was replenished by air before the vehicles set off for the planned location of Depot 480, with the dog teams leading the way. Hillary reached that goal, not without difficulty, on 25 November. Once supplies had been brought in by the Beaver to establish the new depot, he left for the planned location of Depot 700 on a journey that was in parts rapid and in parts slowed by crevasse fields.

Along the way his solitary Weasel proved troublesome and Hillary lightened its load by establishing another store to be known as Midway Depot roughly half way between Scott Base and the Pole, but this didn't prevent the Weasel breaking down irretrievably soon after, so it was abandoned. Despite the near loss of a tractor down a crevasse, he reached the site for Depot 700 on 15 December 1957. He was then roughly 550 miles from the Pole.

With the establishment of Depot 700, Hillary's crucial work for the TAE had been completed. According to his instructions, he should now wait in order to greet the Crossing Party and guide them to Scott Base. However, the obstacles encountered by Fuchs' team meant that they were well behind schedule. In order to operate within his brief, Hillary now had three options: wait at Depot 700; return to base and then fly out to join the Crossing Party when they arrived at the depot; or remain in the field and, by laying an additional depot close to the Queen Alexandra Range, support the exploratory work of Miller and Marsh. To the intense frustration of the surveyors, he discarded all three options and chose, instead, to make a bid for the Pole.

In his diary entry for 18/19 December, Roy stated that the Advance Party learned of Hillary's plans only when Halley Bay alerted them to the contents of a radio broadcast. At that time direct contact between Hillary and Fuchs was impossible because of the distance separating them; however messages could be relayed via the USA's Amundsen-Scott South Pole Station. Even if this process lacked immediacy and atmospheric conditions exacerbated delays, there could be no credible excuse for the fact that it was not until Christmas Eve that Hillary himself confirmed the nature of his plans. The New Zealander consistently asserted that the lateness of his notification resulted from radio problems – but his radio operator, Peter Mulgrew, told a different story. According to a letter Mulgrew wrote some twenty years later, Hillary 'carefully planned the radio messages that I sent in such a way that should we receive an instruction from Fuchs or the Ross Sea Committee not to proceed, it would be too late as we would have passed the point of no return'.[92]

As both parties were roughly the same distance from the Pole at that time, there was, perhaps inevitably, talk of a 'Race to the Pole', but any race would have been a very one-sided affair. Fuchs had never agreed that Hillary should go beyond the original plan and when he did so of his own accord, Fuchs was too far behind schedule to compete – even had he wanted to. In fact, he considered Hillary's journey to be utterly pointless, though he never said so publicly. Besides, Fuchs' work also incorporated a scientific programme that was hardly conducive to racing. Fuchs' race was always against time, not Hillary.

The outcome was that Hillary became the first man ever to drive a motor vehicle to the Pole, and leader of only the third party ever to make the overland journey by any means. He arrived with three tractors and almost no fuel on 4 January 1958 with Mulgrew, his two engineers, Jim Bates and Murray Ellis, and the photographer Derek Wright – though Hillary was the only member of the party to have covered the whole distance as the other vehicle operators had been replaced en route.

Why did he do it? Perhaps he felt that New Zealand, as an emergent nation with an evolving independence, was entitled to more than what he perceived to be the crumbs of the expedition. An overland journey all the way to the Pole, undertaken by an exclusively New Zealand party, would certainly attract more attention worldwide than a mere depot-laying expedition – no matter how crucial that work might be. But personal ego also played a very large part in his decision-making. Yes, the completion of his journey constituted a great achievement, particularly with such poor equipment, but it did nothing to further the expedition as a whole. Moreover, his independent action simply ignored the fact that this was not his expedition. Fuchs had fought for it and gathered funds for it and spent five years planning it and to undermine him in this fashion seems, by any standard, to be ungracious to say the least. If, ultimately, Fuchs had failed in crossing Antarctica, Hillary's actions would have amplified that failure greatly and unfairly.

---

[92] Peter Mulgrew in a letter to Paul Dalrymple, 9 July 1979. Quoted in Haddelsey, *Shackleton's Dream*, p. 209.

In his own published account of the expedition, Hillary freely admitted that he had begun to entertain thoughts of making his own polar journey long before he reached the Antarctic.[93] Initially, he assumed that he would use dogs, but once the reliability of the tractors had been proved with a series of trial journeys, he became convinced that his fleet of tractors could do the work – but only if he could obtain the necessary fuel. No provision for such a journey had been included in the original consumption calculations and even Hillary baulked at using supplies vital for the TAE's success. This left him with only one recourse: the Americans. Given that he wouldn't be able to carry enough fuel for a return journey, and would obviously wish to avoid the embarrassment of having to ask Fuchs for a lift back to Scott Base, he would also have to rely on the Americans to fly him from the Pole to their huge logistics facility on Ross Island.

Already, and on more than one occasion, Hillary had asked for and been given help by Admiral Dufek – his assistance taking the form of loans of vehicles and helicopters. Now Dufek provided the extra fuel without demur, perhaps unaware that Fuchs and his expedition committee were anxious to minimise American input into what was billed as a Commonwealth endeavour. In addition, and embarrassingly for both Fuchs and his committee, the use of Dufek's fuel breached their agreement with British Petroleum, the TAE's most important sponsor. BP had donated all of the fuel needed for the expedition's ships, aircraft and vehicles, plus £50,000 in cash. In making such an extraordinarily generous contribution to the success of the expedition, the company's directors naturally anticipated a great deal of good publicity. It was crucially important, therefore, to avoid any action that might detract from the benefits BP derived from being the TAE's sole supplier of fuel and lubricants – and Hillary's actions risked doing precisely this.

But Hillary's offences did not end there. Indeed, if Fuchs was disconcerted by Hillary undermining the achievements of the expedition by becoming the first man to drive a motor vehicle to the Pole, he was probably even more irritated by his lieutenant's subsequent proposal that he should simply abandon his goal of crossing Antarctica in one continuous traverse.

---

[93] See Hillary, *No Latitude for Error*, pp. 17-18.

It began during Hillary's final approach to the Pole. On 3 January he sent Fuchs a detailed message stating that, in his opinion, travelling so late in the season was unnecessarily risky with 'increasing bad weather and winter temperatures, plus vehicles that are showing signs of strain';[94] he also advised that his mechanics, Bates and Ellis – both of whom had been asked by Fuchs to provide assistance to Roy and David Pratt for the remainder of the crossing – would not risk the journey. He concluded by suggesting that the Crossing Party should stop at the Pole and ask the Americans to fly them out so that they could return to civilisation for the winter with a view to resuming the journey the following spring. Fuchs replied:

> Appreciate your concern, but there can be no question of abandoning journey at this stage. Innumerable reasons make it impracticable to remount the expedition after wintering outside Antarctic. Our vehicles can be, and have been operated at minus 60 but I do not expect such temperatures by March. Whiteout and drift will be our chief concern. I understand your mechanics' reluctance to undertake further travel, and in view of your opinion that late season travel is an unjustifiable risk I do not feel able to ask you to join us at D700, in spite of your valuable local knowledge. We will therefore have to wend our way, using the traverse you leave at the Pole....[95]

Was Hillary being solicitous or duplicitous or did he simply wish to avoid risking another winter in Antarctica? One way or the other, it was an extraordinary thing to do. Fuchs' diplomatic but loaded snub of Hillary saying he need no longer join the Crossing Party at D700 shows just how annoyed he was, and when the exchange was leaked by the Ross Sea Committee in New Zealand the newspapers had a field day.

Was Hillary's state of mind irrational due to exhaustion – or even, as has been mooted, the effects of carbon monoxide poisoning from his tractor?[96] If so, he hadn't improved a couple of

---

[94] Hillary to Fuchs, 3 January 1958. Quoted in Hillary, *No Latitude for Error*, p. 218.

[95] Fuchs to Hillary, 4 January 1958. Quoted in Haddelsey, *Shackleton's Dream*, p. 215.

[96] Stephen Hicks, 'The Commonwealth Trans-Antarctic Expedition 1955-58: How the crossing of Antarctica moved New Zealand to recognise its Antarctic heritage and take an equal place among Antarctic nations'. PhD thesis, University of Canterbury, Christchurch, New Zealand, 2015, p. 237.

days later when he audaciously sent an appeal direct to Fuchs' committee in London, asking it to order Fuchs to stop at the Pole. Not surprisingly, the committee gave the suggestion very short shrift.

Fuchs managed the incident with admirable restraint, treating the whole episode as an undesirable distraction. Conversely, Hillary later paid a price for his actions when, contrary to his wishes, he was never again offered a formal position with the New Zealand Antarctic programme.

Much more cheering was the news that the RAF contingent comprising John Lewis, Gordon Haslop, Peter Weston and Taffy (Ellis) Williams had successfully completed the first-ever trans-Antarctic flight in a single-engine aircraft. They had started by flying the Otter to South Ice and from there they set off on the long leg to Scott Base, completing the 1430-mile journey in exactly eleven hours.

Tuesday 7 January, 1958
... Writing this the next day. Didn't feel well enough to write this when I got to bed, but nothing much happened anyway. We did our thirty miles in spite of starting at 1410hrs GMT. We stopped for camp at 2100hrs. Allan carries me from the back of the Sno-Cat to the tent as soon as it is up and my sleeping bag is inside. (Ralph has stuck a red cross on each side of my Sno-Cat)...

Both the London Committee (from Sir John Slessor) and the New Zealand Committee have stated their complete confidence in Bunny and any decisions he will make and, as Bunny intimated in his reply, that should be the end of that and Ed has been asked to leave decisions concerning the trans-polar journey to Bunny.

There is pretty strong feeling here of 'to Hell with Ed' (and worse) and wish we'd never heard of the man. I have always felt that trouble of some nature would come of him.

We were all pleased a few days ago when Massey-Harris-Ferguson sent congratulations to Bunny for his brilliant leadership on Ed's reaching the South Pole with [the] 'Fergies'.

Wednesday 8 January, 1958
... We did our thirty miles today finishing at about 2120hrs. I was determined to be up and drive by halfway through the afternoon. I was feeling pretty fit again. What nearly made me hand over to Allan was an early stretch of most dreadful close-packed heavy

sastrugi. Luckily it was all over in about three miles and we got onto, not ideal, but pretty good going.

After the first three miles Geoff was in a spot of trouble with a broken A-frame... We were right by, having fuel troubles, so were able to assist in rigging up a wire tow rope...

The dog teams find it tiring with thirty miles each day but they are doing well. I'm not surprised it is thought a one pound block of Pemmican per day is insufficient for them. No wonder, though tired, with twenty-five miles already done today they had two general fights when starting from a rest to do the last five miles. They must be damned hungry, and tired, to be that irritable.

Peter, the New Zealand party radio man, staying on in the caboose at the South Pole to deal with our [radio] traffic, has sent a personal note to Bunny to say he is not of the same mind as the others, and will, if required, accompany us all the way.

Ed is not now going to fly to the Pole to discuss the situation with Bunny, but will fly to D700 to meet him. Bunny's recent message to the Committee suggested Ed and his party might return to New Zealand without waiting for us as their presence would be only helpful rather than essential...

Thursday 9 January, 1958

... A satisfactory day, I should say. It was planned to make it a maintenance day up till 2 p.m.; as in all undertakings in this cold white world, it took a little longer...

We got some work done though and it was a very fine day for it. Sunny with only a slight north-east breeze. Quite a change. Hal had rigged up a set-piece of anemometers and had obtained a 15 metre core, leaving the hole for Geoff's seismic work this morning. Hal was crunching around outside till the early hours. Various other instruments were out including Hannes's flux plate.

While these sciences were in progress, Geoff set out his geo-phones and had two very nice bangs at 25 feet which shot ex-tremely high and straight columns of snow into the air. I tried to photograph one but was stuck at the end of the film...[97]

---

[97] Pratt used his geophones to monitor the energy waves generated by controlled explosions and reflected by the subsurface geology. In a manner similar to echolocation, this process enabled him to calculate the thickness of the ice. Undertaking a series of seismic shots at regular

We had a pretty good journey of twenty miles, mostly over quite good surfaces. We were over medium and heavy sastrugi to start with and by two miles later it had got thicker and was very bad and heavy. At five miles was the cairn built by the dog teams which left us this morning (with a couple of fights of course) and a mile past that the going got better. Another mile on and we were travelling over light sastrugi and light whale backs fairly comfortably at about 4-5 m.p.h. From then on the going improved a lot and it became pretty smooth with only light whale-backs with soft snow between. We did very nicely and caught up with the dogs and Ken and Jon's tent at twenty miles at 2120hrs GMT. It's still a lovely day and only a light breeze with almost no drift all afternoon until at present (0030hrs) a very fine snow crystal falling like tiny floating ice flakes.

Geoff will do a seismic station here tomorrow morning and then we hope to do another thirty miles over smooth surfaces. His last ice depth (this morning) showed roughly 2000 metres which leaves several hundred to 1000 feet of land underneath it above sea level...

At this point, assuming we can now take on its sledge load of petrol, we abandon Wrack-and-Ruin whose main fault lies in her incurable thirst for engine oil.

Late telegram from Enid – sailing [for New Zealand on] 17th January, 1958...

Friday 10 January, 1958
Turned out to be rather a long day where I had at one time hopes of camping at a reasonable hour.

Fortunately, I over-slept this morning – not having heard the alarm clock, (after taking Horlicks!) and didn't wake up till 9.40 a.m. or nearly two hours after I should have woken up to make breakfast. We went without breakfast, though we weren't late as seismic still had to be done and some slow people were still pottering around lashing bits and pieces on sledges...

We got away at 1235hrs while Hal, David Pratt and Geoff lagged behind. After seven miles Bunny stopped to wait for them while David Stratton took a shot. We were having a bit of a rough

---

intervals during the traverse was vital in proving that Antarctica is a single land mass and not a collection of islands.

wind, probably around 25 knots with -24°C (low for our journey so far). Anyway, the change was much noticed and everyone felt cold.

After our first eight miles we started into some medium sastrugi which quickly changed to heavy stuff and pretty closely formed. Three miles of this rough going gave way to smooth hard dunes and a mile or so later we were entertained with a new interest in travel. The smooth hard dunes turned into huge smooth hummock dunes and were closely knit. It reminded me of the Britannia Glacier[98] *(or any other steep glacier wedging down between mountains in polar areas). This, after a short time became mixed with heavy sastrugi and thank goodness, three quarters [of a] mile of it was all we got, the surface changing to fairly good going quite suddenly and then it was only medium sastrugi...*

After doing fifteen miles we caught up with the dogs who had left about two hours before us. The strong wind and low ground drift were still going and it wasn't very nice outside. I wish it could be the worst we shall get. I'm expecting strong winds and -40s°C the other side – and even lower temperatures.

We went on another six miles to make 30.3 today and camped about 2205 hours.

During the run Hal's Fire Engine, as I call Weasel B, was getting rid of a lot of oil, having had four pints in about fifteen miles. I was able to locate a doubtful pipe connection and tighten it way down under the exhaust manifold where my hand could only just reach. It seems to have done the job. A lot depends on these things in the decision about which Weasel to abandon. We were to have dropped Wrack-and-Ruin last night but couldn't take on its fuel load. So it was to be dropped tonight. However, Fire Engine seems such a shoddy thing that it is thought better to take both on a bit longer in case one develops a bad fault. At present the old Wrack-and-Ruin would stay with us if its oil consumption wasn't so high...

Saturday 11 January, 1958

Dreadful weather. Last night's wind increased during the night and brought a northerly blizzard with it, so that we had nothing to do but stay in our tents.

---

[98] The Britannia Glacier lies between Ymer Nunatak and the northern end of main Queen Louise Land, Greenland.

At about 3 p.m. it started to let up a little and the clouds began to break, so we were able to start packing up at 4 p.m. Tents, vehicles and sledges had got well drifted up and thick snow filled every gap between stores on the sledges. Some had got inside my Sno-Cat through driver's and rear door and through windows along the left side, which faced the wind. Some had got all over the engine because I had forgotten to cover it in under the bonnet with sacking. But none of it was too bad...

We eventually got away about 1815hrs and Bunny and David Stratton had been round re-fuelling the Sno-Cats, which was jolly fine of them... We fitted 8000 feet jets to the Sno-Cat carburettors as we attained something over that height yesterday.

We had sunny weather to start with but clouds and fog later accumulated to north-east and spread along that horizon to south-east. By that time we had gone up a hill and were in time to meet the fog as it came over. Then it cleared for a short while and then once more enveloped us, soon to bring light snow as well and the wind began to increase.

Then Bunny had the inside of his carburettor iced up so we all stopped. When they went off again Ralph had a radio schedule with Peter at the South Pole so we remained behind in fog, wind, and snow for twenty minutes. We couldn't see the others and we could hardly make out their tracks, when quite suddenly, there they all were, just ahead, with tents up, only a quarter mile from where we had all stopped. It was the right thing to do for very soon our second blizzard had started only seven hours after the first one had ended. The wind now is howling past the Sno-Cat and through its aerial, and the tent walls and door flap violently in and out with a noise like distant thunder. Inside the Sno-Cat the wind can be felt to rock its body.

As to the surface, well, we only managed to do 15.1 miles and it started off promisingly with fairly smooth going. After three miles we relieved Jon of some of his sledge load as his team of eight huskies weren't doing very well. The altitude must make a great difference to them. Poor old Ivik who always used to look very much the King dog now looks sick, thin and scrawny. Soft old Bouncer has got bad tempered and several others don't look the same dogs. Young Marø still looks fit and well and so do some of the others, but on the whole none pulled as well as they used to and all are a bit done up. We hope they will be flown out at the Pole...

Sunday 12 January, 1958

We woke up with the northerly blizzard still blowing, so not many were astir.

Hal [had] stayed up till 3 a.m. to do some glaciology and took 2½ hours to core down to eleven metres… He didn't get to bed till 4 a.m. and was up again at 8 a.m. to take temperature readings. Ralph was out at about 10 a.m. and wrote down some measurements for Hal's Rammsonde, while Geoff and Hannes got seismic work going…

At about 1300hrs the wind eased and about an hour later extra faces began to appear and the plan was sent round to be ready to move in about a quarter hour. I dug out my sledges and the tent was packed up and I moved out of my drift half an hour later.

It wasn't taken very kindly when I invited one or two to warm up their engines while they packed tents away. I offered to help pack Geoff's tent while he started his engine but he said he wouldn't be ready for at least an hour and a half… I dug out his sledges and Sno-Cat and also helped on someone else's sledge.

Well, we moved at 1625hrs GMT, five and a half hours after the blizzard had stopped! BNGE was never like this!

It continued to snow lightly. We had hard going through deep soft snow over heavy sastrugi, so there was much low gear work… We have done 15.9 miles…

Monday 13 January, 1958

Unfortunate day of illnesses which prevented us doing our thirty miles in good time…

We started at 1200hrs, though Bunny went off about 1030 a.m. expecting Hal and Geoff to follow after. David Pratt, George and I were to remain while David and I fixed a new right-hand rear inner bogie wheel and a new screwed pin through the yoke bogie arm. Something held Geoff up for about an hour and a quarter, while Hal was held up with Allan repacking his Nansen dog sledge of medical gear which Hal draws along behind his Maudheim. George spent the time re-lashing his sledge of drums – three of which he'd used instead of using it off the Sno-Cat sledges as he should have done. He no doubt wishes to make his own load light. The Weasels are supposed to keep as much load on as possible in order to help the Sno-Cats with their loads as they must go the full distance. I am drawing three sledges while George should have twelve drums instead of the eight he now has.

After I had gone 3.2 miles over pretty rough going I discovered I had lost my third sledge and had to go back a mile to collect it from David Pratt who had started dragging it along on a nylon rope.

We had been going slightly uphill and then it steepened and at the same time we started losing most of the heavy sastrugi... It was a seven mile uphill climb all told. After 3.5 miles we stopped to pick up Ken who was ill with vomiting and diarrhoea.

George took his dogs and Ralph took George's Weasel and we came on with my Red Cross bus carrying Ken stretched out in the back with a plastic wash bowl beside him. He was sick five times and had to get out three times. He was quite ill, alright.

The sastrugi got heavier and thicker so I had to go very slowly and carefully. After five miles the sastrugi was really heavy and close, and Ken was very thankful to learn, when I got up with Bunny who had stopped, that we were to camp as Jon was ill too.

We had done 21.5 miles and it was only 6.30 p.m.... Allan is tonight doing the third of four days imping on Bunny and has the two patients to care for as well...

Tuesday 14 January, 1958

... [Weasel B] was abandoned and good riddance to a huge waste of Expedition money on a junk box. It had run a big-end. For some days it has not been decided which Weasel to abandon, so this has decided it quite definitely. Hal is quite glad, for it has always been a lot of trouble to him and also to us on repairs of it. Hal will now be taking over Wrack-and-Ruin...

Our journey today slow, laborious and short, being only 10.4 miles to where we stopped at about 3 p.m. It was mixed going, with first, 2.4 miles to get out of the heavy sastrugi, then, as we got a bit further up the slight hill, it got smoother. After 7.7 miles from the heavy sastrugi it was almost smooth and I was able to get into third gear. After 0.3 miles we stopped and this is where we camp...

Wednesday 15 January, 1958

Thank goodness we've managed to do thirty miles at last, although for the first part I had my doubts about it happening.

We delayed again getting away in the morning, but this was mostly due to packing gear away that had come out of Weasel B and off its sledge. Hal had all his glaciological equipment to stow away in Wrack-and-Ruin and on his sledge.

We abandoned a Nansen sledge that had been towed and also a Maudheim propped up against eight empty drums, plus several boxes of Weasel spares. The sturdily constructed Maudheim was a skeleton when we left it for we had had a couple of strong cross-members and all the longitudinal members off it.

We got away at 1230hrs with Hal having taken over Wrack-and-Ruin. Jon was still a convalescent in the back of my Sno-Cat and Ken had a few hours with his team before getting back to the comfort of Bunny's Sno-Cat. So David Stratton and George have had the dogs. George gets in a terrible state with his skis and gets dragged along on his rear, so mostly he sits on the sledge.

Hal had a bit of trouble getting used to his new vehicle although luckily we started in light sastrugi – almost smooth. After 3.4 miles we got light sastrugi and 4.7 miles on we had medium sastrugi mixing in. Very soon the medium sastrugi became thicker and it remained like that for nineteen miles when we started up the gentle foot of a steepish hill. Half mile on the medium sastrugi got a bit rougher and turned into heavy stuff. One and half miles further up the hill it was quite heavy sastrugi where we stopped for camp after 29.9 miles.

With the altitude now over 9000 feet we have loss of power and vapour locks[99] in the fuel lines. If I stop I either have to switch off both engine and fuel or else keep the engine running fast...

The two dog teams have kept up with the slow moving vehicles over this bumpy stuff. Pity is, if we do get one hundred miles good going to the Pole, our length of daily travel will be limited by the dog's capacity for travel over thirty or forty miles in a day in order to reach the Pole on 18th January (my birthday). I hope we shall be there on 19th, though. Admiral Dufek wants to fly to the Pole to meet Bunny...

We got in at 2245hrs so now, after having made and eaten supper and prepared for tomorrow's meals and written this, the time is 0140hrs. Outside, we've lost today's sunshine, though we started in thick cloud and we've got pretty nearly a whiteout, with fog-like cloud everywhere...

Tonight Hal took some photos in Kodachrome of me, my Sno-Cat and its nameplate. Should get a few mayoral dinners on that in Kent! ...

---

[99] At very high altitude liquid fuel can turn to vapour causing vapour lock. This can result in loss of power or stalling

Thursday 16 January, 1958

I'm afraid we certainly won't get to the Pole on 17th and nor on my birthday, but there is a good chance of getting there on 19th January.

We didn't start away till 1425hrs this morning, but of course Geoff had to do his seismic; on top of that, he and Hannes don't seem to know a very severe season will start before we can get to the other side. I don't think anyone tries properly to get a move on except me. Even a suggestion to Bunny this morning that the vehicles push on and leave the dogs to catch up on one day's run only, wasn't accepted. My point was that we'd have one day earlier to start vehicle repairs. He thought it would mean we would be there an extra day, whereas we would be leaving a day earlier.

While Geoff did his seismic shoot, David Pratt changed his fan and I changed the thermostat on Wrack-and-Ruin and put in an 8000 to 12,000 feet altitude jet.

We had medium sastrugi for the first three miles with a long levelling out on the top of the hill. There was another rise to south-east of us. We got mostly light sastrugi with some medium and after three miles, I found I'd lost my third sledge again, half [a] mile back. At this point I had to fix up my double safety steel rope from under the sledges to use as a tow rope between first and second sledges as one side of the hairpin under number two sledge had snapped.

Then a whiteout came on and I followed the trail of the others till I had them in view again. After about four miles it began to feel pretty smooth. I couldn't see what the surface was like. Two and a half miles on it began to feel a bit bumpy and I was obviously going over medium sastrugi now and again although I couldn't see it. Another two miles and the fog came on denser, so that Wrack-and-Ruin and David Pratt were lost in it behind me, a mile back. Hal had run into an enormous sastrugi and his sledge was partly buried in it, so Allan, from David Pratt's Sno-Cat, was digging him out when I passed. I made for the vague shapes of Rock 'n Roll and the two dog teams until I caught up with them as Bunny had stopped to tighten his front steering rod nut.

Here it was decided to camp as time was 2100hrs and visibility extremely poor, having done nineteen miles. I carried on to do a modification to Bunny's steering platform and nut. I made and fitted a plate to stop the nut turning...

We are now about 88°, 45min south and have eighty-five miles to go to the South Pole.

Admiral Dufek arrived today in McMurdo Sound from New Zealand and hopes to meet Bunny on 18th or 19th when we arrive.

John says it won't be possible to land on or take off from the plateau after mid-February and Slessor recommends four dog teams be at Depot 700 in case vehicles breakdown or other trouble. Decisions taken by Bunny will be backed by the Committee. The dogs will be flown out from the Pole by two special American aircraft flights and they ask for one dog handler with each nine dogs. I am glad about this…

Friday 17 January, 1958
Well, we've done our thirty miles today, as near as dammit.

We started at 9.30, being outside at 8 a.m.… I'd only gone half a mile when I lost my rear sledge again. This time the wire rope had broken and we had to Bulldog grip it together again. We had pretty good weather to start with and light sastrugi with some medium sastrugi. At 1300hrs GMT we went into fog after having done thirteen miles. Due to very poor visibility Bunny stopped after further two miles to wait for everyone to collect together again. This was from 1350hrs to 1420hrs GMT. Wrack-and-Ruin wasn't pulling too well, so his two drums of fuel were pumped into Geoff's front sledge drums. We got going again at 1450hrs (with Hal taking a dog team, as both Allan and David Stratton had started their turn of tummy trouble. Allan lay in the back of my Sno-Cat and David in Bunny's)…

We stopped again after 4.9 miles and waited for everyone to collect together and then moved off at 1620hrs. At 1700hrs the cloud and fog were clearing and the sun was coming out, so everything was much cheerier. Luckily we had only light sastrugi in the fog, but occasionally we ran into a medium one… Our position is 89°, 12' south and we have now fifty-six miles to the Pole.

Geoff and Hannes have laid out the seismic spread ready for the morning and Hal, with assistance, has cored down to eleven metres, which is some job.

I sorted out some clean underwear for 'my shower at the Pole' and had a wash to celebrate my birthday tomorrow. Also cleaned my teeth and wrote a letter to Enid.

At the Pole, Peter Mulgrew says he has already received congratulatory telegrams for us 'on reaching the Pole'. For the

19th, a plane flies to the Pole with Admiral Dufek, nine reporters, Ed, John Claydon and some others...

Heard Donald Milner's BBC overseas programme on the Expedition journey so far, Ed's side, the difference of opinions, the telegrams concerning it, Sir John Slessor on that topic and Edward Shackleton[100] on our future prospects. A very fine programme I thought...

Saturday 18 January, 1958
Ah! Another thirty miles – for my birthday...

At about 0810hrs GMT we heard the sound of aircraft engines and we both rushed to the door to see who. There were two very sleek looking black planes with orange tails and wing tips with beautiful sounding engines, and they came over us from the south, one after the other. They were two American planes, P2V Neptunes.

All on the passenger list were there: Admiral Dufek, Ed, nine reporters, John Lewis... George came out of the next tent presently and waved. I suggested he get his cine camera but he said, 'There's no great point in it'. What a beetle brain! When it was almost too late he decided to take film. I had reminded him that this was polar history, and marked a point in our progress. By this time the people in the planes had learned that it was our early morning as opposed to their evening, so perhaps that's why they circled us at a distance, so George had lost close views with a foreground of tents and vehicles...

We got away, in good weather for a change, at 1230hrs... After today's thirty miles, we are camped at 89°, 39' south (approximately 30° west) and have twenty-five miles to go to the South Pole...

My batteries have been so flat and cold today that three times I had to use the jumper lead to David Pratt's Cat. The mighty radio schedules thump my batteries badly and they won't take even a fairly decent charge while they are cold. Sometimes I feel that I could seriously sabotage the radio set. Also, I had a dynamo belt break. But I didn't lose my rear sledge today. George has got along a lot better today with his ignition done up with new plugs. Pity he gets fed up with things. Doesn't want the Weasel now and tries to get rid of it. Poor old Hal was expected to drive it today after working late last night and being up doing a Rammsonde before

---

[100] Younger son of Sir Ernest Shackleton, and a keen supporter of the TAE.

George had breakfast. This goes on at each camp, so of course Hal needs a bit of a 'zizz' during the day. Similarly, Hannes drives for Geoff when they've worked late putting out the seismic spread and been up 'fairly early' to do the shot. George gets enthusiastic about a novelty but has no exuberant stamina for a long drudge of a job. He understandably feels it is boring just sitting on your arse all the way – or something like that!

I took much pleasure in searching out and reading Enid's birthday letter for me. Poor girl, in October 1956 she was naive enough to write of my birthday – 'I should imagine you are very near to the end of the Crossing'.

The next letter, though (poor Enid must have believed it would have been read before my birthday one), is for when I get to the South Pole, which will be tomorrow...

I had a small bottle of Napoleon brandy from Surrey Tavern which I shared... I also have a bottle of whisky left! David Pratt gave me some Hong Kong Young Stem Ginger, Ralph a tin of Player's (a luxury!) and David Stratton a rubber mouse, which I think I shall mount on the vehicle nameplate.

I made a miniature mast for my miniature Union Jack which I can mount in the bonnet rubber bumper that I recently fitted. This was done tonight ready for tomorrow's entry into South Pole Station. Bunny won't fly the official Union Jack out of political respect, though he sees no objection to personal flags of New Zealand, Australia, S. Africa, Bristol, etc. being flown.

Admiral Dufek, Dr Houk,[101] Ed, Peter [Mulgrew] and Cdr McBane[102] will meet us in their Weasel on the ten mile staked route to escort us in and a Press Conference will be held 'in the hall' shortly afterwards. Then we have showers, then a meal. Peter has been sorting our mail ready for us and has a whole heap of congratulatory telegrams and some more to come from Scott Base.

Minimum [temperature] -24°C...

---

[101] Lieutenant Vernon N. Houk, of the US Navy, was the South Pole Station medical officer and the officer-in-charge there for the 1958 winter.
[102] McBane served with the US Naval Construction Battalions, or Seabees, during Operation Deep Freeze.

Sunday 19 and Monday 20 January, 1958

Actually today is 26th January! And I'm trying to catch up on my diary. Not an easy thing to do on such a journey and especially so when it involves several days at the South Pole Station.

Well, we started off with twenty-five miles to go to get to the Pole. We left at 1345hrs GMT and went slightly uphill over light sastrugi. After twelve miles we went slightly downhill and then slightly uphill again after 1.7 miles. After another 1.4 miles we stopped. We had gone twenty-five miles... From the roofs of the Sno-Cats we could just see, (but with glasses quite clearly), the South Pole Station about 150° and probably eight miles away. We had been asked to come in along the ten mile marked route, but we had missed it, having come too far west.

Our object was to go east till we met the cairn or the marked route. The cairn could just be seen through glasses a long way off. We altered course from 176°M (vehicle compass) to about 120° up a slight rise. After 1.4 miles we stopped to view cairn and South Pole Station. Again we altered course to the cairn on 56°, and again altered course to 100° to the cairn. After six miles from when we first saw the South Pole Station we stopped to view cairn at about 70° about a mile or more away. A mile on we came to the marked route and turned towards the South Pole. After 4.6 miles we stopped in order to all collect together. Soon we came across Weasel tracks which had come up the route, turned west to intercept us and had then turned back. We had seen the Weasels coming across to us a long way off.

A few miles on we could see the station and about twenty-five people lined up waiting. We had to keep together and arrive to-gether and George had to keep close to Bunny so as to hop out and take film. So after 2.2 miles from the Weasel's tracks turning back, we stopped to wait for George who had got a bit behind. Then we started on our entry in funereal fashion, doing about 2 m.p.h. with even the dogs strolling. Jon's team were so whacked that they were having their sledge pulled for them while they quietly walked along in their traces...

We finally pulled up in a bundle with Press and cameras surrounding Bunny's Sno-Cat, the rest being ignored. After some time of this we were conducted to a parking place where we drew up abreast and sorted ourselves out.

We were astonished to see the size of the place which was certainly nothing like a hut. It was several huts, all covered over with wire mesh and canvas supported by beams and trusses. We were delighted to learn that we were to eat and sleep there without the necessity of erecting our tents. We were also offered a hot shower and a meal was ready to be served when we were ready too. At this meal we had all the reporters and photographers – about ten of them. We were twelve and there are eighteen people on the station. The reporters, Admiral Dufek, Ed and Commander McBane were to go back [to McMurdo Sound] that night... after all the reporters were gone we were to have a drink.

Little did we think what delay there would be. I can't remember any times, but it must have been pretty late when the P2V was getting ready to take off and nearly everyone was out to see its departure with JATO (Jet Assisted Take-Off). Sixteen bottles [were] strapped around the aircraft – necessary at high altitude...

Everyone had clambered aboard for the warm-up and I was going about half [a] mile up the run-way to photograph the plane's approach with JATO bottles burning... It took fifteen minutes to get up to a likely spot where Jim (James Burnham)[103] had taken George and here we waited while the plane still warmed up. When it started up the snow runway, (kept smooth and clear by a D2 with wide tracks and a D4 engine)[104] it got all it could from its two engines before firing its JATO. Only eight jets went off and the plane leapt ahead of a huge swirling storm of smoke and drift – straight off the runway to the left of the marker flags.

It came back down the runway and then turned round into its original site. I guess it took about three quarters of an hour to fix on four more JATO bottles and warm up again, but I didn't trouble to walk up to take photos again.

Of the reporters I remember, there was a pleasant chap, [Stuart] Heydinger, photographer of The Times, *[Douglas] McKenzie Associated Press, New Zealand, and also supplying* The Times, *Noel Barber... of the Daily Mail, [Bertram] Jones of the Daily Express who Peter Mulgrew told [us] was a rotten so-and-so for trying to stir up trouble in his press message. He had written the last part of his message about Fuchs and Hillary who were sitting at one end of the table opposite each other, not smiling and not saying much to each other. After Peter told him, with other*

---

[103] James B. Burnham, American ionosphere physicist who wintered at the South Pole station in 1958 and 1961.
[104] D2: a tractor manufactured by Caterpillar Inc.

reporters present, what he thought of him, he asked Ed to speak to him too. Ed did and Jones asked for his press message back to amend the last paragraph. It had already been sent, so he sent another short message to amend the last paragraph...

The angry confrontation with Bertram Jones of the *Daily Express* indicates that, no matter what he might think of Fuchs privately, at this stage of the expedition Hillary was still willing to paint a picture of unity for the world's press. In his diary, however, he admitted that his return to the Pole to meet Fuchs had been the result of 'some fatherly advice' from the diplomatic Admiral Dufek and that he considered the trip to be 'a nuisance!'[105] For his part, Fuchs greeted his lieutenant in a very civil manner and when asked by journalists about Hillary's dash for the Pole, he played it down, even going so far as to call it a 'jolly good show'.[106] In reality, it seems highly improbable that either man was looking forward to sharing the cab of a Sno-Cat during the onward journey to the Ross Sea.

The plane, being ready to take off again, once more tried. It roared up the runway, fired its JATO bottles, sent up a huge whirl of smoke and drift with the plane glowing through its thick dark shroud from JATO flames, but it didn't get off. It came back, but this time there were no spare JATO bottles. He tried taking off with his twin engines and twin jets, but couldn't. Only thing to do was to wait for the second P2V to arrive with a load of JATO bottles. Originally there had been two P2Vs but the other one had to turn back with engine trouble.

Everyone came back into the mess where some Bourbon was already well underway. Admiral Dufek, just came back in, clapped me on the shoulder and wished me Happy New Year. Didn't seem at all perturbed. The second plane arrived with the JATO bottles and I should think it was around 4.30 a.m. (p.m. in GMT) that both planes got away. I wasn't out there, but I heard them.

Something funny [has] happened with the time around here. We had been working on GMT but now we were going ahead twelve hours. Our midnight at the Pole Station on our arrival day was their midday for 20th January, so we stayed up to get our hours in

---

[105] Hillary, diary, quoted in Haddelsey, *Shackleton's Dream*, p. 225.
[106] *Daily Express*, 21 January 1958.

line with theirs... Consequently, we got no sleep on what would, as previously, have been our night time. We had arrived at Amundsen-Scott Base around 0130... so there had been a good many hours between our arrival and the press departure about seventeen hours later...

The shower was wonderful and afterwards David Stratton and I bundled our clothes into a washing machine and made a helluver mess several times. By the time Geoff came along and knocked over an open packet of 'Tide' [soap powder] into all the water on the floor we were beyond caring anyway.

When the planes had gone it was well into 21st January – and their night time. Far from having an early night we had stayed up through our own normal night and mostly through our following day, which was their normal night. I think I got to bed about 5 a.m. local time.

Tuesday 21 January, 1958
I've now got myself into 21st January, I think, and this is where we tried to get down to some work.

I started unloading my three sledges to make up loads on two. I was able to get rid of five empty drums so it looked promising. Ken and Jon carried on with the job for me while I serviced the Sno-Cat. This kept me going till fairly late in -27°C and a bit of a wind. The others had gone to the mess hall to see a terribly corny film about Red Indians, while David Pratt was repairing A-frames and had gone onto arc-welding battery pads...

Wednesday 22 January, 1958
... I'm not sure about today, but I know the Station gave us a party, starting at 5.30pm.

I believe it was yesterday that a plane (a different sort to the P2Vs) had taken off to come and collect the dogs. It had developed an oil leak and had been forced to land in heavy sastrugi. In doing so it had crumpled up its undercarriage and another plane came out to assess damage and take back the people on board. We heard later that the damaged plane is probably a 'write-off'.

In the morning I took off my badly buckled 'A' frame and started straightening it in the workshop... In the afternoon for about one and [a] half hours some of us were out collecting snow shovelled into parachute bags... As required it is emptied down a short chute into a tank where the generator exhaust pipes run to melt it. Then I

258

got back to my 'A' frame and fitted it to its attaching arms and cut a beam of elm (from the way back abandoned Maudheim) to fit between the 'A' frame and stop it buckling inwards. I had to leave it now because of our party.

Everyone was washed and spruced up and started off with Bourbon, fruit juice, orange peel and ice. With thirty-one of us (including Peter Mulgrew who missed the plane earlier on) in the mess hall, it was comfortably packed. Some, of course, came and went from their radio and scientific jobs. Dr Houk and Major Mogensen[107] gave speeches and so did Bunny. He later produced an old flag in blue with white cross of St. Andrew and white lettering of Bruce's expedition in the Antarctic with Scottish National Antarctic Expedition 1901-1903. It is rather fragile now and parts have been skilfully backed. Bunny also produced R. F. Scott's chronometer (Smith's) which the makers had asked him to carry across. Unfortunately Bunny fell on it during crevasse prodding and it hasn't gone since. He also showed the Queen's autographed photo. Many people had cameras, cine cameras and flash and Major Mogensen had a very small tape recorder.

After the dinner I helped wash up and then we had a film, The Man Who Came to Dinner.[108] *We all sat around gossiping and drinking lots of coffee, smoking cigars and enjoying small bottles of medical brandy, which I believe Admiral Dufek had left for us.*

Eventually, apart from the night staff, only Dr Houk, David Stratton, David Pratt and myself were left talking... I didn't get to bed till 6 a.m. and consequently didn't get up till 11 a.m.

Thursday 23 January, 1958

Big day of disappointing work. The weather, too, turned nasty with wind and drift. Bunny was anxious to get away and David Pratt and I had a lot of work to do on battery heating systems...

I was anxious to try welding the aluminium battery pads so I started on that. It looked very promising... But the day was wasted. Even the faces of the pads started to show perforations and when they were welded, others in other areas appeared. We were bound to make copper pipe affairs. We worked on till 5.30 a.m. and then

---

[107] Major Palle 'Mogy' Mogensen, Chief Scientist at the Amundsen-Scott South Polar Station.

[108] *The Man Who Came to Dinner* (1942) was directed by William Keighley and starred Bette Davis, Ann Sheridan and Monty Woolley.

had one fitted in Geoff's and enough for replacing the other pads. We did break off to see a bit of a good film with Allan Ladd... and the break with coffee was welcome. The night-staff generally run one in the early hours of the morning.

Getting to bed at 6 a.m. and being up for breakfast was too much so I lay dozing from 8 a.m. to 9 a.m. From six till seven I didn't sleep and after that, not deeply. I really felt like death.

Friday 24 January, 1958

I still had quite a lot of odd items to pack onto my sledges and into my Sno-Cat and also had to trace an electrical fault on Bunny's Sno-Cat. Nothing at all worked. It was rather a bitter day with a brisk wind and my fingers nipped so frequently that I spent very much more time warming them than on working. The fault was traced to a main wire from the starter solenoid to ammeter so I just duplicated it...

We stayed for lunch, but [by] then we had stayed an extra day and a half with our hosts...

Admiral Dufek had asked us to do a seismic shot at the Pole to compare with the depth found by his seismologist. Geoff said his came out pretty close.

We got away at 0500 GMT which is 5 p.m. local time, and our present working time. There was much waving and photography and sorting ourselves out and picking up ropes dropped by vehicles in front and we had got a sledge caught up in an olive drab parachute which was dragging along behind. Jon got out and put it on my second sledge. The area all round the station to the north and east is littered with parachutes which were used to drop supplies including Caterpillar bulldozers and Weasels.

A few hundred yards on we were at the Pole itself. There are erected the UN flag and the US flag. On the exact spot is a large crate on end, looking rather like the Cenotaph. A great circle of drums (157?) encloses the area. All of our vehicles did a circuit of the drums in order to qualify for the 'Round the World' certificates completed and signed by Dr Houk and presented to each of us at the party. The certificate says 'on his own two legs' but due to urgency we were allowed to drive.

I re-set my trip-reading here from 932.5 miles (from Shackleton) to 000.0. I had driven County of Kent all the way except for the two days when I was sick... At 24.7 miles we camped, time being 1225 GMT...

9

THE FINISH LINE

According to County of Kent's odometer, the Crossing Party had covered 932.5 miles since its departure from Shackleton Base – less than half of the journey's predicted total. However the expedition now had a number of things in its favour that should allow better progress: there were no dogs to limit speed or range as the Americans had offered to fly them out and thereby save them from being destroyed; there were fewer vehicles to maintain, which meant that the engineers could focus their attentions; seismic soundings could now be spaced more widely, with none being needed for the last 290 miles; and the route had already been established and provisioned by Hillary; finally, the last Weasel would soon be abandoned, enabling the Sno-Cats to travel faster.

Nevertheless, Antarctic summers are short and unpredictable – as Captain Scott had discovered to his cost nearly half a century earlier. It was late January, with some 1250 miles to go before Roy and his eleven companions reached Scott Base. Travel in the Antarctic is never free from risk, and the success and safety of the expedition now depended on vehicles which, for all the brilliance of their design, were becoming increasingly decrepit. This reality meant that, while most of the party had been able to enjoy some respite from their labours during the halt at the Pole, this had not been the case for Roy and David Pratt. They had worked throughout the night before they resumed the journey and they felt utterly exhausted.

Despite his tiredness, Roy kept his diary meticulously. Indeed, it may be that the extraordinary level of detail contained in these final entries is, in itself, a product of his exhaustion: knowing that a moment's relaxation could result in a loss of continuity in his scrupulously maintained record, Roy forced himself to make a note of absolutely everything that occurred, no longer able to differentiate between the essential and the purely ephemeral. Only in his haphazard and often inaccurate notations of daily mileages did he allow his guard to slip.

Saturday 25 January, 1958
I was so washed out in the morning that I almost didn't care if I got up or not. Both David Pratt and I, yesterday, were constantly falling asleep over the wheel and once he ran into the Nansen behind my two Maudheims.

I did get out [of the tent] a bit late, and walked straight into a hole being drilled for seismic. This action knocks lots of snow down the hole which makes the drillers angry...

We got going at 0230 GMT... and... stopped after 35.1 miles at 0110hrs in the morning. By the time the tent was up and food cooked and eaten and we were in bed, it was 3 a.m. and I had to wake up at 9 a.m. to cook breakfast...

Sunday 26 January, 1958
I have been getting depressed about not having written my diary since 18th January, so I took a drastic step and plonked Ralph in the driving seat. It's really driving in one gear all the time in a great wide open space.

Anyway, over the hours, I caught up. All I have to do now is catch up on some letters and some sleep rhythm cards.[109] *We've been trying to hustle up our daily progress by not so much waiting when vehicles stop for meteorology, gravity, radio, etc. It is better to let David Pratt or me hang back and then catch up on our own. If the leading vehicles do wait further on it is not necessary to wait till the backward boys are right up and stopped; the others should go on when the catcher-uppers are about half a mile away.*

Another point about making everyone stop is that at this altitude (around 10,000 feet) vapour locks readily occur in fuel systems, so another delay ensues while cooling off. Also, to enable Geoff to get his gravity done without the interference from moving vehicles, those within half a mile of him stop when he puts out a flag. Otherwise he has to sit and wait till other vehicles are all past him by half a mile.

---

[109] Analysis of sleep patterns was a part of Allan Rogers' physiological programme.

We got away at 1140hrs NZ time... and it was quite uneventful. Surface was pretty smooth and we had one part for two or three miles slightly uphill about 1.6 miles after we started.

At 99.6 miles from the Pole, or about forty miles for the day, we camped at 2310...

Minimum [temperature] -28°C...

Monday 27 January, 1958

Pretty good day again for surface and progress. Started 1320hrs (NZ) with pretty smooth going and isolated patches of medium sastrugi. I was able to get into third gear. What a pleasure. We had passed the highest part of something over 10,000 feet.

All uneventful till we'd gone 19.3 miles when, surprise, we saw Ed's abandoned gear about 17° west of our course... All the others had visited it and gone on...[110] *The only thing I collected was a one gallon polythene bottle to put my Imiak in. I have three bottles and now that they are frozen the stuff is forcing out past the corks. My Sno-Cat today, after -29°C for a couple of days, smells like a pub cellar grating in a pavement.*

We moved on without incident, except George lost interest again and was going slowly in first gear, reading a book. This is very wrong because David Pratt or I stay back with any vehicle having cause to delay, especially so in the case of the Weasel as it is more liable to have trouble and frequently gets vapour locks. If he doesn't try it means all have to stop and wait for him and so we lose precious time, miles and patience. Anyway, he was only doing 2 m.p.h. so I got annoyed and pushed off leaving him right behind. Of course, Bunny and everyone else had stopped after doing very well on good surface in third gear. When we got up with the rest, Ralph told of the trouble and why we'd left George. Hal took over the Weasel and followed Ed's tracks, going something like 5-6 m.p.h. so that Bunny could hardly catch up to tell him to stop as we'd done our forty miles... We had been able to follow Ed's tracks all the way from his depot in spite of drifting over.

We stopped at 2430hrs (NZ) after doing 42.2 miles and were 141.8 miles from the South Pole.

---

[110] This equipment had been abandoned by Hillary's party on 31 December 1957. Deep soft snow had seriously hampered his progress, leading him to jettison all but essential items. See Hillary, *No Latitude for Error*, pp. 210-211.

We had heard... that Peter Mulgrew, Griff[111] and the dogs had arrived just after midnight last night...

Tuesday 28 January, 1958
We all had great hopes of a great day today of fifty miles, but a hard blow has been struck against us to prevent it. It may, however, mean a speeding up to Depot 700 but also, it may mean a slowing down.

The seismic spread was all laid out ready and the shot down the hole. There were two misfires so the detonator was replaced. Then Geoff fainted. His face was discoloured and he was carried unconscious to his tent.

David Pratt turfed gear out of his Sno-Cat and rushed over with a light-weight welding oxygen cylinder whilst shouting at me to come. He came round gradually but was far from well and was soon asleep but still has to have oxygen.

Although exhaust fumes come up through his air heater, he hadn't run his engine and he hadn't used his Primus, so I reckoned it was due to a sustained period at high altitude and low oxygen content in the air. We all pant heavily if we move fast or lift any- thing heavy. Even lying in bed I find myself gasping a little and having to take some quick deep breaths to put things right and feel comfortable.

So it seems Geoff is allergic to heights; this being so, he will get worse and possibly suffer a heart attack if he stays. Bunny and Allan decided he would have to be flown out to Scott Base and join us later at Depot 700.

Ralph tried and tried and eventually broke in on a schedule between McMurdo US station and another station. He kept sending the two call signs and 'urgent-medical' until they received him breaking through their schedule. Then, of course, they dropped everything to listen. They were unable to transmit the message to Scott as the telephone line was out of action so a Weasel took it eight miles to Scott Base. I expect a Neptune will come with Griff as our Otter would first have to fly to Shackleton Inlet for fuel,

---

[111] Dr Lewis Griffith Pugh, a British physiologist, had been invited to Scott Base in order to carry out research into carbon monoxide poisoning in huts and tents, the adaptation to and tolerance of cold, and the warming effect of solar radiation. He had previously served as physiologist on the 1953 Everest Expedition.

while a Neptune carries plenty for the round trip and had JATO for take-off at high altitude.

Allan will probably do the seismic shoot here if Geoff is able to direct the business. Whether Allan will continue seismic stations to Depot 700 I don't know – nor about the gravity.

Writing this two days later; I know the answers to above questions.

We did get away, (but I had a much more sensible plan) at 2100 hours! We were able to follow Ed's tracks still, over light to near medium sastrugi in third gear all the way.

After 9.2 miles we had an air drop... We expected them about 1045hrs or after and SARAH[112] was put on to guide the Neptunes to us. For some time we could talk to McMurdo Sound and hear the aircraft... but the aircraft were not hearing us too well. Then, almost suddenly, the aircraft could hear us a lot more plainly and louder and one pilot (Capt. Coley) said they must be getting nearer. We had about 7/8 cloud around 700 feet so they hadn't much chance of seeing us. They were unable to pick up our SARAH beacon but suddenly Capt. Coley said, 'I've got you. You are right ahead, about ten miles away.' He had flown dead on to us from the position information we had given and had at last picked us up with his radar.

First one and then the other plane flew dead overhead but we didn't see a sign of each other because of the cloud. Ralph, on the radio said, 'You've just flown right over the top of us.' Having given them an estimate of the cloud height they came in under it and did a few circles while Griff and Allan talked. Then one of them flew over and dropped a parachute and a large oxygen bottle and then again a second one. Then they dropped a minute parachute with a box containing spare radio crystals for Ralph... This operation was going on from 11 p.m. to 1 a.m. local, including checking the state of the items. We moved on, but only 0.9 miles, when fog came on, so we camped.

I had Geoff in the back of course and he was able personally to thank the pilots over the radio. At camping, I had to do a circuit of the area in order to arrive with the back of County of Kent outside his tent door. With his bedding inside he had to be lifted bodily out

---

[112] SARAH: Search-And-Rescue-And-Homing beacon. SARAH had also been used during the search for Haslop and Rogers when their Auster was downed during the flight to Halley Bay in September 1957.

(200lbs) in his sleeping bag and hard board (Bofors) stretcher. Then one of the huge green oxygen cylinders was laid outside the tent and a channel dug for the pipe to go under the tent wall. Inside, Geoff lies with his head near the doorway and wears the oxygen mask.

Anyway, we did only 10.3 miles and wasted a lot of sleep time. If we had stayed put we could have had a long night's sleep and started early, dispensing thereby of one camp site which uses up about five hours in camping, cooking, decamping and packing sledges and warming up, etc. The other way we lose time, sleep and yet do no more mileage. It angers me because it is so clearly wrong and I don't understand how others don't comprehend it...

Wednesday 29 January, 1958

This morning we were supposed to be out at 1030hrs and apparently everyone was slow except Bunny who must have been in a self-conscious mood over yesterday's farcical waste of time and came round to remind us that the time was twenty-five minutes to eleven. Only 'outside-men' have to get out at the decided time, the day's cook staying in to finish packing and cleaning and making the day's travelling refreshment. I'm afraid a bad mood pervaded the insides of the tents and I was incensed enough to bawl-out some hooliganism (as you might say).

Anyway, as always, we all had ourselves well organised and we were all out and ready in a very short space of time. In fact, Ralph and I were packed up, engine warmed and County of Kent round to pick up Geoff before Bunny and David Stratton had their tent on their sledge. Apparently one or two... made rude remarks to Bunny like, 'Come on, get a move on you lazy b------s' and this was darkly resented. Feeling that it would be overdoing it to go and make more remarks about being all behind I located my whistle in County of Kent and gave a long blast on that.

We had to wait till 1207hrs before moving! An hour's wait! This was largely due to Allan, his patient, the oxygen administration and their tent packing. Allan has mentioned to me that Griff had said that, in his view, Allan's speedy use of oxygen had, undoubtedly saved Geoff's life. Sounds a bit dramatic. Something about cerebral effects had started. David Pratt had, in fact, rushed in with the oxygen from the welding equipment right at the start.

Roy's scepticism regarding the danger of Pratt's condition seems somewhat misplaced – particularly as Griff Pugh was one of the world's foremost experts in the effects of carbon monoxide poisoning in expedition conditions. During the Heroic Era of polar exploration, a number of explorers had come close to being asphyxiated, usually when their hut chimneys became blocked by drift snow, allowing toxic fumes to accumulate. Pratt's poisoning was simply a modern twist on this old problem, his vehicle's heater having pumped carbon monoxide into the enclosed cab. But the danger was no less significant in 1958 than it had been in 1908. In particular, the rarefied atmosphere at high altitude increased the risk of heart failure and brain damage. The swift application of oxygen substantially reduced these risks and Pratt made a full recovery, being able to resume driving in a matter of days.

We started in thick fog over pretty smooth going with light sastrugi in line with our course... After going 10.2 miles we decided to lighten George's Weasel sledge load in order (a) to reduce his vapour locks, and (b) increase our speed. His sledge was too heavily laden at the front too. We each took about 200lbs... From then on we made much better progress doing about 6 m.p.h. instead of 4-4½ m.ph. Also, no vapour locks...

After doing, so far, 34.5 miles we felt it was pretty good and that we would go on, so we re-fuelled. The fog had lifted while we re-lashed George's load twenty four miles back. We went OK too for twenty miles, then George had fuel trouble. He stopped dead... I got air from the system, then his plugs got wet and the carburettor leaked. All these things I looked at and we tried tow-starts. Plugs still wet. It was rather late and we were tired and didn't bother about taking the plugs out again and finding a blow lamp, so David Pratt towed the Weasel behind his two sledges while I towed my two sledges, George's sledge, my dog Nansen sledge and George's Nansen sledge.

George, in an appreciative mood, photographed my train of five sledges...

Thursday 30 January, 1958
Today was a maintenance day and although we had planned to travel as well, we did not as things went on too late, mostly with seismic delays.

On calculating our petrol stock against requirements it was found we would have enough petrol to take Wrack-and-Ruin on to Depot 700 but not sufficient, even with the depot petrol, to keep it running after that. So it was decided to abandon it. So there it stands, about 210 miles from the South Pole...

Friday 31 January, 1958
Our finest day yet. Seventy miles! With pretty good surface, good visibility and no Weasel, nothing can stop us. Hope we are spared serious mechanical failure on the Sno-Cats. I don't think the crevasses some way ahead before Depot 700 can hurt us and we can still do substantial mileage over sastrugi...

Sunday 2 February, 1958
I can't remember much of this morning... We got away at 1305hrs in thick fog which soon became whiteout.

After five miles David Pratt and I... came across Geoff stuck, with his left-hand rear track jammed under the bottom rail... By lifting his A-frame he was able to back far enough to allow the rollers to run into their channel again. Then David and I tensioned both his front tracks, sent him on and started on our own vehicles.

Bunny was a long way ahead. I did both my fronts, then it was schedule time, so I started on the back ones and pressed on to finish them. We were there about three hours. Track adjustment entails bending the track connecting links. Unbelievable.

The need to frequently tighten the links in the Sno-Cats' tracks was a perennial problem for the members of the TAE. In his official account of the expedition, Fuchs would state that 'to tighten all four tracks, 592 steel links had to be bent by hand with a special tool'. The engineer must then 'make, by eye, an equal adjustment all round' with 'no means of bending the links back if one should go too far'. But not to do enough adjustment would mean that 'the operation would have to be begun all over again'.[113]

We got going and after five miles found David Stratton and Bunny working on their l/h front track. When Geoff had caught up with them and told them of his trouble, they had a look at their tracks. There were two broken track bar link pins and they were having

---

[113] Fuchs and Hillary, *The Crossing of Antarctica*, p. 275.

quite a job removing them. It took time but eventually it was all together and being tensioned when another link broke! By now it was 8 p.m. and the sun had at last appeared. Bunny decided to make it a camp...

Tuesday 4 February, 1958
This was our maintenance day and we couldn't have picked a worse one. It was cold, windy and with quite a lot of low drift. Luckily Ken helped and did all the roller greasing and some of the chassis greasing. It was a miserable job for him. We had to heat the grease and grease guns to get them operating. I had the pop-pop in bits to replace the ignition lead and my fingers went through much discomfort: drift got into all the exposed parts and I thought I'd never get it clean. Anyway, it did work alright.

Geoff did seismic...

We got going at 2035hrs in partial whiteout, and after two miles complete whiteout was with us, but luckily it was a pretty smooth surface. At 10 p.m., after a further 2.2 miles, it cleared slightly. We were still going uphill from the previous day. Whiteout came back again and the surface was hard. When it levelled out after 2.4 miles it got bumpier, but this was accentuated by the hardness. A mile on it cleared a bit and we were going slightly downhill and we had low mounds of medium sastrugi in patches.

Four miles on we levelled out with sastrugi the same. 3.3 miles on, the right-hand rear track of Haywire rode under the bottom rail and turned the rail up into a coil about half way back. I had to saw and chisel this away after the Cat had been reversed back onto the rail. Then the track was tensioned and we set off again, three of us, to catch up with Rock 'n Roll. 2.9 miles on I noticed a one foot crevasse opened up by previous vehicles but it was the only one. Then we went downhill over hard surface to camp at 0255hrs (NZ time).

Wednesday 5 February, 1958
A few points of interest of late. On 1st February we learned the joyful news that Admiral Dufek has suggested the USA purchase our Otter for $70,000. That just about scrubs out our present deficit

and still [we have] the book sales and film to come in. It would be nice if we got a bonus one day.[114]

We also learned from Scott Base that the Savoy Hotel had sent a message offering to fly out a full meal to us on arrival at Depot 700. John Lewis replied that it would be a bit difficult cooking a meal in a two-man tent and suggested having it in more convivial surroundings after our return (wives too, I hope!)...

Today we started at 1215hrs over hard surface with large low mounds scalloped by the wind with occasional single, or patches of, heavy or near-heavy hard sastrugi...

After doing seven and half miles we stopped to wonder why we hadn't found Ed's first lot of crevasses. We decided to go on a bit and 3.2 miles later I passed a small crevasse across our route about 4-6 inches wide. 1.5 miles on we altered course at where we thought we were near to Ed's Corner Camp for Depot 700. Then we were crossing medium dunes at about 45°. 2.6 miles on we broke open a crevasse about three feet wide and deep. 0.2 miles further on Rock 'n Roll had stopped on the edge of a twenty-foot-wide crevasse about one and half miles long on the side of a hill across our route.

We decided to camp at 2120hrs after Bunny and David Stratton had prospected ahead and found a lot of wide crevasses across our route and stretching a long way each side. This was the area where Ed had seen 'curious ice knobs'...

The crevasses encountered here were formidable. Ken Blaiklock is reported as saying that some were so wide that a Sno-Cat and its sledges were on the bridge at the same time and that the bridges had sunk to such a degree that the vehicles had to drive down a slope onto the bridge and then up a slope on the far side.[115] In addition, narrow open cracks could be observed between the solid snow

---

[114] The TAE did wind up with a surplus. This money was subsequently transferred to a newly formed organisation, the Trans-Antarctic Association, which still funds Antarctic programmes. See Stephen Hicks, 'The Commonwealth Trans-Antarctic Expedition 1955-58: How the crossing of Antarctica moved New Zealand to recognise its Antarctic heritage and take an equal place among Antarctic nations'. PhD thesis, University of Canterbury, Christchurch, New Zealand, 2015, p. 265.

[115] From a conversation between Ken Blaiklock and Dr Peter Clarkson of the Scott Polar Research Institute.

surface and the bridge. Hillary and his tractor party had crossed these bridges safely some weeks earlier, but Hillary's tractors were far lighter than the giant Sno-Cats.

Meanwhile, the newspapers at home continued to follow proceedings closely, with the much-publicised, if utterly spurious, 'Race to the Pole' now superseded by discussions regarding a 'race to the coast' – a race given the necessary frisson of excitement by the risk that the expedition might not reach McMurdo Sound in time to be relieved by the waiting ship.

Thursday 6 February, 1958
We started over the wide crevasses at 1040hrs leaving Geoff to pack up his seismic gear.

David Pratt's Sno-Cat remained too for both Allan and David were out probing with the rest. They found all the wide crevasses well-filled and solid, though sunken… The only route-finding really necessary was round the curious ice hummocks and ridges and finding suitable slopes down onto the crevasses for some parts of the lips were small cliffs. David went back to bring up his Sno-Cat while we were starting over the crevasses. They didn't catch us up until we came up against the next, different, sort of crevasses…

At this point in the diary Roy lists forty-six crevasses encountered over the next three miles. One he describes as extending 'as far as the eye can see', while another he dismisses as 'only' 25 feet. They surmounted these obstacles 'with no difficulty but plenty of interest', but without finding the safe route established, and supposedly marked, by Hillary.

At 485.8 [miles from the South Pole] we were at the top of the hill looking at [a] downward slope and another rise beyond. In between 479 and 485 we had more frequent medium sastrugi with surface not quite so hard, then we were forced to wind between medium and heavy sastrugi. Then conditions eased and we levelled out.

We had the 1730hrs Scott Base schedule at 485.9 miles and were able to tell them we were over the wide crevasses… At 494.55 miles a six foot crevasse was broken through by Rock 'n Roll but it managed to bump over.

I was directed to a spot which seemed to be narrower and went over. Both front pontoons broke through and so did my rear ones –

heavily, but it crawled out of it alright and I stopped to inspect for damage. I found it too. On the rear steering platform the right-hand spring connecting arm was fractured and bent upwards by the stop on the pontoon.

We stopped there at 1950hrs and I worked on an emergency repair while the rest, except Allan, who lay reading in my Sno-Cat, got scouting ahead and Ralph assisted with my repair. In the meantime Haywire and David Pratt arrived and didn't like the look of our crevasse, so started looking along it to the north for a place to cross. David was about half [a] mile down that way when Haywire returned to say David's rear steering arm, rear swivel ball-pin had sheared. I had just about finished lashing on my cut-to-shape wood block between the axle and steering platform to take the weight of the spring and spring arm, so I was ready to assist...

We unlashed my second sledge to get at the two spare steering arms and removed the left-hand threaded ball-pin. It was decided to leave Haywire and David there to do the repair while we turned south along our crevasse in the hope of picking up Ed's cairned route through. We started at 2340hrs NZ time.

On my compass... we altered course from 220° to 339° at 494.6 miles, turning right. We had long crevasses now on both sides of us, sometimes closing in towards us, but always giving us a fairly decent route through between them. Without a break they continued for 6.2 miles until we decided to camp at 500.8 miles at 0140hrs. We now felt that Ed's route must have been behind us. It had all been a beautiful sunny day.

Friday 7 February, 1958

At 1125hrs we started, making our own course to Depot 700, going east. At 500.9 miles we turned away south from [an] 8-10ft crevasse and followed along for 0.25 mile to cross the crevasse over a strong bridge of mound sastrugi... Then we turned left along the other side of the crevasse before turning right over the next at 501.48 miles, the two crevasses being only one hundred yards apart...

Then at 503.95 miles I stopped to book for Ken's sun-sight as it seemed we were over all the crevasses. Anyway No. 22 of that lot wasn't found and they had been getting less conspicuous by surface indication, though they had got progressively wider, being, in the later ones, up to about fifteen feet of surface indication. We had crossed them all, over the most solid looking mounds of sastrugi while still keeping as well as possible in the general direction of our course. We started away from the area at 1520hrs pretty confident of a crevasse-free run to Depot 700...

We stopped for the Scott Base schedule from 1730 to 1800hrs NZ time and they were very pleased to hear of our progress...

We started up a gentle rise at 523.5 miles, which got slightly steeper with light sastrugi. 0.6 miles on, it got smoother and we had a hill still running along above on our right. David Stratton viewed the distance from his Sno-Cat through binoculars and said we would go on a bit but would do a box search if Depot 700 didn't show soon. We had never doubted his navigation so were a little bemused. At 527.7 miles we stopped almost on the top of our rise to view, 3.3 miles away, two masts sticking up above the brow of our rise. These we could see only through binoculars. Here was Depot 700 very nearly dead ahead.

At 528 we started downhill over medium dunes towards the Depot and we stopped at 531.0 miles at 2125hrs NZ time. Here we straight away had a weather schedule with Hannes and passed it on to Scott Base for their flying use. Unfortunately, although we'd a glorious day of sunshine, Scott Base was having snow.

We had camped and began to wonder by 0130hrs why the other two Sno-Cats hadn't arrived. David Pratt only, at about 0220hrs, turned up to say that Haywire was out of action nineteen miles back with exactly the same trouble as David had had – a broken rear ball-pin! Of course he had no spare.

We had him and Allan in for a cup of tea and talk, so it was about 4 a.m. when we settled down to sleep. Ralph and I had a couple of tots from my bottle of whiskey and also tried the Imiak which had been thawed out on the engine.

As we had approached Depot 700 we could see to the left, about a mile from the depot, a large snow cairn, then half a mile from the depot another cairn, and between that and the depot four drums spaced out. The depot was in two dumps – the old original dump of eight drums rigged with ladders, 20ft length of 8 inch x 8 inch timber and a flag and the new dump of four drums with a yellow wind-sock flying above it. They had left quite a bit of food on the original depot like fresh sliced bacon, chocolate, apple rings, sultanas, soup packets, cigarettes, etc....

The expedition had achieved another major milestone, reaching Depot 700 – the southernmost of Hillary's planned depots. It was here that Hillary was to re-join the party by air.

Saturday 8 February, 1958
I'm writing this on 10th February and this time have no vehicle survey log to help me. I remember that last night I wrote a couple of letters, then twelve pages of diary and after that decided to celebrate our arrival here with four-fifths of a bottle of whiskey I'd saved since last January (it was full till South Pole!)...

David Pratt got away in the afternoon [at] 2.30pm to return to Geoff with the other spare steering rod swivel pin. Otherwise, apart from a bit of sledge unpacking, I don't seem to have done very much. Weather at Scott has been too bad for flying...

I had a good wash in an old large cocoa-tin after getting the water good and hot on the Primus. I set the tin up on my Sno-Cat track out of what little wind there was and in the sunshine washed hands, arms, face, neck and hair. Long before I'd finished drying my face, my hair was cemented with ice and large blobs and icicles festooned the lower areas of my hair. I felt very much better after it, especially as I had trimmed my moustache.

David Pratt got in [bringing] Geoff's Haywire at 6.30 p.m....Poor Geoff had been vomiting and wasn't too well...

Sunday 9 February, 1958
Ralph spoke with Scott at 6 a.m. this morning and found their weather pretty bad and ours pretty good but it was decided to wait till later and see if improvements would come...

I wrote thirteen or fourteen cards or letters and twelve pages in this diary. I had an hour or two [of] sleep in the evening which was very refreshing and I was able to rush off another quick letter to Enid before dressing for the arrival of the Beaver (about 2310hrs NZ time).

John Claydon and Derek Wright were with Ed and they had picked up our SARAH beacon about fifteen miles away... The plane was offloaded and newspapers, magazines and mail were inspected. Ralph and I had John and Derek in our tent for a cup of tea and something to eat, then I helped John refuel and brought the heater over for starting his aircraft in the morning. John had decided to stay overnight for the change and also because they had been flying through eight-eighths cloud a lot of the way up. Ed joined Bunny in his Sno-Cat, together with David Stratton and Hal.

Apparently all Ed's team were not in favour of his ambition to go to the Pole. They all thought his intentions were obvious during his last winter's preparations and even back in New Zealand. I had openly stated the same thing during winter of 1956 in Shackleton – and earned abuse from others. David Pratt said he knew from as far back as the Sno-Cat trials in Norway.

Further, not mentioned in here so far till I heard something more definite, some days ago Ed shot all of our dogs except eight, notwithstanding our desire to have them adopted into zoos or homes if possible, or otherwise to leave them till the last minute. He said they didn't look fit. The rotten self-opinionated louse. It is more unfortunate that the dogs had been adopted by schools and that Admiral Dufek had flown the dogs out to save them from being destroyed at the South Pole and that the RSPCA had offered to pay the cost of the dogs' fares home and in quarantine and then find them homes.

The depots of fuel he was supposed to lay and [is] generally supposed to have laid, were flown in by John Claydon who flew 56,000 miles! The fuel used by Ed to get himself to the South Pole was flown in by John. His survey report of his route, terrain distances, etc. is almost worthless I am told by our navigators; and Ed himself has not known where his crevasse areas are as we have gone along. He's being known as 'Big-Ed'.

Some time ago most of Ed's people went back to New Zealand on the US icebreaker Akto (or something) including our RAF lot except John Lewis. It was thought the US airstrip on the barrier ice might break up so that they could not be flown out later.

Ralph and I got to bed about 4 a.m.

In his autobiography, *View from the Summit,* Hillary would defend his shooting of the dogs on the basis that 'due to agricultural regulations the dogs would never be permitted to return to New Zealand'. He claimed to have lost sleep over the job and blamed Fuchs for not having 'thought of this problem at a much earlier stage instead of leaving the task to me'.[116] Of course, destroying sled dogs that had outlived their usefulness was nothing new, but many of the Crossing Party felt angry at Hillary's decision.

---

[116] Hillary, *View from the Summit* (New York: Pocket Books, 2000), p. 183.

Blaiklock and Stephenson probably had the greatest cause because they had planned to use the huskies to survey the Horlick Mountains the following spring, but, when interviewed half a century later, Roy could still hardly contain his fury over the slaughter.[117]

As for Hillary's survey of the vehicle route, Blaiklock was dismissive: 'Ed could claim that he had proved that the route was passable – but against that he took no trouble, took no survey detail whatsoever; did nothing. He just travelled southwards and that was it. So we didn't actually find his route all the time... there was quite a significant amount where we couldn't find his tracks because they'd faded away and he had no traverse'.[118]

Monday 10 February, 1958
There was a lot of packing-up still to do still this morning... We got away at 1000hrs NZ time... at 1155 hours Rock 'n Roll broke open a crevasse eight feet wide but got itself and sledges over safely. County of Kent turned back to cross further along and got over safely.

After Rock 'n Roll had broken open the crevasse we other vehicles stopped and David Pratt complained of vibrations and grindings. I couldn't see anything while we were stationary except a broken main leaf on his left-hand rear spring. This spring we changed straight away in about one and half hours...

Mileage today thirty-two miles.

Tuesday 11 February, 1958
Seismic in the morning – and it made the most colossal bang. The blast came first, pushing in the tent walls and giving an instan-taneous pressure on the body immediately before the bang arrived. After the local noise had subsided there was a rushing noise through the air like four or five steam trains disappearing into the distance...

They were a bit behind with packing up and Bunny pushed on so I followed leaving David Pratt to accompany Haywire.

We got away at 1245hrs over a fairly hard surface and after one mile we were going up another hill, pretty smooth with some medium sastrugi and dunes. One and half miles on we went

---

[117] Roy Homard interviewed by Stephen Haddelsey, 3 July 2009.
[118] Ken Blaiklock interviewed by Stephen Haddelsey, 1 June 2009.

through some very large dunes and 0.4 miles on I saw three people walking ahead of Rock 'n Roll; Bunny was probably driving while Ed, David Stratton and Hal looked for some of Ed's crevasses – which were non-existent (such was his previous survey – and now trying to guess). We were now going about level with light sastrugi, medium dunes and scattered heavy sastrugi. 0.7 miles from where they started to walk ahead the three of them stopped and got back into Rock 'n Roll...

Haywire [broke] in on the 1730 Scott Base schedule to inform us that David Pratt was in trouble with his steering cross-shaft broken. I turned back with the one spare one leaving my sledges there while Bunny went on. I had to go back 6.3 miles...

The weld between the arms and the shaft had broken allowing the whole thing to collapse and twist. His rear pontoon and axle had swung right round and locked against the rear tow frame. He, Geoff, Hannes and Allan had straightened them by jacking up and swinging the axle. We had the job of fitting the new one. This took about five hours including travelling, mostly due to Tucker's way of fitting things. Allan did a couple of brews in the tent. Ken, Jon and Ralph did my Sno-Cat maintenance...

Another 6.4 miles brought us to my sledges. Here we invest-igated more trouble in David's Sno-Cat. I rode in with him... After a while I came to the conclusion that a grinding noise was due to a broken front output-bearing in his transfer gear case. He remained unconvinced and thought it was in his front left-hand pontoon. Anyway, I went back to my Sno-Cat...

At 632.2 miles (less 12.7 for the recovery job) we came across the abandoned Weasel of Ed's. Before that, however, on the hilltop, after the crevasses, we had a new sensation – one of the great many that travel in the Antarctic can bring. The atmosphere was charged with a hazy dream-like unreal quality by the fog, the smooth white icy areas studded by ice hummocks and pinnacles and a feeling that little moon-men should appear from behind them. It was a grand feeling of adventure and excitement in the unknown. New shapes looming up in the fog with all distance lost in the cloud leaving us in a little moving sphere of near-clarity with an opening right up in to the sky.

We waited at the abandoned Weasel for David to catch us up. We were there an hour before he came. He was sure his pontoon bearings were breaking up and wanted to camp, but I didn't approve of that spot for we were still in cloud with a brisk icy wind bringing along ground drift. The surface was sastrugied, hard and downhill. He agreed to go on a bit. Another 1.4 miles further found us in a much nicer area, so we camped and I said I'd help with the grinding noise tomorrow...

Wednesday 12 February, 1958
... As we didn't get to bed till 7 a.m. we weren't up till 3 p.m.... We learned later that Bunny and Co didn't camp – eighteen miles further on – till 4.30 a.m.

We did a few tests on David's transfer case, but right at the start I said I was 100% sure it was the front output bearing and that I would bet £100.[119] Not taken of course, but later he said he'd pay me eight pints of beer in New Zealand. The subsequent tests showed it to be in the T/case and later, when we had it off, the broken balls could be seen from outside without stripping. It took a long time to remove the old and replace the new, so that it was about 12.30 at 'night' when we jacked in.

We had whiteout with fog and snow and so it was fortunate that we had the repair to do at that time when the other two vehicles, on ahead, were unable to travel for the weather. Also fortunate was the fact that they had maintenance to do anyway and Sno-Cats 'A' and County of Kent had already been done. We understood by radio that the others would wait till we arrived and that they would not want to move anyway if the weather was bad...

Thursday 13 February, 1958
Around 9 a.m. we had fairly decent weather with sunshine but by the time we got on the move at 1100hrs NZ time we had the whiteout with us again. David Pratt's old ruin was alright, so we decided to move on. Bunny had said that if we had any doubts about the vehicle being sound we should go back to [Ed's] Weasel and put the new roller race in the back axle.

We would have liked to have done so but we were anxious to proceed and not anxious to have more Weasel troubles, although it looked to be in very good condition... In fact it would have eased the passenger conditions and been warmer than in the other Sno-

---

[119] An output bearing is a heavy duty bearing installed in the transfer case of a four wheel drive vehicle. The transfer case transfers power to the front and rear axles.

Cats. Mine gets reasonably comfortable after a couple of hours with the blower going...

I had tried to get Haywire on the radio at 10 a.m. but no luck. Scott Base relayed the message to me that they weren't moving with the whiteout but Scott Base couldn't read me, they only heard my carrier. Guess I wasn't properly tuned in. Anyway, we were just ending a couple of days of radio blackout.

In the whiteout it felt that we were going uphill, with fairly soft surface and light sastrugi and some medium dunes.

The Speedo read 633.6 miles when we moved. At 637.7 we started on small crevasses about six inches wide which gradually got up to about five feet. We crossed them all safely but could see where the previous vehicles had broken them open. By 640.5 miles the crevassing had ceased and we'd crossed sixteen of them.

We managed to follow the tracks of the other vehicles all the way in the whiteout and at 650.4 came across a good Weasel track with a flag. It loomed up out of the fog but no sign of the vehicles and camp. There was a grey glare just beyond, however, and this turned out to be the [Midway] camp and cairn only 0.15 miles on...[120]

People emerged unsuitably dressed to greet us. Ed was wearing long johns, shirt hanging outside with a sweater over it. It should make an interesting colour slide if I guessed the exposure correctly. He hurled some invective at me with a big grin...

I didn't hear the New Zealand [radio] tonight but I'm told the repair story of Sno-Cat Able was read out and that County of Kent with Roy Homard had gone to her assistance. Apparently they interrupted the Expedition news item to insert the news flash. They have us on every night in the news, but we rarely think of stopping to hear it.

Friday 14 February, 1958

... Valentine's Day, when I started the day by reading Enid's letter.

We got away at 0930hrs with Bunny, Ed and Hal looking for Ed's old tracks in a whiteout. Some medium sastrugi and dunes for 22 miles, when we started to go downhill to the sunlit plains below.

---

[120] Fuchs recorded the Crossing Party's arrival at Midway Depot, roughly half way between the South Pole and Scott Base, as having occurred on 11 February. See *The Crossing of Antarctica*, p. 282.

Three miles on it was pretty smooth with some light to medium dunes and 2.5 miles further it got level. We altered course... and then I realised we were on Ed's old track again. After doing 50.3 miles for the day we camped at 2240hrs.

Saturday 15 and Sunday 16 February, 1958
Starting at 1330hrs we followed Ed's tracks across some very flat territory that reminded me of dried-up mud flats. It seemed that we would get to normal surroundings again once we'd crossed the flats and climbed out. The flats however, go on for miles and miles.

In our case we'd gone only 18.8 miles when Rock 'n Roll came to a halt with its front and rear pontoons at very odd angles. The weld had broken on the steering cross-shaft where an arm is attached which operates a steering pushrod which moves the rear axle. Also, a support tube on the same assembly had broken next to its weld. It was the same trouble as David Pratt's, but not quite as twisted up. With no spare, the only thing to do was to repair it.

Fortunately David Pratt had got an electric welding plant... It's quite a business underneath getting the cross-shaft off, there being various attachments and obstructions to deal with. The assembly has to be pre-heated before welding and for this two blow lamps were used. Our large green Terylene shelter came in very handy as a work shelter and wind shelter. After stopping I inspected my steering cross-shaft and after a false alarm, due to a cracked coating of flux, found it to be sound. I inspected Geoff's and found his was cracked at a main weld and the support tube broken next to an end weld, so I took the assembly off. David Pratt was able to nearly complete welding Bunny's then the belts started to slip. There was a lot of messing around underneath to shim up to tension the belts and this lasted a while...

In the meantime, with assistance from Bunny, his steering gear was all rigged up again. With Geoff's cooled down I fitted his with assistance from David Stratton, while David Pratt prepared his broken and twisted one ready for welding and carrying as a spare. At this point the belts slipped again, so we said to hell with it, we'll repair it (the shaft) and the welder only if the necessity arises.

This brings me to the end of the next day's work, (Sunday 16th) which saw us packing up at 1.30 a.m. (Monday). Our Saturday's work ended at 5.30 a.m. Sunday morning, so we were straining ourselves as much as we could... Saturday night we had -37°C, too. We knew it would be a moving day in the morning so it was no good trying to do the welder and the spare part in our tired state, especially if we had a long day's driving ahead.

Monday 17 February, 1958
At 1030hrs we were following Ed's tracks again, though in some places they were rather vague. The surface was a little softer than a couple of days ago when we stopped. It was pretty smooth with some light and medium sastrugi dunes... We arrived at Depot 480, to camp at 2245hrs.

I had seen a snow cairn first from about four miles away, then another further to the left, then the black speck of the depot on the horizon straight ahead from three miles away. We were all glad to be there and I looked forward to bed very much.

At Depot 700 Ken and Jon had sent a letter to Admiral Dufek explaining that they wanted, next year, to do a dog team survey of the Horlick Mountain only a couple of hundred miles from our route this side of the South Pole, (or something equally vague). They wanted to know if Dufek could transport them from New Zealand to McMurdo. They were keen also to have IGY at Scott Base keep two dog teams for them.

Savoy Hotel have sent a case of Bollinger champagne and 3lbs of caviar to Scott Base for us.

Tuesday 18 February, 1958
Progress today was made under adverse conditions when travel would not normally be undertaken.

First, however, there was seismic to be done and refuelling for all... There were ten drums of petrol at Depot 480 (2½ each), six ration boxes and four of odds and ends rations, five tins of grease and some oil, etc. We left the engine oil.

By the time Geoff was packed up and fuelled it was 1435hrs – starting off time. Conditions were as bad as they could be almost: complete whiteout, snow, wind and drift and visibility fifty yards. After a quarter mile on compass Bunny gave up as the magnetic compass response was too weak, so it was decided to wait in our vehicles to see if the weather improved.

At 1600hrs it was still the same and someone had the idea that several people with markers (ski stick, flags, etc.) could mark a route from a line of three sticks set up by compass. Each new stick would be stuck in when the last two were still just visible. This was done for eight miles when the sun re-appeared so David Stratton set up his sun-compass. This was at 1905hrs NZ time.

At 1920hrs we started. Then the sun went in, so after 0.2 miles, (mostly 90° off course) we went back to the marker method. The system was speeded up by the marker bearers not walking ahead to fix the route, but riding on the sledges of the leading vehicle and dashing off now and again to shove in a stick, while Ed (later Hal) directed the vehicle left or right from his vantage point in the roof escape hatch. Like this we did another 7.5 miles, making our total for the day 15.9 miles up to the time we camped at 2140hrs...

Soon after we camped the sky started clearing, fog and cloud broke up and the sun came through with a mock sun either side and a sun pillar forming above it. Later it had nearly all cleared, leaving a blue sky. Hope for fine sky tomorrow.

Message from Admiral Dufek supports plan of Ken and Jon and will give them passage from New Zealand to McMurdo. Cannot promise any details yet. IGY at Scott are prepared to look after two dog teams for them if seal meat for winter is cut up before we leave. Tall order for around sixty seals...

Telegram from Enid tonight to say she arrived safely and had a very enjoyable trip. Wonderful to get my letters. See me soon.

And very nice too.

Wednesday 19 February, 1958
It was bad luck that last night's promise of fine weather wasn't fulfilled for it closed over again about 1 a.m. and was just as whited-out as it could be in the morning. There was a delay when Geoff discovered a broken track link and the whole track bar had to be removed to effect repair.

We got away at 1030hrs with marker flags being put out again. The method is now speeded up by David Stratton leaning out of the door steering and Ed using the accelerator. David was able to keep on course by the markers behind while two bodies on the sledges stuck in more markers at intervals varying from one hundred yards to four hundred yards according to visibility. These were each sighted up on the earlier markers. The tail-end vehicle picked up all the markers and brought them up to the front again when two fresh bodies took over the job of sticking them in. In this way we got along at 3-4 m.p.h. and covered 41.7 miles! ...

Tuesday 20 February, 1958
Nasty day again but we still got in a pretty fair run, in spite of maintenance and seismic, with whiteout for travel...

As I was cook last night and this morning I should have been awake at eight. I awoke, feeling that I'd beaten the clock but found the time two minutes to nine. The alarm had rung and run down and I hadn't heard a thing, though the clock sits only eighteen inches from my head when it's inside the sleeping bag... This over-sleeping and not hearing the alarm sometimes happens, but we have always been on time for moving. A seismic morning is always a safe one because it invariably involves 4-5 hours before we can get away.

This morning we had vehicle maintenance. That leaves only one more maintenance to do before Scott Base. Of course it was a rather windy morning, but compensated for by temperature of only -22°C. The wind-chill was quite bad enough for filling and air-bleeding grease guns and getting grease on hands and gloves and clothing, crawling under vehicles to grease hundreds of track rollers, etc. It all got done of course and we were ready about one and half hours before we moved. The seismic takes the time and they have their last cuppa and pack up tent when it's all over.

We started in whiteout at about 3 p.m., I think. We used the stick method with Bunny driving hanging out of the door to keep course on the sticks. We had a soft snow surface which slowed the vehicles to third gear and there were unseen hard medium sastrugi dunes. After about 1.2 miles we stopped to set the sun compass when the sun managed enough light through the clouds to cast a faint shadow. About three miles on the sun disappeared again, so out came the sticks. Bunny had driven for a mile or so on compass...

The sun came out again at 2050hrs but soon went in and at 2130hrs Bunny stopped with petrol trouble. I had a go at the rather complicated system and it was murder on the fingers. However, after an hour (which seemed to me more like half an hour) all seemed well and he has had no more trouble, though we only did 1.9 miles after that, then camped at about 11 p.m. or after.

It was too bad to go on with the surface appearing a flat grey, but with the Sno-Cats suddenly nosing at an alarming angle into the air over an invisible large sastrugi or a whaleback. We had done twenty-five miles and that's not too bad...

Friday 21 February, 1958
Our fourth day of whiteout, cloud and snow. Fourth day running that is...

We camped at 2135hrs, having done 38.6 miles – all on sticks. I shall ask Bunny tomorrow to let me take the lead as I can do it faster with my sliding window (not having to lean on an open door to steer) and also can see much more easily as a consequence, so that I shan't wander all over the ice sheet as they do in Rock 'n Roll. He'll probably refuse...

Just remembered that Peter Yates (radio operator at Scott) said they're fixing up a surprise for us when we reach Scott. My guess is someone dressed as Diana Dors! I'm sure it can't be wives!

Saturday 22 February, 1958
A change in everything today: seismic finished in record time, sun most of the day, change of terrain and – mountains! ...

We left at 1205hrs. I had offered to go ahead with the sticks, being comfortably able to keep a straight course by looking out behind from my sliding window while still being able to drive. Bunny hedged and said David S. was doing the navigating and would want to do the course himself. Damn it. Keeping in line with sticks already laid out is not navigating! Nothing happened of course, except, as usual the leading vehicle continued to wander all over the ice sheet and the chaps on the sledge had to run as much as fifty yards left to put in the next flag.

Fortunately the sun came out enough to make the sun compass usable and it was just about good enough all day as the clouds had a good tendency to break up and thin a bit. Everyone was happy...

We camped at 2230hrs NZ time, the going having been fairly smooth for the last sixteen miles or so. My trip reading from the Pole read 956.6 miles and from this is to be deducted about fifteen miles in extras I expect.

Sunday 23 February, 1958
The big question of the day is, 'do we fly back to UK from New Zealand by RAF Comet, or not?' A message from Transpolar suggests, (from the Committee), that for publicity and financial reasons we fly by RAF Comet, taking only forty-eight hours. Bunny not very enthusiastic. He too looked forward to a month's cruise holiday and a chance to write some of the book that the publishers want out in six months.

Started at 1250hrs over pretty smooth surface. After I'd gone only 0.9 miles Jon remembered his cameras that he'd left on my left rear pontoon track. We went back to the camp and they were squashed into the snow but unharmed.

Bunny had started off ahead of the rest of us, so we were all behind. We got even more behind when Haywire stopped with steering trouble twelve miles or so after starting. The front steering rod had become disconnected at the front steering platform and had plunged into the snow where it dug in and bent backwards round the hydraulic steering cylinder. We had a new rod, so were able to fit it, with some difficulty... It was very painful on the fingers in the wind. (It also meant a busted lip for me where the end of the drag link hit me and pushed a tooth through inside).

We soon were going uphill which got steeper after 0.8 miles from the breakdown and 1.3 miles further I had to change from third gear into second. The hill steepness lessened for a short distance then I had to go back into second four miles on from the last change down. The hilltop came 1.5 miles later with light soft sastrugi. The hilltop didn't last long for it got slightly steeper and 3.2 miles from the level I had to change into second again. 0.6 miles on I was just able to make third gear. 0.4 miles on we were on another hilltop... 0.2 miles later we were going down a fairly steep hill over soft medium sastrugi. Only 0.4 miles later we were going uphill again, having cut down into and then up the other side again of a well-defined little snow valley. We knew we had beautiful flat-topped snow covered mountains on each side of us but part of the time huge surface undulations prevented our seeing them and most of the time the fog and cloud did the same.

After 0.2 miles up the valley slope I had to change down again into second for 0.3 miles and then back into third again. About 0.7 miles on we levelled out again – roughly. 0.2 miles further, slightly downhill, then we turned sharp left in the thick fog to arrive at the Plateau Depot 280, 1.4 miles later.

Here we found not only the Depot, but Rock 'n Roll, (whose tracks we'd followed), our Otter and the Beaver. We weren't surprised to see the aircraft there for we'd been in touch with Scott Base about the weather and flying during the day... We were about four or five miles from the depot when John Claydon zoomed over us in the Beaver. We'd left Haywire and Sno-Cat 'A' well behind and they had SARAH beacon on. John then flew up to them as well. Before we saw him coming towards us we heard him talk to Scott

285

Base. 'I can see a second plume of steam, so they can't be far behind,' and 'they're coming along in huge balls of steam,' and 'hands are waving out of the windows like nobody's business'. That was Ralph and me.

We piled into the plane where everyone else had congregated and had a swig of bottled beer. John Lewis and John Claydon were there, also their aircraft chap, Wally Tarr. Outside was a geophysicist on magnetism. Everyone was full of high spirits and a lot were taking photographs...

Both planes were in the air at 2330hrs, taking their two bods, also Ken and Jon, who were going back to deal with the seal meat job...[121]

The planes had brought two fresh eggs each, a steak each, ham and cooked beef already cut. Beautiful. Trouble was, one steak and one egg were too much for me now that my stomach has so far contracted with small nutritious meals!

Another significant milestone had been reached: the Plateau Depot marked the end of the Polar Plateau and, from this point, the Crossing Party would begin their long descent of the Skelton Glacier. They could also look forward to more interesting scenery. They had made good progress since leaving the Pole – much better than they had in approaching it, and infinitely better than the journey from Shackleton to South Ice. Nonetheless, time remained tight if they were to avoid another winter in the Antarctic.

Monday 24 February, 1958
Not a nice day at all... Seismic did one of the big noises with bundles of Nobel 704 hung in holes about three feet and eighteen inches deep dug in the snow (three of them). A huge 'crack' and blast and a great swirling pall of white smoke goes up. Yesterday's sent up a spinning smoke ring, up and up and up and kept going long after the main cloud of smoke had stopped going up and was drifting away with the wind. Today's bang we took for the usual

---

[121] Blaiklock and Stephenson flew to Scott Base in order to prepare seal meat dog rations in for their planned survey of the Horlick Mountains. Sadly, after abandoning their chance to be among those who completed the crossing, the promised support of Admiral Dufek was withdrawn due to a change of priorities and their new adventure never materialised.

signal to pack tents, but when we were nearly finished another big bang went off. Anyway, we were later than we hoped... leaving at 1430hrs...

We started downhill but after only 4.5 miles of pretty good going, Haywire stopped. I was behind, so I pulled up alongside and found a repair job to do. The left-hand rear pontoon outer-bearing had broken up and disappeared in dust. The damage had continued and the big brass nut had broken into several pieces; also the extension axle was badly worn on the thread. With the necessary spare parts we were able to get on with the job behind a canvas screen. It is necessary too. On this occasion we had -34°C and a strong wind.

We started away from there at 1640hrs... Visibility was nil... I tried, (just succeeding) to follow the previous vehicle tracks through the open window. It was cold and windy and I got covered with drift. Another three miles and we met Rock 'n Roll and Haywire who had stopped to wait for us. David Pratt, without the advantage of a door sliding window, was following close on my trail. Windscreens were frozen over inside of course.

Ed thought we could have a go on sticks, but we all thought that something below -34°C with a strong wind was a bit much. He walked on ahead while collecting flags from Rock 'n Roll. The flags had to be stuck in about every thirty yards. Like this we progressed for another 1.7 miles and packed up. Camp, 2050hrs NZ time.

Tuesday 25 February, 1958
Start 1020hrs in very poor visibility with drift and wind. But, this was going to prove to be about the most wonderful day of the expedition.

After poor visibility to start with we were able to see the mountains ahead and start downhill towards them after doing six miles. The biggest lump called Mount Huggins was the point we were aiming at. A line of them started unfolding very invitingly. After about two miles we turned right to run alongside the mountains on our left, about ten miles away. We went uphill, downhill and uphill over undulating ground and after five miles from our turn right along the mountains we went down again. In the next six miles we went up and down twice more and then Ed walked ahead marking the route with ten flags in the next 1.5 miles.

Our beautiful journey was about to open to us. The change of terrain brought a sense of expectancy, curious excitement and alert interest as we started to traverse around the side of a hill which

287

rose to our right. On our left were such beautiful snow-covered mountains bathed in sunlight. A large peak that we had passed earlier, before we turned right along the main range had, beside, it a most dark and craggy tall ridge next to it. In the next 3.2 miles we went downhill, uphill, downhill and uphill, before traversing slightly uphill around the side of a hill rising to our left. There was quite a fresh wind with drift rushing down the hills and it probably helped give effect to some of the very many photographs we took.

All this time we were overawed and delighted with the wondrous beauty of the snowy mountain scenery, not only on our left so slowly passing our view, but also ahead and to our right when the hill in that direction didn't obscure them. The surprise of a sudden breathtaking view brought new joy after we'd turned left around the side of a hill rising to our left. We were going up it at an angle and suddenly we reached a ridge where it dropped very steeply away below us. At this point we had to turn sharp right to run down the spur with the steep slope on our left. Before doing so, we stopped at the turn for some time in order to take in the sheer beauty of the scene. The steep slope led down to a wide basin far below which was ringed with mountains in light and shadow caused by a low sun. It was quiet, immense and altogether wondrous. There were very many photographs taken here, but they could never do justice to the whole scene…

We stopped to camp in most appalling wind and drift! This was midnight and what a devil of a job pitching camp in that wind.

Wednesday 26 February, 1958
Still windy in the morning… Our time for leaving was postponed in the hope that the wind's fury would abate. There were about three spells when it was fairly calm for about ten minutes, or less, otherwise the wind remained generally much the same.

We decided to move as soon as possible after 1230hrs. We did get away an hour after that; unfortunately I had gone only a few yards when we came onto hard ice and my first sledge, without a rigid tow-frame, shot forward, up onto my right rear pontoon and got carried in under the body on the track. I came to an agonised stop. On the front of my sledge the pop-pop, Sno-Cat spare gearbox and a case of radio spares were right under the body and the fuel drum centre beam, which sticks out a couple of feet in front of the sledge, was right through the back of my Sno-Cat. The jamming of the sledge between track and body had forced the body up and the

288

strain had snapped the fractured steering platform spring attaching arm. It looked pretty bad but I hoped a crowbar would save the situation.

David Pratt drew the sledges backwards and, the front one, being caught on my track, drew the vehicle backwards too as the track went round. This left everything nice and tidy with the tow ropes taught again. By the rearward pull, the ends of the broken arm were about in line and it needed only the broken end levered up to come into position with the two broken faces together again. Then, with a thirty inch crow bar between the rear spring shackle plates and slipped along under the broken end to hold it up in place everything looked much rosier and it only needed the crowbar to be lashed in position tightly. This Hal did in good seaman fashion.

The hole in the back of the body was beaten flat and canvas Bosticked on the inside, so that it didn't look quite so much as though a four inch shell had passed through. I gave it a few left and right locks over a couple of hundred yards to test it and all seemed satisfactory except for a crunching noise where the broken ends of the platform arm ground together.

We seemed to go a bit uphill over hard ice after 0.7 miles, but for that 0.7 miles downhill I had a three inch rope as a brake under the runners. Another 1.8 miles and small crevasses started in the hard ice. Most were easily seen, but snow had bridged-over some of them and Bunny broke open two, one three feet wide and one five feet wide. They didn't last long and weren't serious. After a further 3.3 miles the hard ice surface became snow-covered again and we had seventeen miles of slippery ice. All this time I had to watch my sledges in my mirror to avoid having them slide into the pontoons again. If I saw them slithering quickly forward with the tow rope becoming slacker, I had to accelerate to escape them.

The snow surface was fairly smooth, but after 0.9 miles it became fairly hummocky which was not nice in the dull light – they weren't detectable until the vehicle was rolling over them at sickening angles. After two miles it got smoother and a mile on we seemed to go uphill slightly. The surface became covered with thick soft snow which was at least a good absorber of bumps.

We knew we were on the route alright because after 1.8 miles (from the smooth part) we came across a half-buried empty dog Pemmican tin. 4.1 miles on I could see a tiny speck on the horizon, about 20° left of our course, which was Skelton Depot. A mile later we altered course for it. We had just about passed Teall Island on our right and were clear of Skelton Glacier and starting on the Barrier Shelf Ice. 2.1 miles after altering course we were at the depot, where we camped at 0132hrs and it was beautifully calm and mild. Well, well Skelton Depot (D180).

Thursday 27 February, 1958

I'm writing this now on HMNZS Endeavour, *so it'll be a bit scrappy, partly through not remembering details, partly with so many days to go back over and partly because this ship rolls and I'd rather be lying down.*

We started the day doing maintenance on the four Sno-Cats. It may not seem worth it with so few miles to go, but it's only fair on the vehicles and any further life in front of them...

Bunny moved off leaving us to follow on. He wanted all the sun he could get to use the sun-compass. I got away about twenty minutes later while the other two were still fuelling. With the amount of drift we had it might have been difficult to find tracks if left too late and visibility was pretty poor. I had started about 1925hrs... We went over medium-heavy dunes, but came later to deep soft snow. At ten miles later we altered course... and the surface was smoother. Two miles on it was pretty smooth and we were going quite nicely at 10 m.p.h. After twenty miles we camped and half an hour later Haywire came in. About an hour later David Pratt turned up...

Friday 28 February, 1958

Our Otter and Beaver would have arrived at Skelton Depot if [the] weather had not been too bad. As it was, we moved on and it was at this next stop that they arrived, with Doug McKenzie of New Zealand press and Broadhead of New Zealand Broadcasting Corporation. Also George Marsh and Jim Adams came up.[122]

Jim Adams stayed to complete the journey with us and do 'imping' on Allan. Both aircraft arrived about 10 a.m. and didn't stay long. We started off about 11.45 a.m., coming to some medium sastrugi dunes twenty-two miles later. Thirty-seven miles later we camped, having done sixty-four miles. We camped 2105hrs NZ time.

---

[122] Major Jim Adams was a British physiologist involved in IGY and working in McMurdo Sound.

Saturday 1 March, 1958

We were up about 7 a.m. to make breakfast and supposed to be ready to go at about 9 a.m. However, we weren't ready to go till 1030hrs NZ time, due to David Stratton deciding he wanted a sunsight in order to find a drum cairn which we should have been at.

Just at this time an American Otter appeared on the scene and Bunny got everyone hustling on to get moving. This was just as the Otter was about to land, but we had started to move. We all felt rather mixed up about not stopping for just five minutes but we could visualise a horde of reporters descending among us, without even the courtesy of prior notification, so on the whole we felt it to be fair.

Unfortunately the plane taxied along for some distance, slowly catching us up and this held everyone's interest so at last Bunny stopped. I was behind and to the right and Haywire was to the left. David Pratt, watching for the plane, was behind Rock 'n Roll and hadn't seen him stop, so, before you could say Jack Robinson, David's Sno-Cat had climbed up onto Bunny's rear sledge. David unhitched his sledges and I mine, then I went round and towed away his sledges so that he could back off. He hadn't damaged himself, but Bunny's sledge wheel was smashed up, so there was a delay of about forty-five minutes altogether, including fixing up a new sledge wheel. All this time the Otter was circling around with its passengers doubtlessly taking photographs.

We got away again at 1125hrs... over light to medium sastrugi dunes... We were passing the mountains on our left while we made our way over the shelf ice. First we came round Minna Bluff with Mount Discovery behind it, then round White Island with Black Island just behind that. Behind again was Brown Island.

It took ages to get past White and Black Islands and even then, with Ross Island clear and seemingly close, we kept straight on as though to pass Ross Island too... After doing sixty-two miles from our last camp we turned left, going in towards Ross Island and [Mount] Erebus. Our total for the day was seventy-five miles when we stopped to camp at 0120 hours.

We had arranged to be in at Scott Base about 1400 next day, so we wanted to get in as much mileage that night as possible...

Sunday 2 March, 1958

Starting at 1055 hours we were a bit later than we had hoped. I guessed our arrival time to be 1445hrs and I was only two minutes out. At five minutes to twelve we were spotted from Scott Base and Peter Yates said over the radio that it would take only fifteen minutes to get the news to London over the special line that had been arranged. Perhaps it was on the late home-news, but certainly it was in time for the early morning papers. We got in at 1447hrs NZ time after doing 21.6 miles.

We had seen several Weasels come down over the pass from the US Base at McMurdo to Scott Base but they all stayed there and nothing was discernible against the snow and moraine background. One Weasel only came out along the ice beside the Island and made towards us as we headed for Castle Rock... The Weasel stopped without coming out far and was flying a flag, which when we got close we could see was reading: 'The World Press Salutes TAE'. This Weasel, greeting us at the start of a flagged route, circled us like a frenzied thing with about five people in it taking photographs.

We found there was no way in to Scott Base except along the base of Ross Island on the shelf ice, using a road between huge pressure waves in the ice. I don't know how far we had to go like that but possibly a mile. All the while the Press Weasel was tearing in and out of the line of Sno-Cats taking pictures.

The surface of our 'Road-of-Triumph' was not altogether smooth and level. Some places had tide cracks and banks across it and at others there were turns left and right and the route was only just wide enough between guiding flags at other parts. Near the end was a turn left down a steep bank and I rather worried about my sledges careering into the back tracks again, but I managed to avoid that and then we were drawn up in the midst of about forty cameras, apart from about another twenty scattered along the moraine as we came in.

We were all grouped by Bunny's Sno-Cat while all the stills and cine were taken to the heart's content of their owners; they, with grim intentness forming a solid curved front of huge deep dark lenses animated only by winding-on, whirring and clicking. Someone was handing around a bottle of Hudson Bay Whiskey. I think it was Jim Adams...

I stayed down by my Sno-Cat for a while talking, while up on the moraine by Scott Base huts, speeches of welcome and responses were taking place. Hundreds of men from Scott Base, McMurdo Sound US Base, HMNZS Endeavour and the press made it a stirring welcome, but there was a surprise to come.

With the speeches well received, it was now the turn of an American (servicemen) band to add noisy colour to the celebrations. They had a variety of musical instruments and did their best [to] play well-known traditional tunes (such as 'John Peel'). These were not readily recognisable at first; then came a heroic effort to play the National Anthem which caused many a grimaced face amongst the audience but we were not without sympathy. Afterwards we spoke to the leader, a top sergeant, to congratulate him and his colleagues.

'Are you,' we asked, in order not to diminish their status, 'the camp, or ship's band?'

'Camp band – ship's band – nothing! Our captain said last night, "You get those musical instruments out of the store. We're going to play these boys in when they get here tomorrow." I said, "Captain, we've never played instruments," and he said, "That don't matter, just so long as you play good and loud."'

This was a never-to-be forgotten scene for many reasons and the band was a highlight.

We all eventually made our way to the New Zealand hut for a good wash, a good meal and lots of talking. I clearly remember that a large tin of caviar, sent by the Savoy Hotel in London, was sampled in variously small amounts by some, rejected by others and finished off in tablespoonfuls by me and one or two others. We got to bed very late, even though tired out.

While we were at Scott Base, Dr Griffith (or Griff) Pugh, an expert on carbon monoxide poisoning and who had assisted in the urgent treatment of Geoff Pratt (28th January, 1958), checked us for health and found that several of us had an unacceptable level of the poisoning. This could account for several of us having had periods of several days of severe vomiting and diarrhoea during the crossing (or unwashed plates and thermos flasks etc?).

We couldn't linger at Scott Base. Captain Harry (Plywood) Kirkwood RN was anxious to get us away to New Zealand in HMNZS Endeavour. We had time only to unpack our sledges and store the spare parts and pack our personal gear. We had arrived at Scott on 2nd March, 1958 and had to leave on 5th March without having found time to look at Captain Scott's old hut at Hut Point.

One Sno-Cat will go to America and one will be on show in the UK. My Sno-Cat County of Kent – (I kept the wooden name plate) was recognisable by being the only one of the four Sno-Cats to have windows in its body. It is left at Scott Base. I regret this as I had come to love it.[123]

I include the sea journey on HMNZS Endeavour *to New Zealand as part of the expedition journey. This sturdy little vessel, had it been forced to wait too long for us, might very well have become trapped in the coming winter sea-ice at McMurdo Sound. If this had happened we would have been spending another winter in the Antarctic. As things were, we had started late and arrived late, but, in addition to the scientific programme and vehicle maintenance, every effort had been directed to speeding the journey in order to be off the ice sheet by the beginning of March.*

We had completed a scientific journey of 2,158 miles in ninety-nine days – one day less than Bunny had estimated.

We arrived at Wellington on 17th March, 1958, (I think) and had a most exciting welcome from many ships, a flight of Royal New Zealand Air Force Vampires, monumental formal receptions and magnificent welcomes from the New Zealand people. Also, Magga Dan *had brought families (including Enid) and friends out to meet us as we entered Wellington harbour.*

Marvellous!

---

[123] County of Kent's post-TAE career came to a tragic end on 19 November 1959 when it plunged into a crevasse near Cape Selborne, killing the driver, Tom Couzens, and seriously injuring the two passengers, including Bernie Gunn, a veteran of the NZ IGY party. For details, see Haddelsey, *Icy Graves: Exploration and Death in the Antarctic* (Stroud: The History Press, 2018), pp. 115-118.

AFTERWORD

The Crossing Party left Antarctica on board HMNZS *Endeavour* on 5 March 1958 and arrived in New Zealand on the 17th in beautiful sunshine. They received a tumultuous welcome from the ships and boats in Wellington Harbour and a fly-past of RNZAF Vampires. The streets were alive with jubilant well-wishers and the explorers found themselves toasted at numerous receptions. It was much the same – apart from the weather – when they reached the UK on 12 May, but following the parties came the more sombre award of honours: a knighthood for Fuchs, Polar Medals for first-timers, and additional medal clasps for Roy and the other more seasoned explorers. It is quite possible that Roy's unremitting labours in appalling conditions might have resulted in a higher award, had Hillary not muddied the waters with the Cabinet Office by pre-empting Fuchs' recommendations for honours – another action that would rankle with many long after the end of the expedition.[124]

Of course, the enthusiastic welcome accorded to Fuchs and his team had very little to do with the expedition's scientific achievements, most important among which was proving definitively that Antarctica is a single continental landmass; it had every-thing to do with the successful crossing of Antarctica – a journey that Shackleton, in the prospectus for his ill-fated *Endurance* Expedition, had memorably described as 'the last great polar journey that can be made'. It was the journey that had captured the imaginations of the general public – just as Fuchs had always known it would.

Taken as a whole, the TAE had achieved the vast majority of its objectives and it had done so without the loss of a single life. And yet, despite its many successes – indeed, possibly because of them

---

[124] Interviewed by Stephen Haddelsey on 1 July 2009, Ken Blaiklock asserted that Hillary had submitted his own recommendations to the Cabinet Office without Fuchs' prior knowledge or agreement. Blaiklock remained convinced that Hillary's action had made it difficult, if not impossible, for Fuchs to submit a further list of recommendations.

– the expedition has long since faded from public awareness. Of course, the diversion of attention to the Space Race might be to some degree responsible for this forgetfulness – but that can be only a part of the answer. After all, while the name of Fuchs is known to very few beyond those directly affected by his fifteen years as Director of the British Antarctic Survey, and Hillary's brief, vital, but highly controversial work in the Antarctic has paled to nothing in comparison with his achievements in the Himalayas, the names and exploits of Shackleton and Scott, whose expeditions were dogged by disaster, remain very much in the public eye, with new biographies, dramas, documentaries and exhibitions produced on a regular basis. But even the suggestion that death and failure sell better than triumph leaves the story incomplete – if it was as simple as that, then Hillary would have been forgotten as completely as Fuchs.

In reality, the TAE was not only a victim of its own success – it was also a victim of the means of that success. Put simply, to many, an expedition equipped with reliable motor vehicles, aircraft, and wireless lacks the poetry of expeditions that relied, very largely, on human muscle. The image of frostbitten heroes slogging across barren landscapes, hauling unbearably heavy sledges towards impossible goals trumps that of men riding across the same wilderness in the supposed comfort of a heated cab. That this comparison is entirely spurious is proved by Roy's diary: he and seven companions endured extraordinary hardship during the first year of the expedition, while the TAE's final victory was achieved in the face of odds that, at times, seemed utterly insurmountable.

Sadly, the memorials to the TAE as a whole are few and far between. On Ross Island, Hillary's mess hut survives as an integral part of a Scott Base that has otherwise expanded beyond recognition, but Shackleton Base disappeared forever during a massive calving of ice from the Filchner Ice Shelf in 1986. South Ice may still exist, but, if so, it is buried beneath an estimated 13 metres of snow and ice at a point unvisited since 1958. More positively, the three Sno-Cats that returned to civilisation can still be viewed: one at the Canterbury Museum in Christchurch, New Zealand, a second at the Antique Gas and Steam Engine Museum in Vista, California, and the third at the Science Museum's storage facility in Wroughton, near Swindon.[125] Roy's County of Kent was

---

[125] The Wroughton facility is open by appointment only.

never salvaged and remains upside down and crushed in a crevasse close to Cape Selborne, Antarctica, while the Muskeg and the Weasels lie mouldering and forgotten at various staging posts along the route followed between November 1957 and March 1958.

Inevitably, the initial gush of public interest in the TAE and the men who took part faded rapidly on the expedition's completion. But the months – in some cases years – spent amid the snowy wastes of Antarctica remained central in the life stories of those who ensured its success. This was certainly true for Roy. In a life that was both long and varied, the TAE remained, in many respects, the jewel in the crown – as is proved by the time that he lavished on preparing his diary for publication, and by his conviction that it should be published in its entirety.

Roy ended his diary with the single word 'marvellous', written soon after he left Antarctica forever. Of course, it could have been just a throwaway word – but somehow it seems to be far more than that: a word loaded with meaning. In part, Roy was probably expressing his satisfaction at a job well done by him personally. While the expedition's successes would have been reduced by the loss of a geologist or a glaciologist, its primary objective – the crossing – would still have been achieved. Without the two engineers it would have failed utterly. Moreover, in his absolute dedication to every facet of his work and to the success of the expedition as a whole, he far exceeded all that might have been expected of him – a fact that Fuchs acknowledged in a note written at Shackleton on the eve of the Crossing Party's departure:

> Roy, after these days at Shackleton I can congratulate myself on not being so foolhardy as to choose one of the other numerous applicants![126]

Roy might also have been describing the team as a whole: recording his respect and admiration for a group of men from disparate backgrounds, and with very different skills and experience, who came together to complete a truly epic journey in one of the most inhospitable environments on the face of the planet. More prosaically, he might have chosen the word marvellous as a final euphoric exclamation at the realisation that he could at last lay

---

[126] Vivian Fuchs to Roy Homard, Shackleton Base, 22 November 1957.

aside his grease-gun: that never again would he face the awful task of lubricating each of the 296 nipples of his Sno-Cat's track rollers in blizzard conditions.

Finally, perhaps Roy was admitting that at last he was satisfied, that he had taken part in an adventure that was truly worthy of the name. This is pure surmise, of course, but it is satisfying to think that this brave and remarkable man who, in his youth, his friends dubbed 'Roy the Romancer', did not just dream; instead, he turned his dreams into a truly exceptional reality.

SELECT BIBLIOGRAPHY

Arnold, Anthea (with Goldsmith, Rainer)	*Eight Men in a Crate, The Ordeal of the Advance Party of the Trans-Antarctic Expedition 1955-57*, Norwich, Erskine Press, 2007
Barber, Noel	*The White Desert, His Personal Story of the Trans-Antarctic Expedition*, London, Hodder & Stoughton, 1958
Fuchs, Sir Vivian	*A Time to Speak*, Oswestry, Anthony Nelson, 1990
Fuchs, Sir Vivian, & Hillary, Sir Edmund	*The Crossing of Antarctica*, London, Cassell, 1958
Haddelsey, Stephen	*Icy Graves: Exploration and Death in the Antarctic, Stroud*, The History Press, 2018 *Shackleton's Dream: Fuchs, Hillary and the Crossing of Antarctica*, Stroud, The History Press, 2012
Helm, A.S., & Miller, J.H.	*Antarctica, The Story of the New Zealand Party of the Trans-Antarctic Expedition*, Wellington, R.E. Owen, 1964
Hillary, Sir Edmund	*No Latitude for Error*, London, Hodder & Stoughton, 1961
Hillary, Sir Edmund	*Nothing Venture, Nothing Win*, London, Hodder & Stoughton, 1975
Hillary, Sir Edmund	*View from the Summit*, London, Corgi Books, 2000
Kemp, Norman	*The Conquest of the Antarctic*, London, Wingate, 1956
Knight, John	*The Crossing: Sir Vivian Fuchs, Sir Edmund Hillary and the Trans-Antarctic Expedition, 1953-58*, Stroud, Amberley, 2018
Lister, Hal	*Ice, High & Low*, Milnthorpe, Privately Printed, 2005

McKenzie, Douglas — *Opposite Poles*, London, Robert Hale, 1963

Stephenson, Jon — *Crevasse Roulette, The First Trans-Antarctic Crossing 1957-58*, New South Wales, Rosenberg Publishing, 2009

Sullivan, Walter — *Assault on the Unknown*, New York, McGraw-Hill Book Co., 1961

Thomson, John — *Climbing the Pole, Edmund Hillary & the Trans-Antarctic Expedition 1955-58*, Norwich, Erskine Press, 2010